Photography of the Age

Newspaper photography in Australia

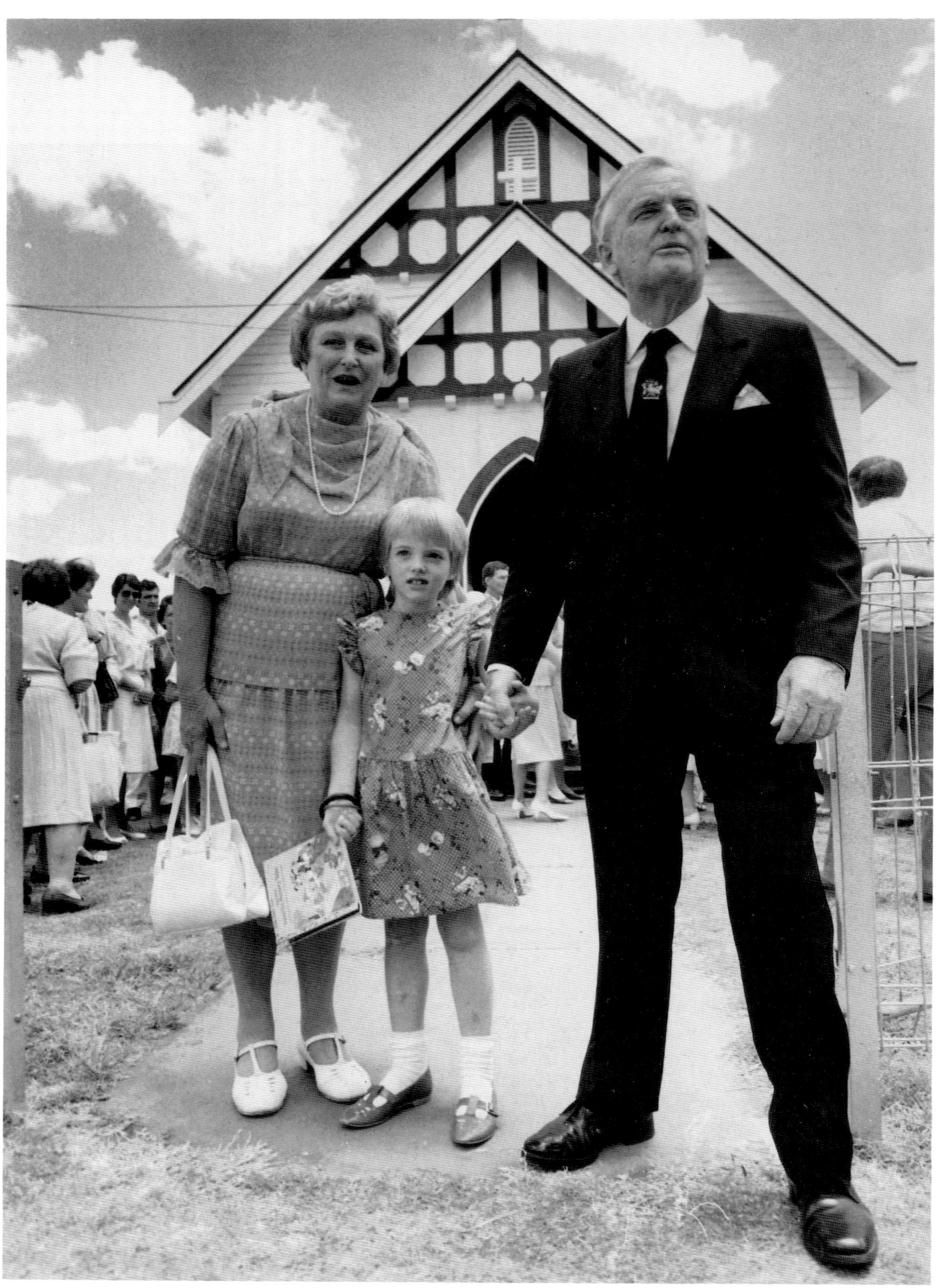

Flo, Joh and grand-daughter, Kingaroy, Qld. (John Woudstra)

Photography of the Age

Newspaper photography in Australia

Kathleen Whelan

Hale & Iremonger

Acknowledgements

I would like to extend my thanks to the following people for their help in making this book a reality:

- Wangaratta College of TAFE and the Victorian State Training Board for their Industrial Release program, which allowed me to work at the *Age*, and to the Art and Design Department for covering during my absence;
- Stephen Jolly, John Cato, Clare Gervasoni, Paul Walker, Terry Cameron, Kristine Beach, Linda Lees, Julie O'Brien, and Steve Roberts for their help in bringing the book together;
- the *Age* Pictorial Department with special thanks to Peter Charles and the library staff;
- the *Age* photographers for their willingness and generosity in sharing their ideas, knowledge, and individual photographs;
- and my publishers, Hale & Iremonger, particularly Kerrie McLeod for her exciting suggestions.

The author

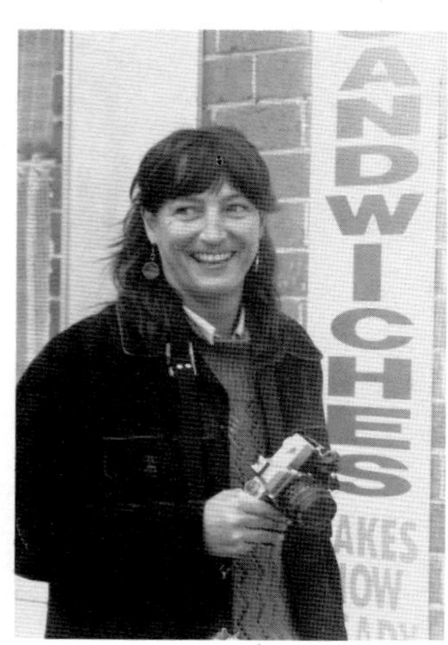

Kathleen Whelan, an experienced educator and photographer, currently lectures in photography at the Wangaratta College of TAFE and is chair of the TAFE Art and Design Statewide Committee. A member of the Australian Association of Professional Photographers, Kathleen possesses a Masters Degree in Education from the Tyler School of Art, Temple University, Philadelphia USA. She has participated in numerous exhibitions, and her work is represented in collections in Australia, the USA, and Peru. Kathleen has contributed to many professional and craft journals *Photography of the Age* is her first book.

Typeset, printed & bound by
Southwood Press Pty Limited
80–92 Chapel Street, Marrickville, NSW 2204

For the publisher
Hale & Iremonger Pty Limited
GPO Box 2552, Sydney, NSW

National Library of Australia Cataloguing-in-publication entry

Whelan, Kathleen.

Photography of the Age.

ISBN 0 86806 484 X.

1. Age (Melbourne, Vic.). 2. Photojournalism — Australia. I. Age (Melbourne, Vic.). II. Title.

070.490994

CONTENTS

FOREWORD

Socially, photography is the most significant visual art of the 20th century.

Such a statement may seem excessive, but when one considers that developed countries consume photographic imagery with greater enthusiasm than they gorge fast food, some inkling of its impact will be obvious. Photography holds a central place in our culture. We hold on to our most treasured memories through the humble snapshot. In science, we extend our knowledge of the world through photography. We decide where to spend our holidays by looking at photographs in glossy travel brochures. We may choose the goods we buy in response to the visual salesmanship of advertising photographs. But, more dangerously, we tend to form our opinions by looking at the images of photo-journalists and their cousins, the press photographers.

Press photographers are in a unique and privileged position. The events of the world take place on a stage which they view from the Royal Box. We, the public, wait outside in the street. Press photographers have a moral obligation to be objective. Pictorial editors and editors-in-chief bear a similar responsibility. But readers have a part to play as well. They must be aware of the risk of being manipulated.

One of the problems of photography is that the medium is transparent. If we look at paintings, drawings, or engraving, the medium is always apparent. We are aware of paint, of brushstrokes, of a line of charcoal or pencil — the craft of the hand, and we accept the finished product as an interpretation of reality. The photograph is different. We do not see the chemical stains, the grains of silver, the dyes on a piece of paper. Rather we see the 'reality' of the thing photographed. It is no longer an 'interpretation' but 'the truth'. After all, haven't we accepted the notion that 'the camera never lies' — that 'seeing is believing'? This power to be believed, no matter what, is awe-inspiring. But, if the camera does not lie, we can be certain many photographers do.

In 1948 the English astrophysicist Fred Hoyle remarked, 'Once a photograph of the earth taken from the outside is available, once the sheer isolation of the earth becomes plain, a new idea as powerful as any in history will be let loose'. Twenty years later one of the Apollo missions made that photograph available. We knew what it would look like long before we saw it. We were accustomed to phrases like 'spaceship earth', 'global village', but seeing the photograph was a remarkable experience. Within 12 months the first Earth Day was held. Within 18 months the Environmental Protection Agency was founded. The first of the European 'Greens' parties was formed. Today those parties hold the balance of political Power. The editor of the *New York Times* commented, 'the picture provides the sobering perspective on man's puny earthly works and rivalries, reminding all humanity that nature is the basic antagonist, not other men'. This was 'picture-power' indeed.

There is an apocryphal story about one of Australia's greatest editors — the late Graham Perkins of the *Age*. It concerns a particularly horrible image from Vietnam of a group of soldiers walking away from a helicopter carrying what appeared to be bundles of skinned rabbits. They were the bodies of Vietnamese babies. An editorial conference was called to discuss whether or not the photograph should be published. Finally, Perkins made a characteristic decision, 'Publish. Let the bastards spew in their Weeties!' We, the readers, were the 'bastards'. There followed a deluge of 'Letters to the Editor', in praise and damnation. But Perkins, and other editors of courage in Australia and the USA, kept publishing such photographs. People in the street screamed their horror. The madness of the Vietnam war was terminated, not by some new super-bomb, but by public opinion stirred by a weapon already 150 years old — the camera.

The pictures were explicit, they did not need captions. By contrast, in 1936, during the Spanish Civil War, a comparatively unknown American photographer, Robert Capa, took a photograph of a man in uniform apparently falling over, right arm outstretched, hand clutching a rifle. Captioned 'The moment of death,' this image is not explicit. Many different captions could be given to it. Capa himself told four different stories about its origin, commenting in one interview, 'if you want to get good action shots, they mustn't be in good focus. If your hand trembles a little, then you get a fine action shot'. Were we duped? Where lies truth?

In the arts, to facilitate discussion, it is usual to categorise. The categories may be by geography or period, so that discussion may turn to twelfth-century Russian icons, or the Italian Renaissance. Or it could be through the 'isms' — symbolism, impressionism, cubism, and so on. But, more often than not, categorisation is by subject matter — the landscape, the portrait, the nude, the still-life. The world of press photography is much more constrained in its choice of categories. I recall days in the 1940s when I was one of that group who carried massive 5″ x 4″ speed graphics, pockets stuffed with flash globes; we had only five approaches to consider — Violence, Royalty, Sex, Religion, Sentiment.

Violence lies at the centre of news. It may be the violence of people — war, a gun-crazed misfit, road carnage, bashing, murder, rape. It may be the violence of nature — flood, fire, earthquake. All may generate good copy, good photographs. (We are fortunate in Australia that, in the main, we have an ethical press that does not intrude too far into the grief that violence leaves in its wake.) Royalty — the important, famous and infamous. What these people do is news, or so we are told. And Elizabeth Taylor's umpteenth marriage becomes the 'Wedding the Whole World's Been Waiting For!' Religion, too, makes a good story, preferably if it involves a fringe group. And if it's Jimmy Swaggart, you've got the lot, because he mixes it with that other obsession, Sex. Mostly the tool of advertising, Sex still has a place in the news. The tabloid's formula for page three may be obvious, but, come the first day of summer, and a pretty young woman in a miniscule swimsuit on St Kilda beach will find her photograph in even the conservative press. And if there just is no news? Let Sentiment run loose. The photographer can always go to the Lost Dogs' Home, the Children's Hospital, or the nursery at the Zoo.

In November 1972, the National Gallery of Victoria staged a major exhibition, 'Fifty Years of Australian Press Photography'. It was a resounding public success and, for the first time, press photographers were acknowledged in Australia as artists whose relevance extended beyond the confines of the printed page. Then about ten years ago the *Age*, in its own gallery, exhibited some of the prime pieces from its archive. It demonstrated, in microcosm, the power of the press photograph and the internationally high standard of its photographers. I hope it does it again. Soon.

John Cato

INTRODUCTION

A newspaper is a very selective look at the world — the end result of what journalists, editors, and photographers, constrained by editorial philosophy, deem to be 'newsworthy'. Only one per cent of the 'news' that crosses an editor's desk each day will be printed.

Editorial philosophies fit roughly into one of two categories: give people what they are interested in; or, give them what is in their interest. Newspapers in the first category see themselves as feeding the public with what it wants; those in the second seek to inform and to educate. In practice, most newspapers contain elements of both approaches — it's the mix that varies.

The editorial philosophy of the *Age* outlines the paper's aims:

- To remain a forum for ideas and talents.
- To be a newspaper of record and to play a positive and creative role in the development of Victoria.
- To continue to be an independent and critical voice in national and community affairs.

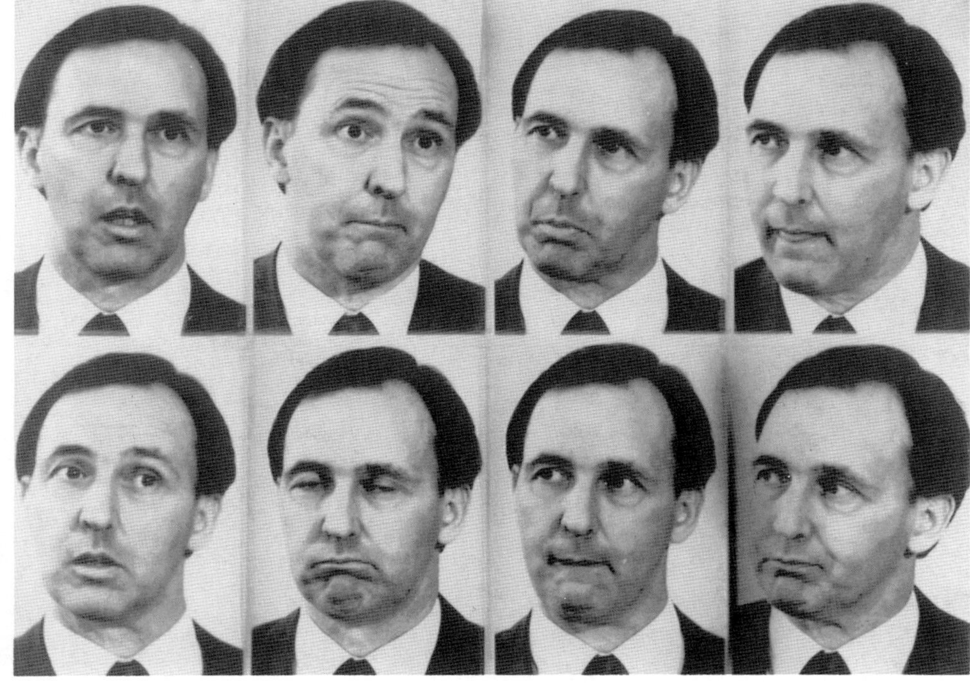

Not all photographs are equally flattering. Those that do appear in newspapers may influence the public's perception of an individual or event
(photographer: Peter Morris)

ACCESS AGE 670 1601

Access letters must be 50 words or less. Lines are open between 8 am and noon, 1 pm and 4 pm weekdays.

So this is having fun?

The photograph yesterday of a steer being roped with a jolt at a rock 'n' roll rodeo at Maldon on Sunday spoiled some readers' breakfasts and sent them to the phone in protest.

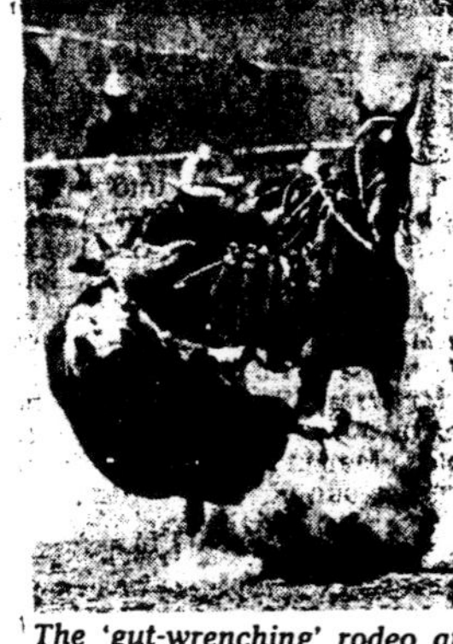

The 'gut-wrenching' rodeo at Maldon.

Gut-wrenching

The photograph on page three ('The Age', 11/3) of the roped steer is a graphic illustration of how we can use animals to keep the Moomba spirit alive. The caption adds the finishing touch, although it doesn't specify whose guts is being wrenched.

Rosemary Hanbury,
Armadale.

Gross animal abuse

Once again 'The Age' (11/3) makes light of gross animal abuse dressed up as entertainment. The lassoed steer pictured at the obscene "rock 'n' roll" rodeo at Maldon warranted this more appropriate caption — "Garotte till you drop".

Tom Perry,
Elwood.

Testosterone junkies

As a rock 'n' roll musician, I find the concept of using this art form to enhance the gut-wrenching action for pseudo-American testosterone junkies shameful and disgusting. Not only that, but the visual shock of seeing one of our bovine friends being strangled spoilt my breakfast.

Dirk Welsford,
Williamstown.

Is the photographer's task to record, to entertain, or to provoke? Readers' reactions to this photograph, which appeared in the Age *in March 1991, are as ambiguous as its caption*

This philosophy informs the political stance of the *Age*, which sees itself as being 'independent of party and sectional interests, socially reformist, financially prudent; but nevertheless innovative'. The paper's identity consists of 'a combination of physical features (page size, typeface and design) and editorial philosophy and practice . . . [that] may evolve over the life of a paper, adjusting and changing with the times and the community it serves.'

Press photography documents our culture — the ideas, attitudes and expectations that we share. Despite this sharing, one person may attach to a scene a significance that escapes another entirely. This may be of little importance when it comes to a beautiful baby contest: some may be more intrigued by the faces of the spectators, others more interested in the appearance of the winner. But, selecting what to photograph and whether to publish it can influence how the reader interprets the world.

Few, if any, photographs appeared in the Western press during the 1991 Iraq conflict that showed the suffering of the Iraqi people under Allied bombardment. Were such photographs not taken? Were they censored by the international news agencies before being released? Would their publication have influenced public perceptions of the justness of the war in the way that images from Vietnam did 20 years earlier? Is the public so accustomed to horrific photographs that their publication generates apathy and indifference?

Editors determine the subject of a picture. But there are many approaches to that subject. How, for example, do the photographer and the journalist portray the unemployed or Lindy Chamberlain? Does one wait for the tearful look or for the gentle smile? Below John Lamb has shown Lindy Chamberlain laughing. The photograph reflects the change in public attitudes to her. No longer is her laughter interpreted as an unfeeling absence of grief.

It says much about the open nature of Australian society that newspapers are free to print photographs of prominent people that may appear to ridicule them. But for every photograph of Prime Minister Paul Keating kissing the soil in New Guinea there are several hundred equally unkind images that will never grace a newspaper's pages. Newspaper policy, the editor's discretion, and the existence of unspoken pressures will all influence just what is printed.

The photographs in this book are an investigation of contemporary Australia, and all, with one exception, were shot in the last ten years. They are powerful and striking images. That their primary purpose was to persuade people to purchase a newspaper in no way detracts from their quality. Rather these photographs reflect the preparedness of picture editors to give their staff a freer rein in order to satisfy the increasingly sophisticated tastes of an educated readership.

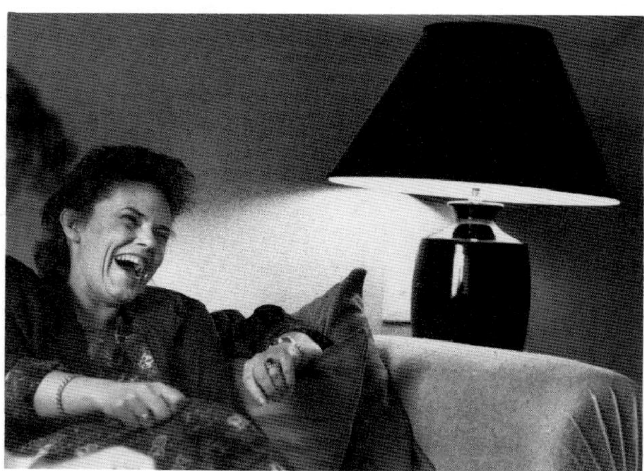

CHAPTER 1

THE PICTORIAL DEPARTMENT

Newspaper circulation

Newspaper sales per household have decreased since the 1950s. This may be attributable both to the advent of television as a provider of news and to the preference for private rather than public transport. (Sales decline by tens of thousands each day that there is a public transport strike.)

To arrest the decline in circulation, newspapers have focused on particular markets. Some have chosen the lower income earner, others the higher. The tabloid press retains a higher distribution overall, but there has been an increased circulation per household to minority audiences that are well educated. The quality press aims to attract such an audience — up-market and politically 'middle-of-the-road'.

Deliberately focusing on a smaller, more select audience has a number of repercussions. One is that fewer newspapers need to be printed, thus lowering costs and permitting more money to be spent on journalists' salaries. (The *Age* and the *Sydney Morning Herald* have the largest editorial staffs in Australia.)

In response to the concentration of newspaper ownership within fewer hands, journalists, and the public at large, have become increasingly prepared to demand editorial independence. The perceived anti-Labor bias of the *Australian* in the 1970s resulted in a considerable decline in its readership.

Readers of both the *Age* and the *Sydney Morning Herald* tend to possess professional qualifications and to be relatively affluent. They provide an attractive audience for advertisers who are willing to pay substantial sums (currently about $34 per column centimetre) to reach them. Advertising revenue underwrites between 60 and 70 per cent of newspaper production costs.

Pictorial assignments — how they originate

At the *Age* there are two conferences daily where the six editors examine the news for the day and where the Pictorial Editor discusses ideas for possible photographs. These conferences provide the basis for the work during that day.

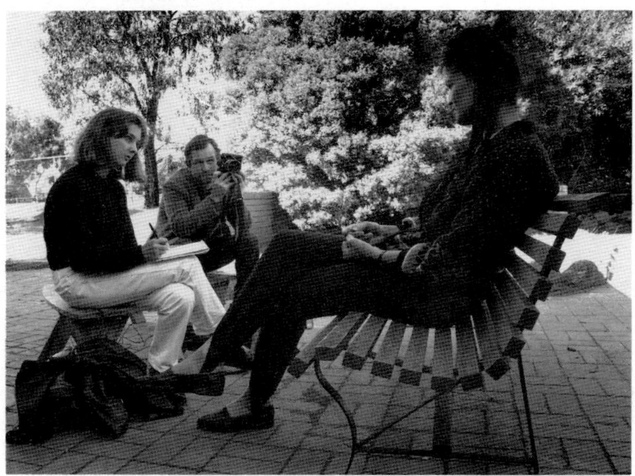

Photographer Andrew De La Rue looks on as journalist Suzy Freeman-Greene interviews a Maori community worker. Accompanying a journalist on a story not only allows more time for photographs to be taken but lets the photographer know the type of article that will be written and to photograph accordingly

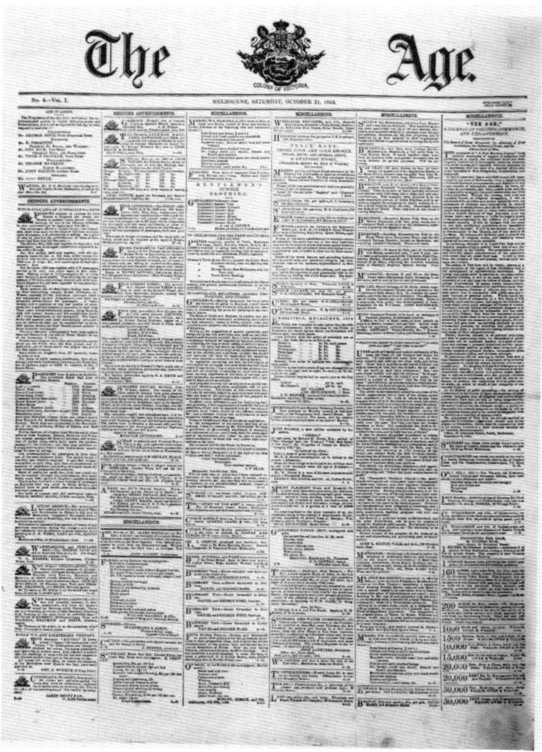
The Age.

No. 6.—Vol. I. MELBOURNE, SATURDAY, OCTOBER 21, 1854.

October 1854

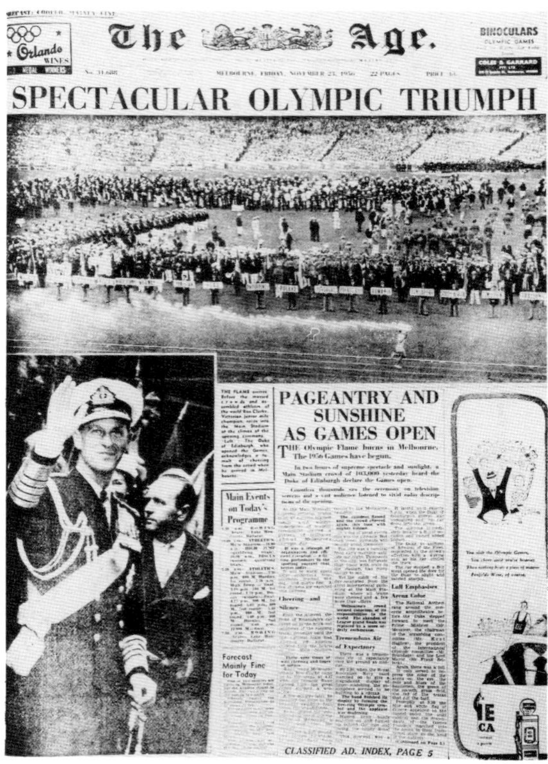
The Age.

MELBOURNE, FRIDAY, NOVEMBER 23, 1956 22 PAGES

SPECTACULAR OLYMPIC TRIUMPH

PAGEANTRY AND SUNSHINE AS GAMES OPEN

THE Olympic Flame burns in Melbourne. The 1956 Games have begun.

Main Events on Today's Programme

Forecast Mainly Fine for Today

CLASSIFIED AD. INDEX, PAGE 5

November 1956

The changing face of the Age: *the dimensions of the page remain the same, but the masthead, typeface, number and width of columns, and prominence of advertising have altered substantially*

April 1962

The Age

No. 33,371 MELBOURNE, SATURDAY, APRIL 21, 1962 38 PAGES PRICE 4d.

Classified Index Page 22

FITZROY EXPLOSION WRECKS FURNITURE STORES

STOP PRESS

Arrest of Salan Confirmed

Hairbreadth Escapes for Many in Shattered Shops Area

Arrest Reported of O.A.S. Leader

First 1962 League Football Today

Restorers Uncover Hidden Paintings

Fell to Death in Bid to Regain Shoe

The Queen is 36 Today

In Other Pages

December 1989

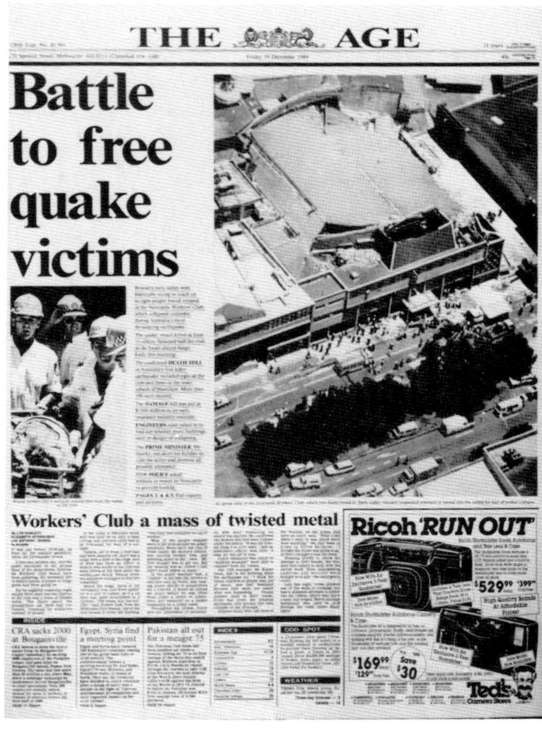
THE AGE

Battle to free quake victims

Workers' Club a mass of twisted metal

CRA sacks 2000 at Bougainville

Egypt, Syria find a meeting point

Pakistan all out for a meagre 75

INDEX

ODD SPOT

WEATHER

Other assignments will come from journalists requesting photographs to accompany a story. It is then up to the Pictorial Editor to allocate a photographer for that job. It is preferable that the journalist and photographer work together to ensure that the pictures suit the article, but this is not always possible. A journalist may need to spend several hours interviewing people, whereas a photographer is usually allocated only one hour for a job. Professional differences of opinion between the journalist and the photographer may also intervene. The journalist may have a particular type of photograph in mind, while the photographer may be more preoccupied by what is visually best for a 'good pic'.

If there isn't much news on a particular day, the photographer is expected to find his/her own photo. That can be a very difficult challenge; driving around the city looking for action; knowing enough about the news to find something newsworthy; or creating the news oneself. John Lamb is very talented at finding his own stories. He looks for the human interest angle and works well with journalist John Leahy. His is a case of the photographer helping to create the news.

The Editor's view

by Michael Smith, Editor, 1989-1992, Group Executive Editor, 1992-

Photographers are key members of the *Age* team and have been since 1927, when Hugh Bull was appointed to the staff to become Australia's first press photographer.

The *Age* prides itself on the quality of its photographers as well as the excellence of its writing staff. Our photographers aim to present news, features and sport in an accurate, informative and exciting way.

The *Age*'s pictorial content must reflect the nature of the paper. The *Age* is a serious daily newspaper and the ultimate picture is the 'frozen moment', the essence of an event, captured as it actually happens. Contrived or set-up pictures would seriously undermine our credibility. This does not mean that humorous pictures or pictures reflecting the lighter side of life are not valued. Quite to the contrary, some of the more memorable pictures published in the *Age* have been whimsical, humorous or downright funny. All, however, must meet the demand that they present events in an interesting and completely honest way.

The ability of the press photograph to freeze the moment in time is the major advantage newspaper pictures have over television film. The television camera, although able to convey images powerfully, still presents only a fleeting view of events.

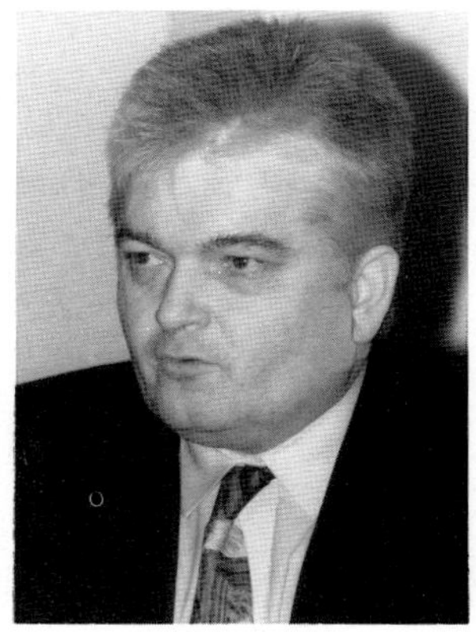

Michael Smith, Group Executive Editor

A testament to the lasting influence of newspaper photographs is the number of them that adorn walls around the world, capturing forever moments in the history of politics, of sport, of life.

Good pictures don't simply happen. As with articles, photographs require planning. The planning process begins at the *Age* with a morning news conference, involving the Editor and his senior executives, at which forthcoming events and story and picture ideas for the day are discussed and their coverage planned.

At the evening news conference the results of the day's efforts are assessed and placed in the paper according to their news value.

This liaison between reporters and photographers is extremely important. Photographs have to complement the stories they accompany; the picture and the story combine to form a complete package, one adding to the value of the other.

A strong story with a good picture is likely to be placed further forward in the newspaper than one with a lesser picture. Conversely, a good picture with a poor story may be placed further back in the paper than a good picture and a good story.

The selection of pictures involves the Pictorial Editor, the Night Editor, and the Editor. All contribute to the selection process but ultimately it is the Editor who has the final say.

It is also the Editor who decides whether or not to publish a picture that may present an ethical problem, such as taste or an individual's right to privacy. There are few hard and fast rules, but the *Age* is careful not to intrude unnecessarily into people's lives or to depict grief insensitively. The Editor must also be aware of the legal aspects of using some pictures, especially when court cases are involved.

More than most industries, newspapers are experiencing enormous change. The advent of colour reproduction of photographs in the *Age* is exciting, but it also represents new challenges in the way we take colour pictures, process the film, and print the photographs. It is the responsibility of the photographic department to provide the highest quality pictures to obtain the best result from the state-of-the-art colour presses at the *Age*.

The broadsheet format of the paper enables us to use bigger photographs than our smaller tabloid competitors. We may use few pictures but our format enables us to design imaginative pictorial layouts.

The *Age* is proud that it has some of Australia's finest newspaper photographers and they are producing some of the best examples of their craft.

The role of the *Age* Pictorial Editor

by Peter Charles

Although the role of the Pictorial Editor is seen by many as being simply one of selecting pictures for publication, there is a lot more to the job than that.

The day starts with the morning news conference which is attended by the Editor, Associate Editor, Chief of Staff, Features Editor, and the Foreign Editor. All the potential stories for the day are discussed, ideas expressed, and the possibility of pictures to accompany these stories is explored.

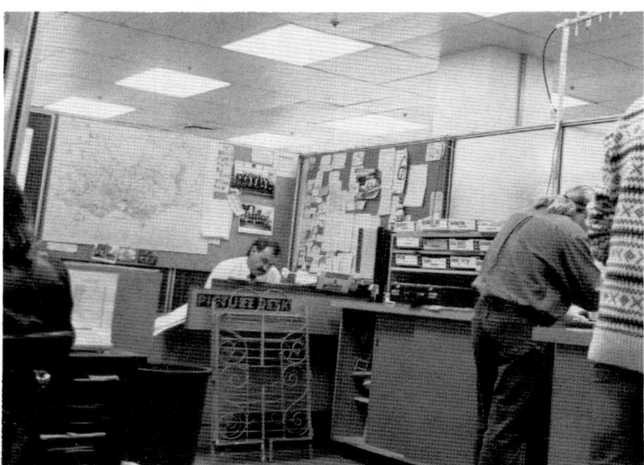

Peter Charles at the Picture Desk

After the morning news conference, the Pictorial Editor then assigns jobs to specific photographers. Although all newspaper photographers are required to be proficient in all aspects of their craft, they all have their specialty fields. One photographer might be good at fashion, another might excel at sport.

It is therefore the responsibility of the Pictorial Editor to try, where possible, to match a particular photographer to the assignment that best utilises his or her strengths. Of course, when a big news job happens, every person on the pictorial staff must be capable of covering the story.

At about 6 p.m. each day, the evening news conference is held and is attended by the News Editor as well as by those present at the morning conference. This conference determines where stories are to appear in the paper. The placement of stories on particular pages is often contingent upon the strength of the picture, that is, a good picture accompanying an average story can often result in that story and picture being moved further forward in the paper. Of course, the reverse is also the case.

After the news conference the Pictorial Editor, Editor, Night Editor, Chief Sub Editor, and Page 1 Sub Editor hold a picture conference to decide which pictures are to go on what pages.

The Pictorial Department of the *Age* is one of the larger departments, having a staff of 57 that includes photographers and dark-room, library and clerical staff. Their administration is an important responsibility of the Pictorial Editor. The Pictorial Manager assists the Pictorial Editor to ensure that the photographic equipment is of the highest standard and well maintained. But the Pictorial Editor's primary concern is always that photographs appearing in the *Age* are of the highest quality.

Sending and receiving overseas and interstate photographs

Newspapers throughout Australia often cooperate and share both pictures and stories that are of interstate interest, such as politicians' press conferences or interstate sports meetings. (The degree of cooperation may alter as newspaper ownership changes.) The *Age* usually sends a few pictures each day via picturegrams to Australian Associated Press for use by regional newspapers, and the Pictorial Editor may ring each cooperating interstate newspaper twice daily to check what is available.

The *Age* subscribes, at considerable cost, to a variety of national and international news services. Australian Associated Press draws on the resources of other news services including Reuters, the UK Press Association (PA), Associated Press (AP) in the US, and Agence France Press (AFP). The paper also subscribes to the news services of the *Independent*, the *Guardian*, the *Los Angeles Times*, the *Washington Post*, and the *New York Times*.

During the day's news conferences, the Foreign Editor will alert the Pictorial Editor to foreign stories that the paper wishes to cover. It is then up to the

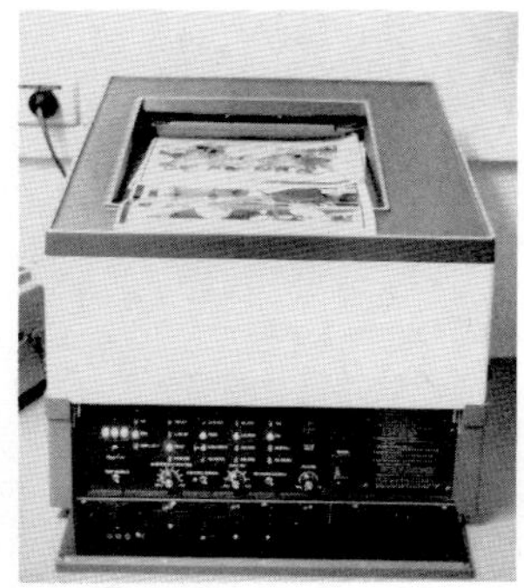

The picturegram machine

Pictorial Editor to monitor the incoming picturegrams for appropriate photographs.

Although the *Age* frequently uses photographs from Associated Press (AP) and Reuters, these world-wide networks carry few picturegrams from Australia. Those they do receive are usually of very newsworthy events only, such as the Hoddle Street Shooting, a Royal tour, or the Melbourne Cup.

Legal constraints

In Australia, for the most part, it is legal to take any photograph on public property with or without the consent of the party being photographed. Individuals who believe they have suffered as a result of a photograph being taken may seek a court injunction to prevent the photograph's publication, although such an injunction may not be granted.

There are, however, some legal constraints on taking and publishing a photograph in this country:

- You may not take a photograph inside a parliament house without the consent of the Speaker;
- You may not photograph the interior or surrounds of any court;
- You may not photograph members of a jury;
- You may not photograph any person whose identity, if known, may affect the outcome of a trial;
- You may not photograph anyone whose identity is subject to a suppression order;
- You may not enter and photograph inside a person's house without their permission;
- You may not identify children who are wards of the state.

Ethical considerations

Ethical considerations are equally important in determining whether or not a photograph will be published. The *Age* is concerned to present factual photos — not tricks. A picture that has been manipulated (double exposed or reworked) will not be published unless the caption clearly indicates the alteration.

Although the *Age* will reproduce photographs of overseas dead bodies if they are not too gruesome, it is reluctant to print photographs of dead bodies of recognisable Australians. The paper does not wish to add to the survivors' grief. A photograph of a funeral taken from a distance may be acceptable, but close-ups, which are often more emotionally charged, are not. (On a more pragmatic level, photographs of

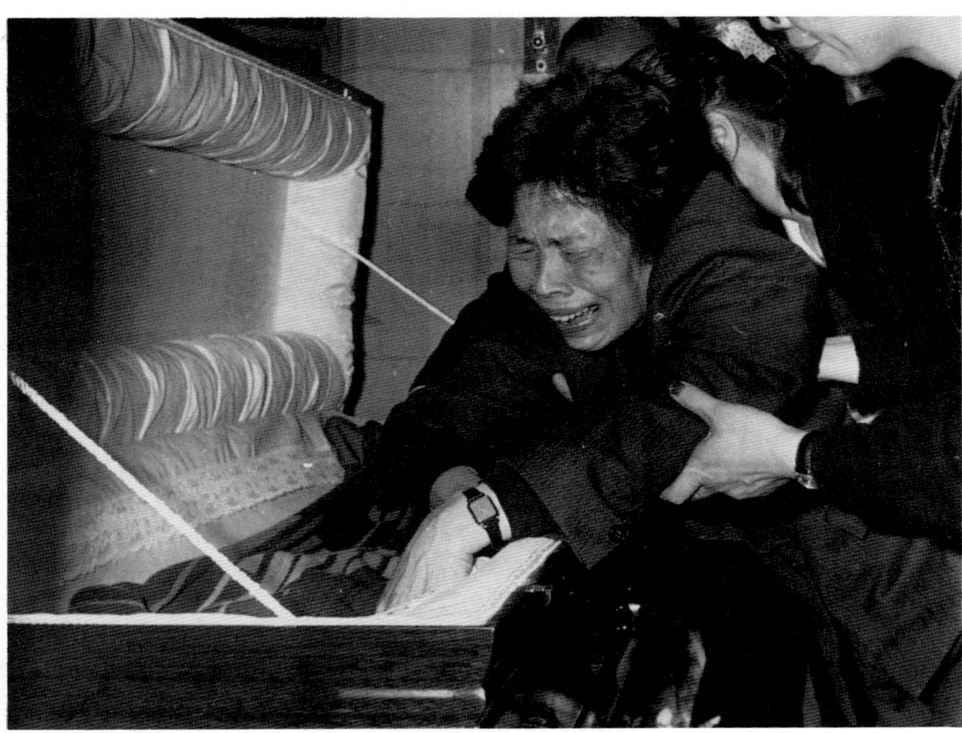

How close is too close? Balancing the public's right to know against the individual's right to privacy is not always easy

animals in distress appear infrequently — readers tend to react strongly to photographs of what could be their own pets.)

But it is often the news-worthiness of the photograph that determines whether or not it will be published. Photographs of the victims of war or of accidents may offend some people but still appear in print. Contentious or sensitive photographs will be considered by all the *Age*'s editors, although ultimate responsibility for their publication will rest with the Editor in Chief.

Ethics and the photographer

Press photographers constantly grapple with the question of how much they should intrude into other people's lives. Do they persist when the subject objects strongly? How close do they get to a funeral? Do they try not to disturb an important meeting or or do they stand up the front, perhaps even using a flash, if that's what it takes to get the best picture? Do they select an angle that flatters or disparages an individual? Should prominent people be photographed in compromising situations? (The *Age*'s view is that politicians, at least, are fair game.)

The Picture Library

The *Age*'s Pictorial Library houses about four million photographs, some of which date back to 1900. All photographs, cartoons and illustrations (from whatever source) that have appeared in the newspaper are filed according to subject. They are cross-referenced by people, country, and other general categories. The negatives are filed separately. They are cut into strips of four, numbered with a white paint marker, stored in cellophane, indexed by number, and filed 'forever'. Unpublished portraits of 'newsworthy' people may also be kept for future use.

The Library exists primarily to serve the needs of the newspaper, and files must therefore be both comprehensive and readily accessible at any hour of the day or night. (The requirement of the last 20 years that the pictorial library staff be professionally qualified librarians has made the system much more efficient.)

The volume of the material handled and the nature of the work demand great accuracy. This remains a paramount concern despite the need for speed.

The library is also a source of revenue for the *Age*. There are many requests for reprints of photographs. Charges for reprints for personal use may range from

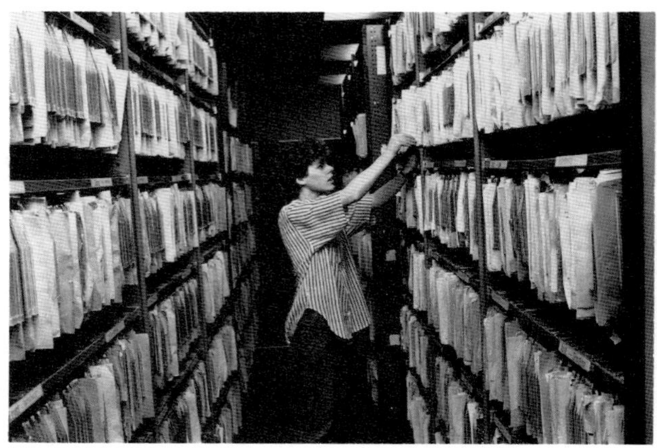

The Age *Pictorial Library*

Before filing, prints are classified and details recorded of when it was taken and the story, if any, that it accompanied

Thousands in city for Palm Sunday

Several thousand people marched though the city yesterday as part of the annual Palm Sunday peace march to support world peace and a healthy environment.

An organiser, Ms Peg Fitzgerald, said the march signalled a new era in people's commitment. "It's a great encouragement to the old-time peace activists to see that more than half the faces are young people," she said.

Ms Fitzgerald said the changes in Eastern Europe had made people realise 'that they had the power to change government decisions.

Marchers gathered in the Treasury Gardens and walked along Bourke Street and Swanston Street, accompanied by live jazz from the Musicians Union motor float and traditional Kurdish music and dancing.

About 1000 people attended a prayer service in St Paul's Cathedral before some joined the peace march. The march was led by Melbourne's lord mayor, Councillor Bill Deveney, and the actor Mr Gerard Kennedy.

Mr Kennedy said that despite the pro-democracy movements in Eastern Europe, Australia's own democracy had failed to eliminate chemical, biological and nuclear weapons, and to care for the environment.

He said that people would have to "make their money talk" by creating a boom in ethical investment (investments which avoided trade with South Africa, uranium mining and environmentally damaging projects) and buying green products.

Youth to the fore: a large number of young people took part in yesterday's Palm Sunday peace march.

PIC 411

PLEASE RETURN TO THE AGE PICTORIAL LIBRARY

Classification AUST: DISORDERS + DEMONSTRATIONS: NUCLEAR VICTORIA: 1990: (PALM SUNDAY RALLY) Published

Date Filed

Neg. No.

Do not cut or fold

$6 to $25. Permission to reproduce a photograph in another newspaper may cost $20, in a book $50, and to reproduce a photograph in an advertisement $100.

As with journalists' by-lines, which credit the writer by name, the *Age* will usually credit a picture to a photographer, but the newspaper retains the copyright (the right to reproduce the photograph). When printed in another publication, the photographer need not be credited, although the paper usually is.

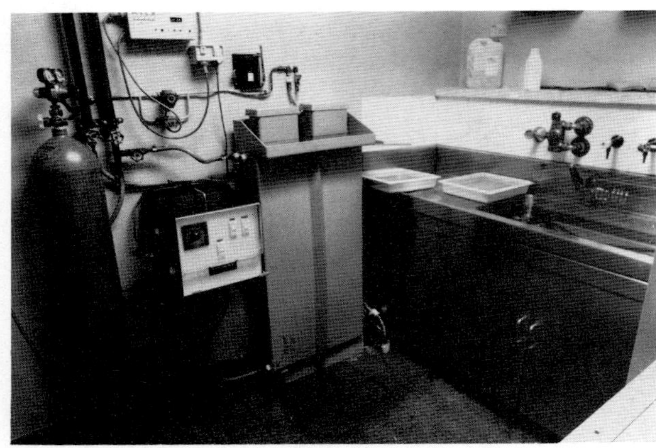

The film developing room. The deep tanks contain developer and fixer which are agitated by gas from the cylinder

The darkroom

The *Age* darkroom, managed by Don Bowler since 1951, has two full-time employees and two cadets. The staff maintains the equipment and replenishes the chemicals and paper. About 10 enlarger bulbs and 50 litres of developer are used each week.

The 12 high-quality enlargers, including Leitz 1C enlargers which are 25 years old and used daily, require little maintenance. The wall-mounted Leitz 2Cs accommodate 2¼ ″ and 35 mm negatives and have been converted to the Ilford Multigrade system along with all the other enlargers. This system obviates the need to use numerous different grades of photographic paper to achieve a range of contrasts.

In press photography, time is of the essence. Therefore, most of the enlargers have automatic focus that adjusts as the size of the enlargement changes. They have two 75-watt globes and the lenses open to f2.8 to increase the brightness and speed of printing.

The photographer may choose between developing trays or an Ilford 2000 autoprocessor which takes 90 seconds from dry to dry. The prints are reputed to have an 18-year archival permanence.

Film processing

The three processing rooms for black and white film boast two TMax developers and one Kodak D76. They are in deep tanks with stock solution that is changed at least weekly. The fixer is also held in deep tanks and is mixed one part to four for strength and speed. There are stainless steel sinks for washing and trays of diluted wetting agent for the final wash.

Outside each room is a timer where the photographer sets the desired developing time. Upon completion a bell sounds that can be heard over the whole floor.

Colour work

Colour first appeared in the *Sunday Age* in 1987 in photographs of the football finals. Although colour film is employed today, in 1987 transparencies (slides) were used.

On Fridays and Sundays all photographers are told to 'shoot colour' in the expectation that a few photographs will make the front or back page or the sports section (the only places where colour is used). For the remaining pages, the photographer, or the platemaking section, will print black and white from the colour negatives.

The colour films used are Kodak Ektapress 100, 400, or 1000 ISO and are developed automatically. The negatives are then processed by a Kodak 'Create a Print' 35 mm enlargement centre which uses the RA4 Rapid Access process with the corresponding paper.

After placing the negative in the machine, the photographer may crop, change the colour bias and/or density and have a finished print within three minutes. The system does not permit any alteration to the image by either burning in or dodging a particular part of the photograph.

The Art Department

Before the selected photographs go to press, the Art Department retouches and scales them to size for the final layout. The captions are also placed on line.

Newspaper art is often used in features and has become very popular. A background in finished art or design is essential for the nine members of the Art Department who may be called upon to illustrate, make diagrams, restore old photographs, or create montages (a combination of images).

Angela Wylie, darkroom cadet, works with a colour enlargement on the Kodak Create-a-Print equipment

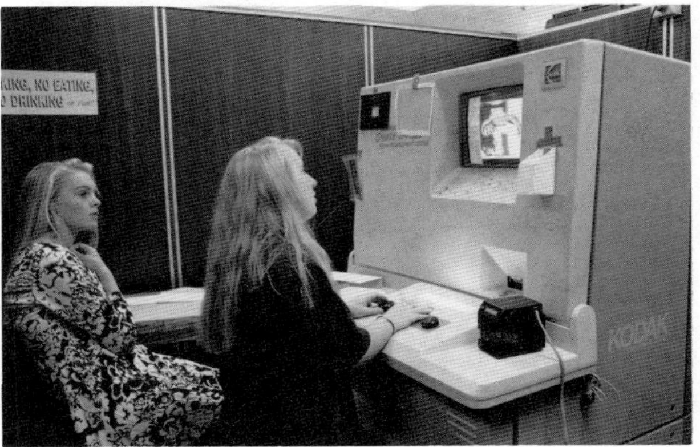

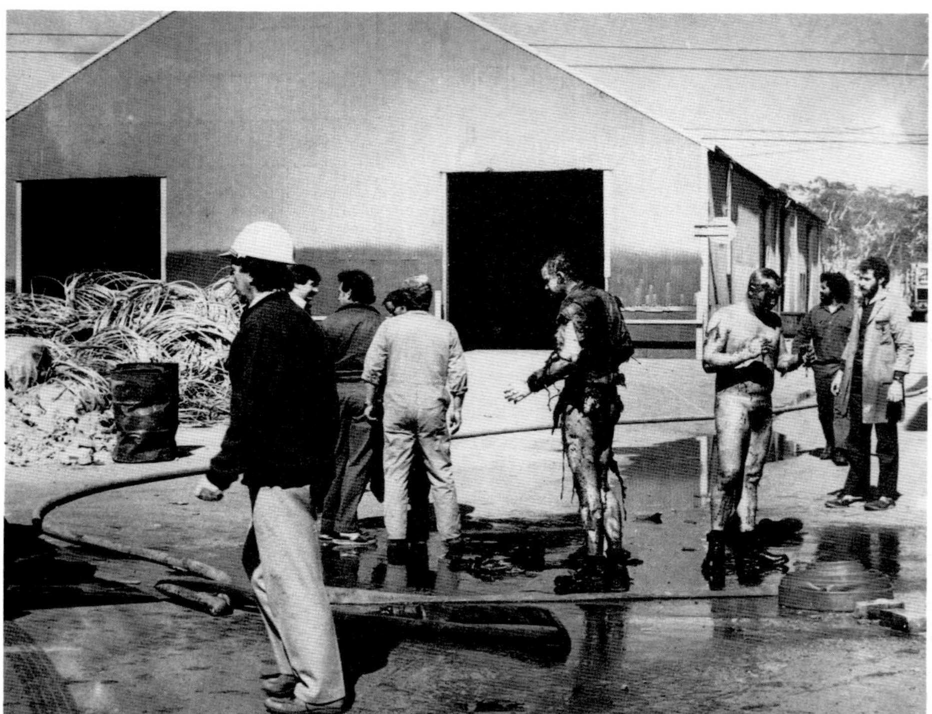

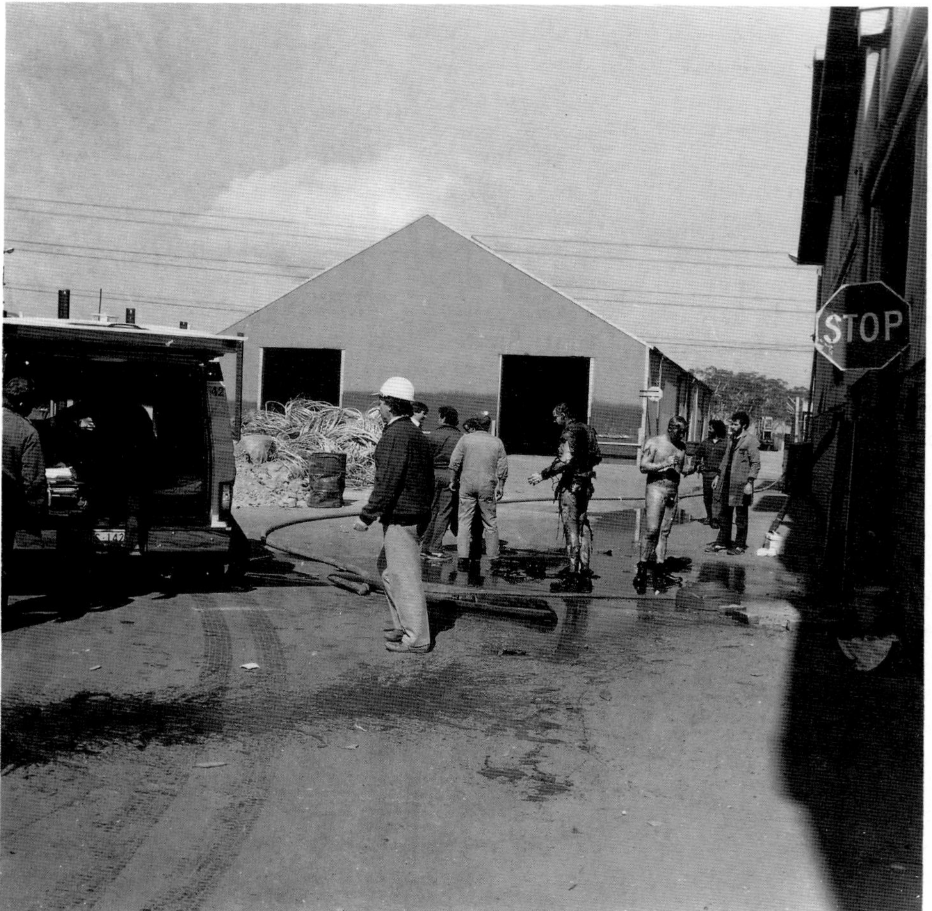

Facing reality

I congratulate 'The Age' on publishing the Simsmetal photo. It is only when we see such happenings we realise the problems encountered. Then too late we do something to stop it happening again. Were the Access writers who were against publication of the photo all women? Can't they face reality?

RAY WOOD,
East Ringwood.

Real life

I support the editorial decision to put the photograph of the Simsmetal blast victims on the front page of 'The Age'. It was a graphic and real piece of journalism. Those who opposed the photo in Access (2/10) should come out of their glass house and learn a little about life outside.

GORDON RIDDELL,
Thornbury.

Do not condemn

We must not condemn an important piece of photojournalism. C. Cozzolino's distressing photo should stop us in our tracks. Let us reassess our own values as employers, supervisors and employees. We can all improve the safety of our fellow worker.

PETER ORMOND,
Essendon.

Improper

I feel it was improper of 'The Age' to print the photograph of the two victims in the Simsmetal furnace accident. I am sure no one would want to be shown naked and in agony. These men would have been unaware that they would be shown in such a state.

ANITA TOZER,
Buller.

Moment in time

Not often do we experience the fragility of human life for the rush of our existence so protects our vulnerabilities. The Simsmetal photograph freezes a moment in our time. It demands some timeless reflection. Remember to take care of that which is irreplacable.

ANDREW BUCHANAN,
North Eltham.

Private hell

'The Age' showed lack of compassion and principle in showing the Simsmetal victims in their distress. We can all imagine what people must suffer in such circumstances. We don't need to see a photo. It is an invasion of a private hell.

KAY SCOTT,
Croydon.

Cropping

Cropping is usually done by the editors, although the pictorial department is involved whenever possible. Photographers would prefer to control the final shape of their images, but this may not be possible when the layout is changed in later editions to incorporate additional news items.

Cropping affects the overall design of the photograph and can sometimes change its meaning. Wherever possible, the editors try to retain the original shape of the photograph.

Layout

The *Age* began publication in 1854 and for the first 50 years had very few illustrations of any description. By the early 1900s, the occasional inside advertisement contained an illustration. It was not until the 1940s that illustrated advertisements (particularly for Capstan cigarettes) appeared on the front page. Most illustrations were confined to features and special supplements, such as the Centenary Supplement of 1934.

The *Age* employed its first full-time photographer, John Bull, in 1927, and from the 1930s quite small photographs began to appear on the inside pages to illustrate news items. Bull's camera weighed 20 kg and produced images on 8″ x 10″ (203 x 254 mm) glass negatives. 'Action' shots were technically out of the question.

As cameras grew lighter and rolls replaced sheets of film, photographs were easier to take and, by the 1950s, had become an important aspect of front-page layout. The use of photographs was further promoted by the change from hot metal to lithographic printing technology.

In the 1990s, the *Age*'s appearance is clean and bold. The design is more organised and geometric than the piecemeal appearance of the 1960s. The type is bolder and stronger than that in equivalent newspapers overseas, and the photographs are printed larger. A particularly good picture will dominate the front cover. It is rare for more than one front-page photograph to appear. As Editor-in-Chief Mike Smith says, 'If it's a good picture we will use it well'.

The *Age* employed its first design editor in 1980, and since then the number of designers has increased to four. They work primarily on the features sections (Saturday Extra, Tempo, Green Guide, and so on). The 'news' pages remain the province of sub-editors who are equally concerned with layout and typography.

Certain elements that contribute to the overall appearance of the paper are fixed. They include: a seven- or eight-column vertical grid, mastheads, straplines (and any other artwork that appears regularly), and per page advertising levels.

Robin Cowcher, the Senior Designer, describes the designer's role: 'A newspaper designer works with an editor, sub-editor and possibly a photographer or illustrator. Our job is to advise on a visual solution, then to determine the suitability and proportions of the photograph/s or illustration in relation to the amount of text, then to select an appropriate heading type. The page should be inviting, not confusing.

'When selecting a picture to lead a section like Saturday Extra or Tempo, we work closely with the editor and look for a shot which:

- tells its own story, but is clearly related to the text it accompanies and has its own visual integrity;
- is graphically strong;
- is a print of high quality. This is particularly important with colour pictures as the newspaper printing process is of a very high speed and cannot cope with subtleties (too dark or too light);
- is unexpected or unusual.

'One of the major problems is lack of time to reflect and improve a layout or picture. Sometimes you have to sacrifice your personal taste just to get the job done and the page away.'

Cropping a photograph may have a dramatic effect upon both image and message. Carmine Cozzolino's photograph, opposite, of a chemical explosion at Simsmetal, taken from a distance, showed an ambulance as well as victims. When the print was cropped, probably to emphasise the drama of the scene, the ambulance disappeared, the victims became more prominent, and the photographer more intrusive. Carmine Cozzolino felt that the cropping distorted his photograph by implying that the victims were helpless and had been left to bleed. Readers' reactions were mixed

CHAPTER 2

THE PRESS PHOTOGRAPHER'S JOB

The *Age* is known for its quality photography. A policy of avoiding such formula pictures as the scantily clad bathing beauty allows its photographers a more creative licence which, in turn, demands more of them. The photographer must take an interesting and visually expressive photograph that will not only catch the Editor's eye but also amplify the accompanying story.

A city such as Melbourne does not often generate hard news. There are few dramatic traumas or tragedies. Yet, every working day, the Pictorial Editor assigns each photographer up to five jobs which may range from a flower show to a political conference to a chemical accident.

Photographers all prefer the more newsworthy assignments. The front page is their aim. Yet the majority of photographs published appear elsewhere in the newspaper — Saturday Extra, the Good Weekend, Home, Epicure, Sport.

Shooting for Tuesday's Epicure section is one of the least desired jobs as it usually consists of photographing empty restaurants and nervous owners. But even an Epicure job has its pressures — making and keeping appointments, organising film and camera gear, finding the restaurant, dealing with the people on the other side of the lens, and eventually taking the best shot possible.

Photographers must succeed on each assignment, sometimes under adverse conditions: weather, lighting, crowds, competition from other news people, and always in the face of that constant enemy, time. They may have as little as 15 minutes to choose from four rolls of film and produce a perfect print before

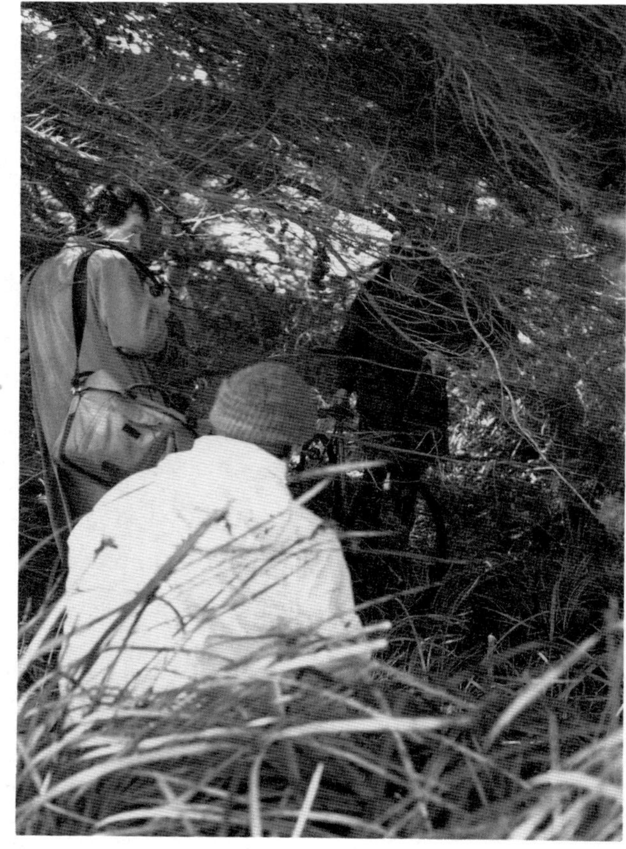

Often the elements are against the photographer. Here, police are searching for the body of a Geelong woman. The dense scrub, and the need not to disturb anything in front of the searchers, compelled the photographer to wait in a clearing until three searchers emerged from the bush

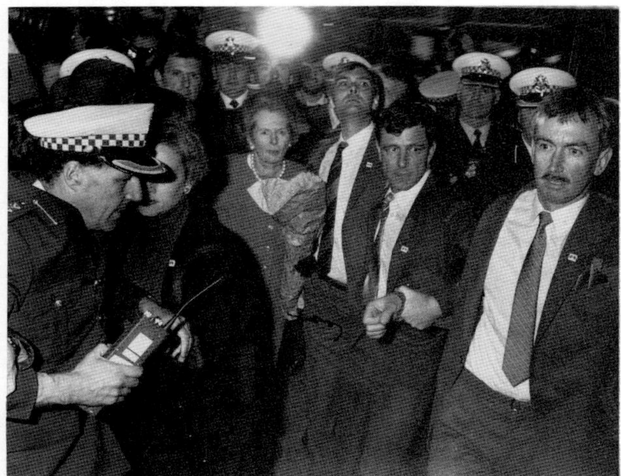

Sometimes simply getting near enough to photograph a subject is very difficult. To get so close to Margaret Thatcher, John Lamb would need to have been quite determined in fending off rival photographers, police and security guards

the 7 p.m. deadline.

There are very few areas of employment where one's work is under such constant assessment. In the course of a week, a photograph in the *Age* may attract the attention of up to a million readers. The 20 staff photographers, as well as the cadets and the darkroom personnel, will all quietly judge the photograph as it is being developed. The editors will huddle around the bench making their selection.

The visual arts are so subjective, so influenced by taste and cultural ideas, that it is hard to know why one photograph is chosen and another rejected. But only about one third of a day's and night's work appears in print.

And when the photographer knows that it is a good picture but has been printed too small or cropped badly or simply does not fit into tomorrow's paper, then a good-humoured flexibility is as much a requirement of the press photographer as technical expertise.

Essential skills

Flexibility The first requirement is the ability to deal each day with new situations, from arranging a meeting to pushing through a crowd to get a picture. The photographer must be able to cope with the pressures of city traffic and constantly changing locations.

Communication The ability to talk with many different people in the course of one day is important. Photographers must introduce themselves and explain their reasons for taking a picture. They must

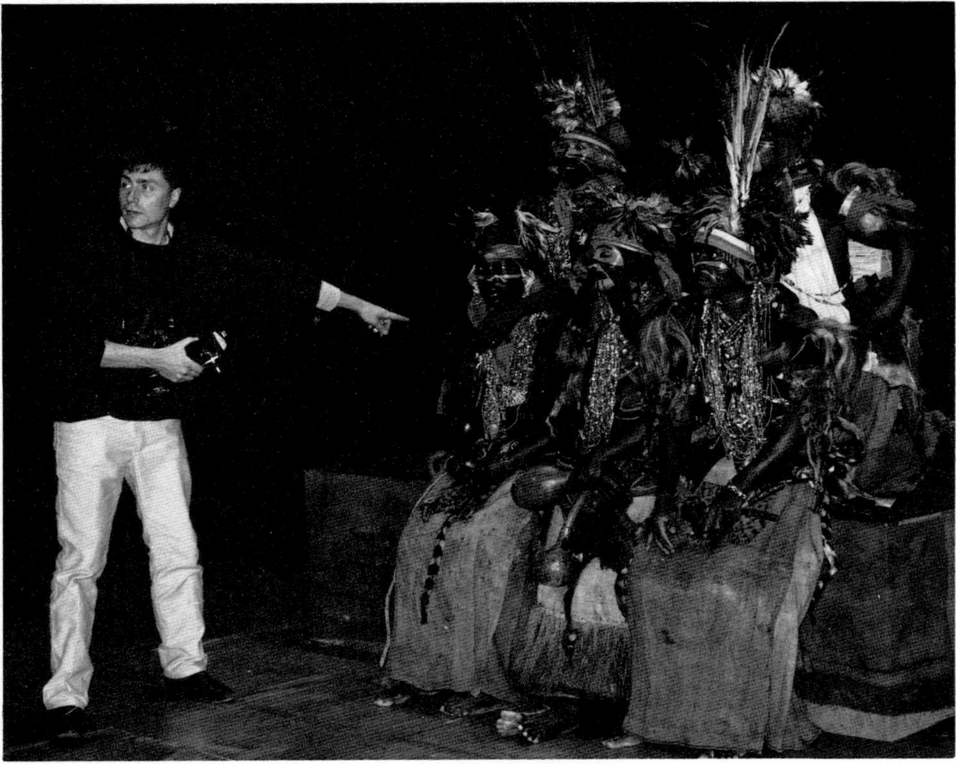

An important skill of the photographer is an ability to communicate with a subject diplomatically but clearly. Here, Sebastian Costanzo asks for help in arranging African Oye musicians who speak a language unknown to him

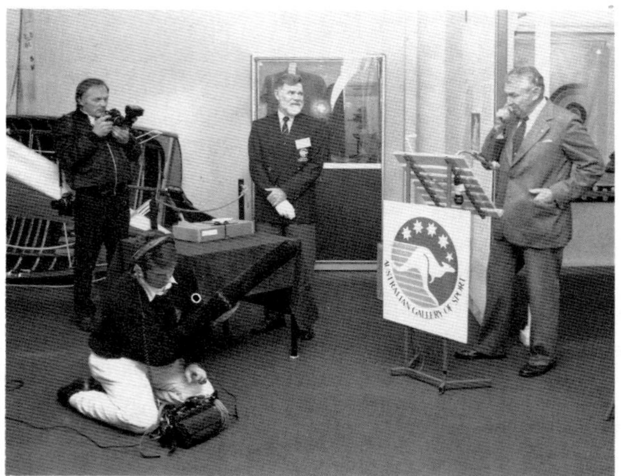

Often the media dominate a situation. Here the 40 guests took a back seat to Bruce Postle and a TV sound technician when Sir Frank Beaurepaire's medals were presented to the Sports Museum by his son

be sufficiently confident to approach total strangers, to negotiate unknown territory and to push their way to the best spot for the best picture.

General knowledge It is essential to have an up-to-date knowledge of such important personalities as politicians, sportspeople, and possibly their near relations. The names of lesser known people must be discovered at the first meeting, recorded accurately and remembered. The photographer must recall whose face goes with each name. Even names of jockeys and horses must be carefully remembered. (A trick that Joe Sabljak uses at the races is to photograph the board prior to each race. This allows him, when he sorts through the negatives of nine races, to identify the horses in each race.)

Preparation Photographers must know their equipment and films and prepare them thoroughly in advance of any job. If possible, they must anticipate the lighting situation and be ready with the appropriate film. (Extremely limited light might require added studio lights or advance checking of flash equipment, although, because of time limitations, photographers try to avoid using either flash or artificial light.)

Seeing On arrival at a job, the photographer must quickly assess all angles and natural light sources. This may involve climbing ladders or trees, crouching, standing tall, or shooting from the viewpoint of an onlooker. Whatever the case, it is essential to find the best position for the photograph.

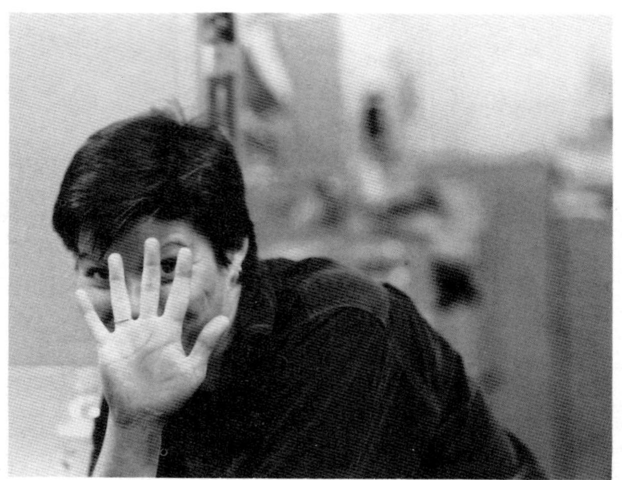

f2 aperture

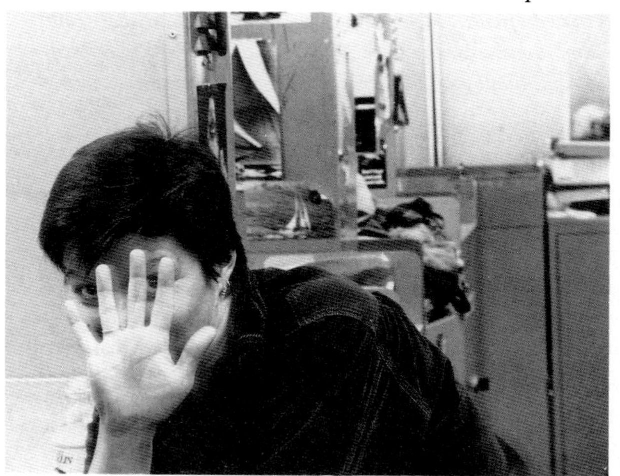

f8 aperture

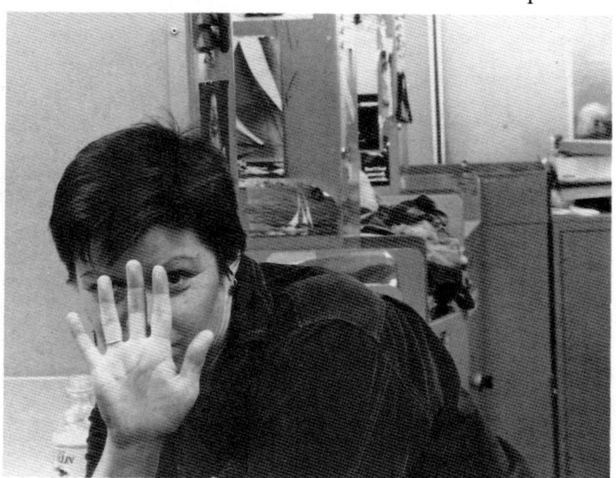

f22 aperture

Three examples of depth of field, or focus, taken by Joe Sabljak of Cathryn Tremain in the Age *Pictorial Department. The depth of focus increases as the aperture closes*

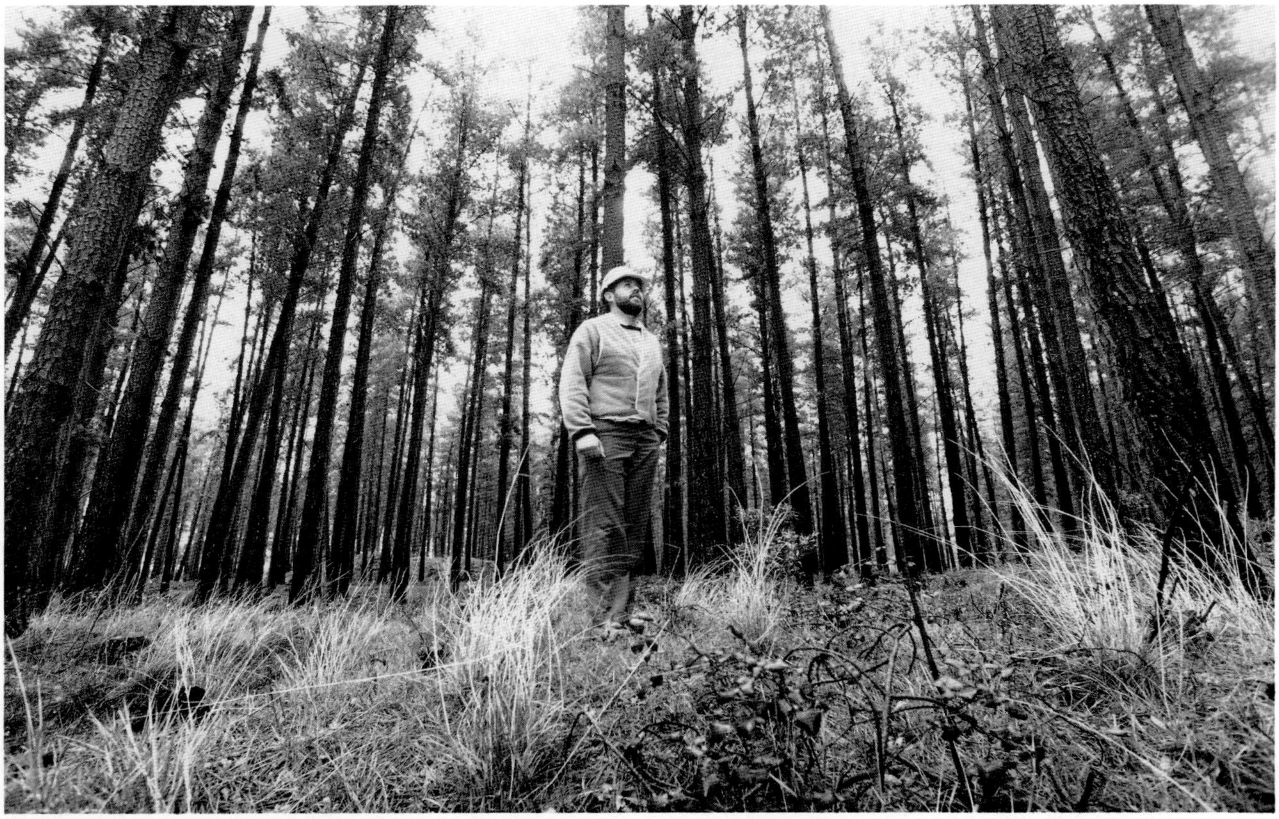

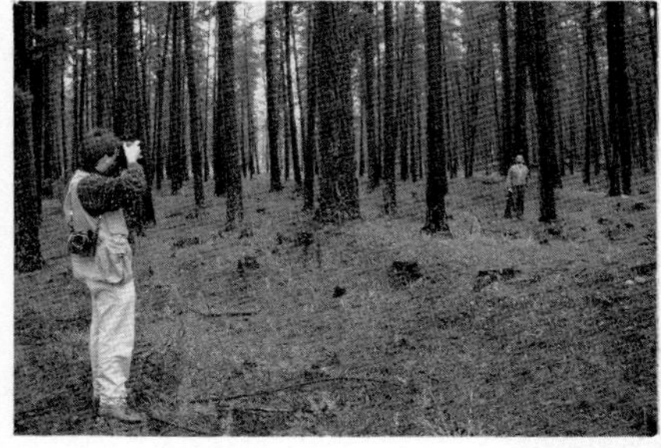

At the top is the photograph that actually appeared in the Age. *Mark Wilson, like most photographers, is prepared to use any and every possible camera angle to get the best shot. This may involve crawling into a hole, asking your subject to do so, climbing a tree, or crouching down just to change the perspective and impact*

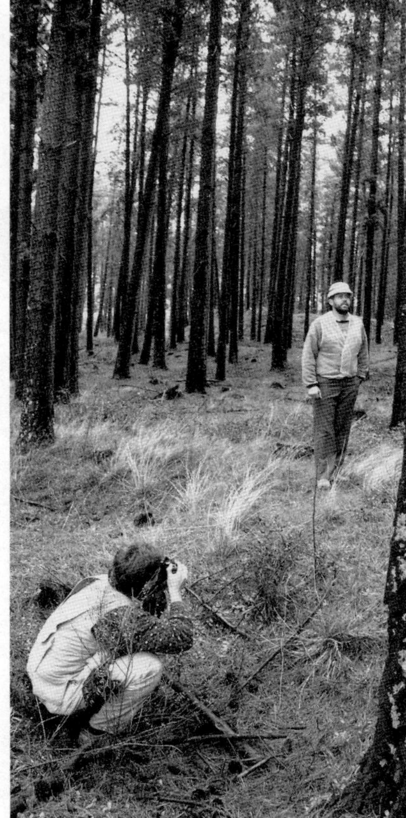

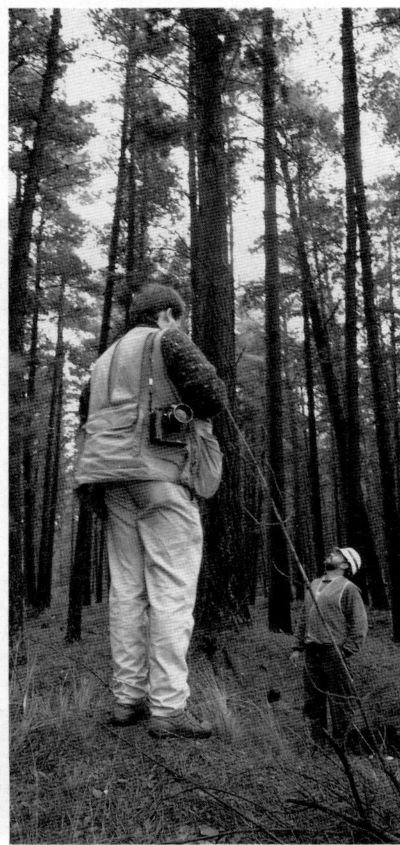

The background should never be ignored — it is part of the picture. There is no way of avoiding background tone, but a change of angle or position may eliminate distracting elements. (There is nothing worse than the limb of a tree protruding from a subject's head. Careful choice of depth of field by changing the aperture will help. A small aperture [f16] will keep details in focus; a wide aperture [f2] will give a background blur.)

Design sense Arrangement or framing of the picture will make or break an image. Using the principles of design will enhance a photograph. The photographer must be aware of the visual elements and organise them in such a way that they interest the viewer.

Principles of design		**Elements of Design**	
movement	rhythm	point	line
balance	harmony	plane	shape
discord	unity	tone	texture
repetition	pattern	colour	form

Camera knowledge It is important to choose the lens best able to produce the shot the photographer has in mind. A lack of space may dictate a wide-angle lens. The angle of view alters with lens focal length. To get the best possible image it is necessary to visualise the final product before shooting.

It is essential to have some acceptable photographs from every assignment to present at the picture conference. To guarantee this, the photographer will usually take a relatively safe and predictable shot at the earliest opportunity and then experiment with more interesting angles or, perhaps, double exposures.

Developing and printing All the *Age*'s photographers develop their own negatives and print the enlargements. They use multigrade photographic papers which enable them to manipulate contrast. If taken in dim light, the photograph may be printed on grade 3½ paper to darken the blacks and lighten the whites. Conversely, lower grade papers (eg grade 1) will be used to tone down sunlight and shadows that are too strong. It is not uncommon to burn in an area such as the sky with a low grade paper and burn in a black-and-white dress in grade 5 to eliminate grey tones. In this way, the photographer can highlight one area and soften another, thus controlling all the tones in an image.

Camera equipment

The *Age* was the first Australian newspaper to change from the larger 120 (2¼" negative) format to the more portable and versatile 35mm format. All its equipment is Nikon 35mm SLR. Even though manufacture ceased in 1979, some of the older F2s are still in use. All the bodies are fitted with a motor drive capable of taking four or five photographs per second. The Nikon lenses are adaptable to both older and newer bodies. There is a pool of special lenses,

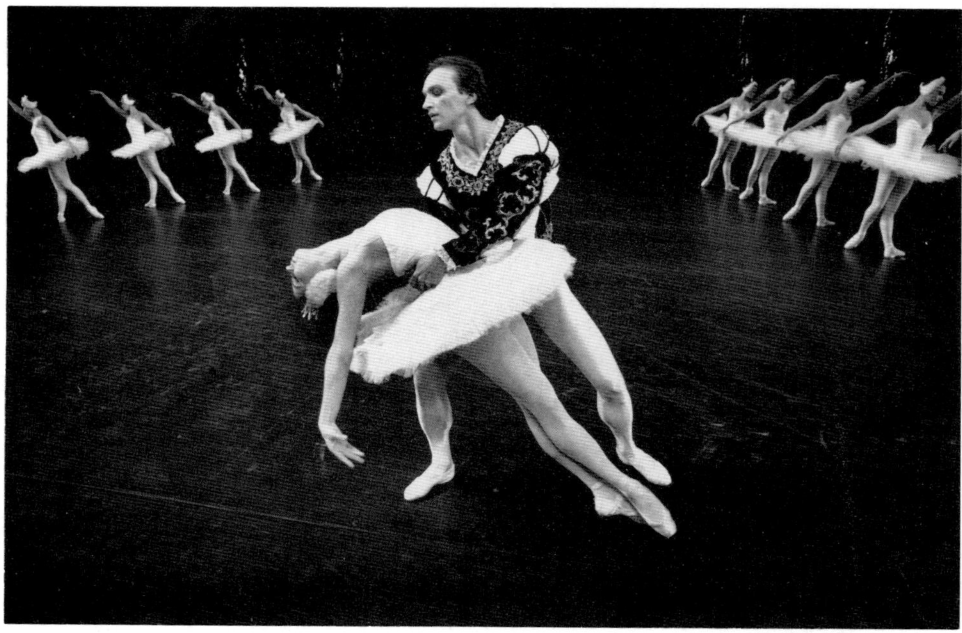

William West used a wide-angle 20mm lens to photograph the Bolshoi Ballet in rehearsal. By having the principal dancers close to him, he was able to capture their expressions while the dancers behind created the atmosphere

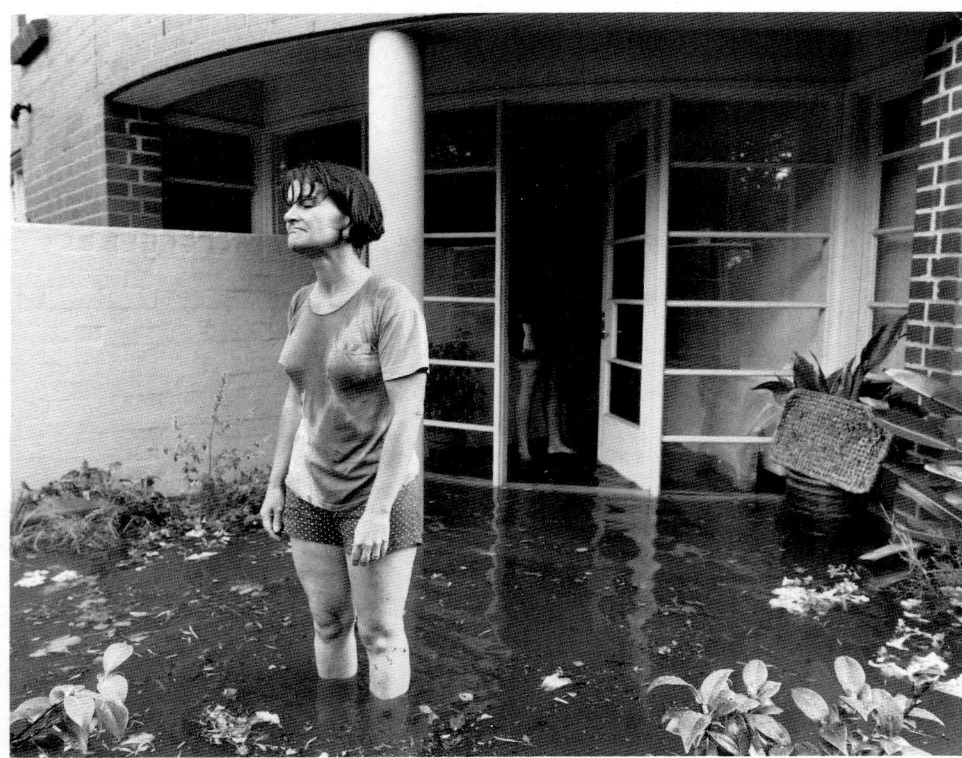

Ray Kennedy chose a 50mm lens to capture the emotions of a Middle Park resident when her house flooded. This 'normal' lens gives viewers the feeling that they are present, seeing what the photographer sees

cameras, and filters that photographers may book out for particular jobs. This specialised gear includes 600mm lenses, filters, accessories, and an underwater camera.

The photographer's basic kit is suitable for most situations and usually consists of two camera bodies and four or five lenses: one wide-angle lens (20mm-28mm), one standard lens (50mm), two portrait lenses (80mm-180mm), and one telephoto lens (300 mm-400mm).

20mm lens This lens is favoured for capturing the surrounding environment and providing a wider and more detailed background. Because its angle of view is 100 degrees, it can be used in a confined space, such as a lounge room or office. The apparently greater depth of field will give clarity in both the foreground and the background.

Most press photographs are of people. The photographer will often move close to the subject (but not so close as to distort the subject's face) so that, when a 9cm-wide photograph appears in the newspaper, detail is not lost. The wide-angled lens still permits the background to have some impact.

The standard lens (45mm-55mm) The standard lens corresponds most closely to the angle of view of the human eye (45 degrees). It tends to produce a flatter image than the wider-angle lenses and is not particularly useful for capturing surroundings or for portraits taken from a distance of more than two metres. (The *Age*'s photographers rarely use it.)

The medium telephoto/portrait lens (80mm-135mm) The 80-135mm lenses are extremely useful for the newspaper photographer. The medium telephoto lens enables the photographer, while remaining at a distance, to capture a detailed portrait without the camera crowding or frightening the subject.

Because the perspective changes with an angle of view of 25 degrees (half that which the human eye encompasses), the background appears to be closer to the subject. The depth of focus is also reduced with this lens. With careful choice of aperture (f2.8 for a small depth of field), photographers can blur the background into insignificance if they wish to emphasise the face.

By choosing a longer depth of field (f11-f22) and focusing carefully, the photographer can shorten the perspective and bring the distant background closer to the subject which remains in reasonable focus.

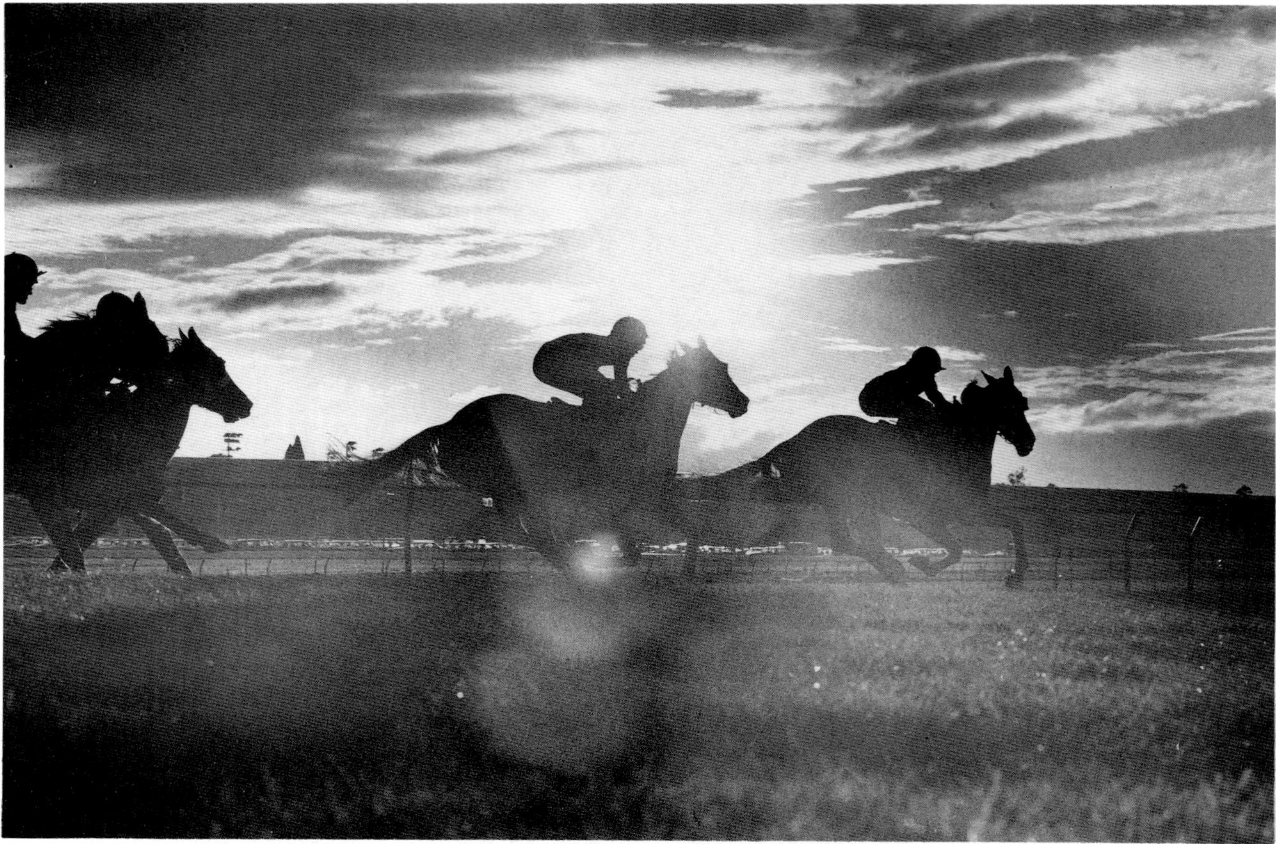

Geoff Ampt photographed the last race at Moonee Valley with an 85mm lens. It allows the photographer to be at a reasonable distance from the subject yet not lose impact

The long telephoto lenses (300mm-600mm)

Although the long lenses are heavy and awkward to use, they are a necessary part of the press photographer's equipment. Without them it would be impossible to photograph a cricket stroke or a politician's expression from a distance of more than 20 metres. These long lenses have changed the way we view sport — we no longer see the whole ground, instead we concentrate on the ball and individual's actions.

The longer lenses weigh between 4kg and 8kg, and photographers may stand for up to four hours seeking the perfect shot. Their task is made no easier by many sporting grounds forbidding the use of monopods or tripods (one- or three-legged stands) because of the dangers of players colliding with them.

The 300mm lens has an 11-degree angle of view; the 500mm lens's is five degrees, so both view only a small area. The photographer must follow a game tirelessly in case something important happens. A quick pace and frequent change of direction obliges the photographer to pull-focus each picture. One hand is usually kept on the focusing ring and the other on the shutter-release button.

The longer lens is not restricted to sporting events. It allows the photographer to remain at a distance and still capture a subject's face. This results in the more natural, unposed image most photographers prefer.

Flash and lighting equipment

Each of the *Age*'s photographers has a Metz flash 45 CT1-4 and a battery pack and chargers. They also have access to a Metz studio portable kit which includes two heads, stands, reflective umbrellas, and a synchronised flash.

When shooting in black and white in limited light, the photographers often use faster films (1000-3200 ISO) rather than flash. But, as the newspaper uses more and more colour, flash and studio lights become more necessary to compensate for poor daylight or for the colour bias of tungsten household lightglobes or fluorescent light (which gives a sickly green tinge). They will bounce the flash off any

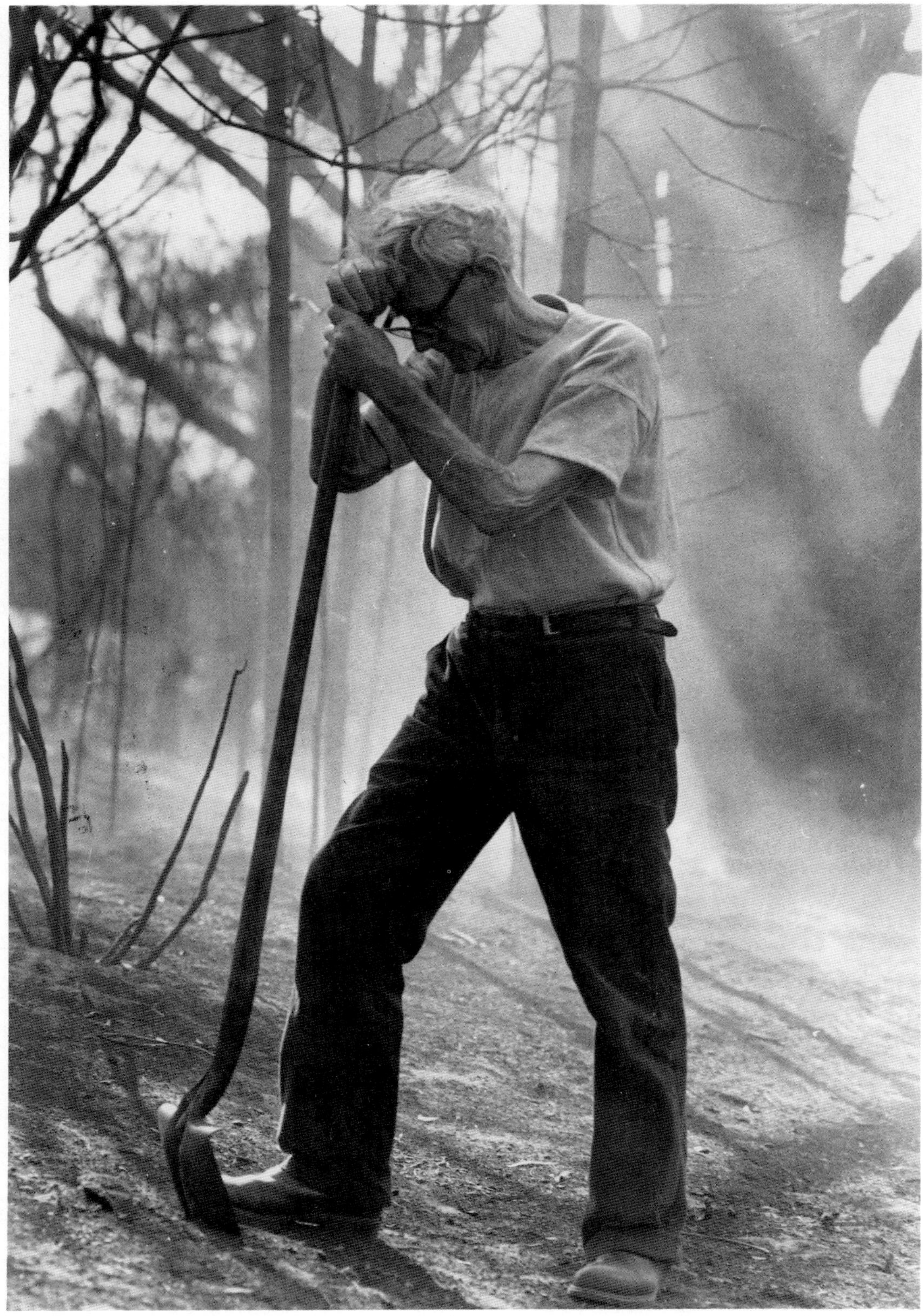

Bruce Postle shows Jack Blackburn's despair as he leans on his shovel when his garden has been reduced to ashes after 60 years of loving labour. The use of the 135mm lens allowed Bruce to remain sufficiently far away so as not to intrude

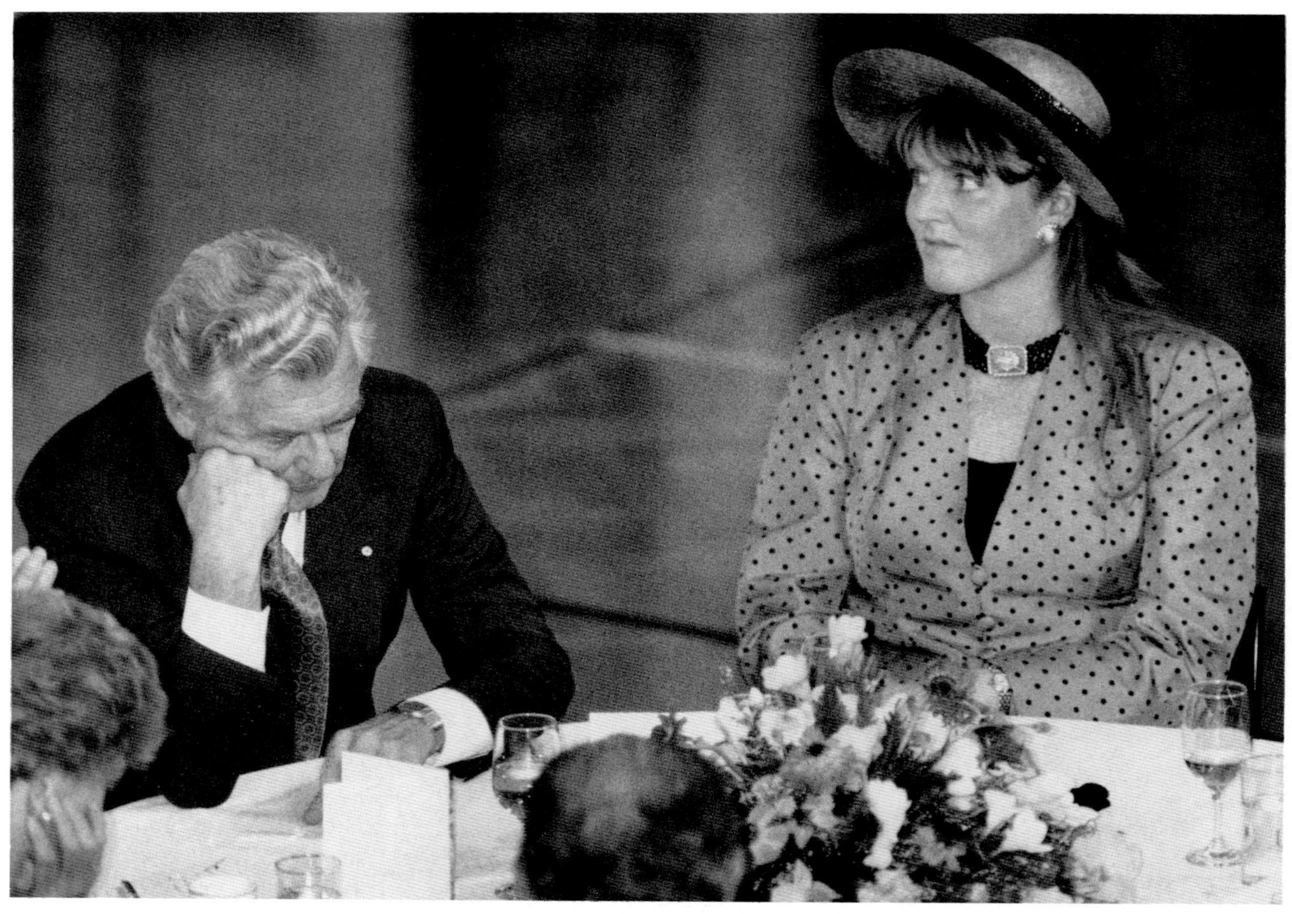

Photographer Cathryn Tremain was able to catch Bob Hawke and Fergie in an off-guard moment by using a 300mm lens from across the room

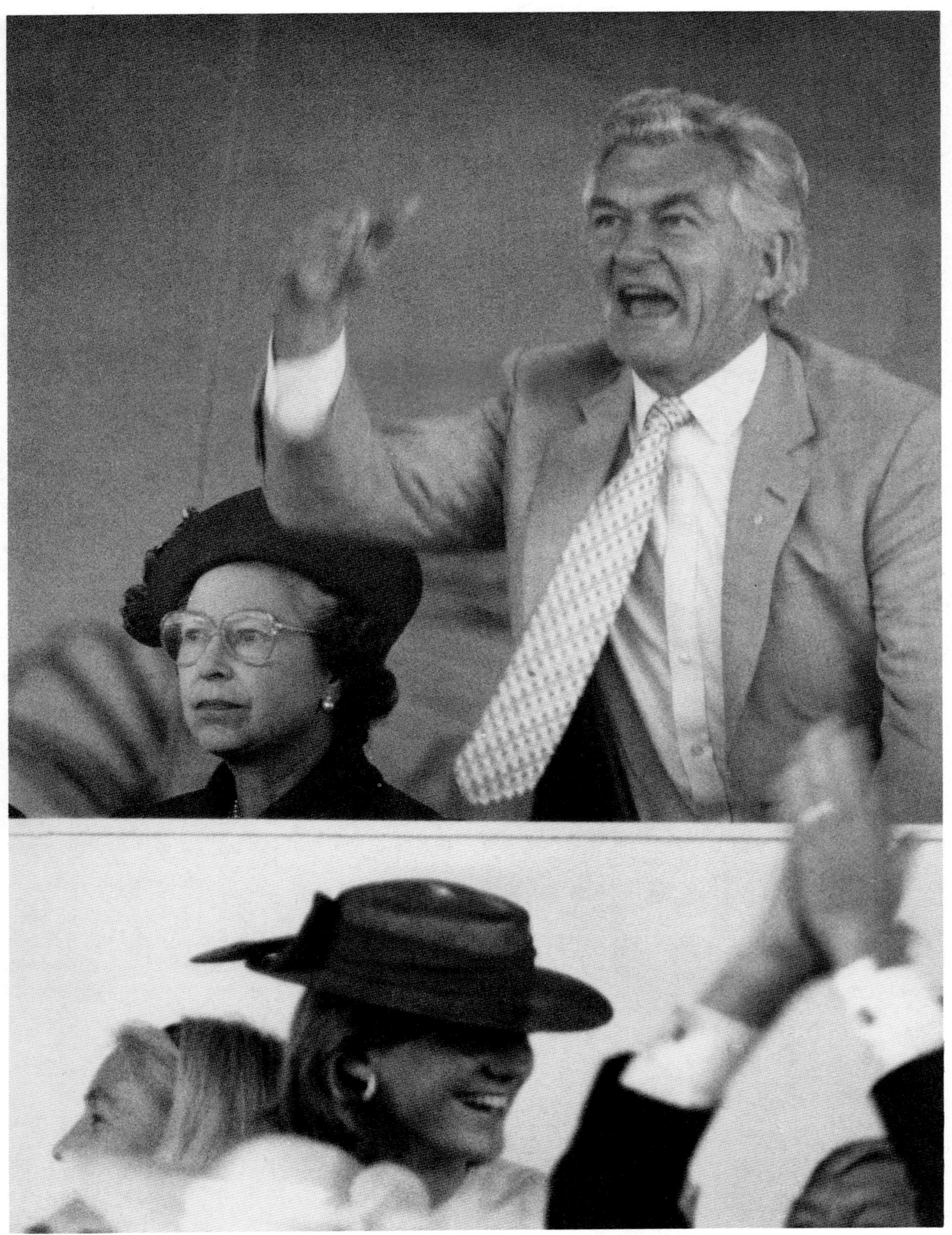

Bob Hawke's money was on the winner, the Queen's on the runner-up. Bruce Postle used a 600mm lens to capture the moment

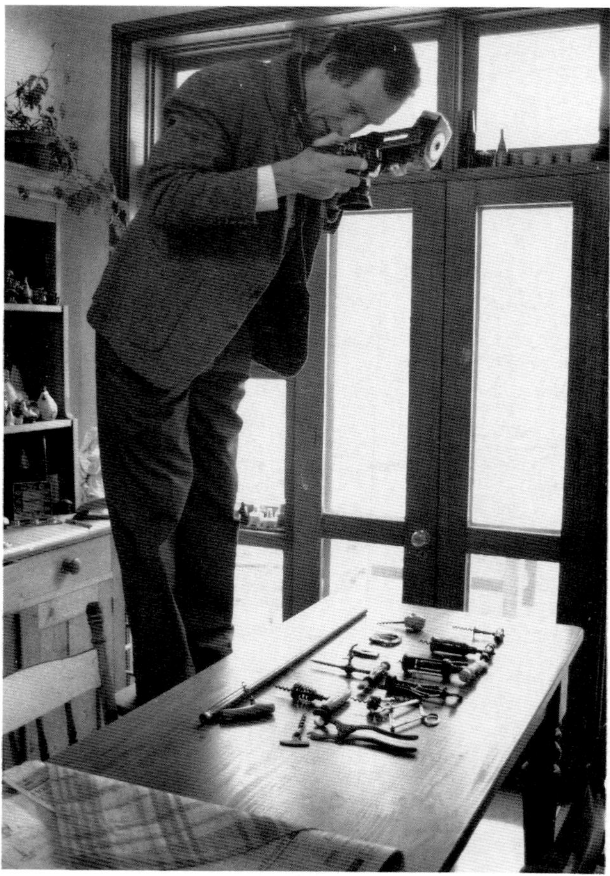

It is sometimes very difficult to use flash in an enclosed area. An experienced photographer such as Andrew De La Rue will use a variety of techniques. Direct flash can be too harsh and create shadows. Here he bounces the flash off the ceiling to photograph a collection of corkscrews. Prior to that he had the owner hold up a newspaper at one side so that he could bounce the flash off that

Cathryn Tremain using the studio Metablitz kit to photograph Rats of Tobruk

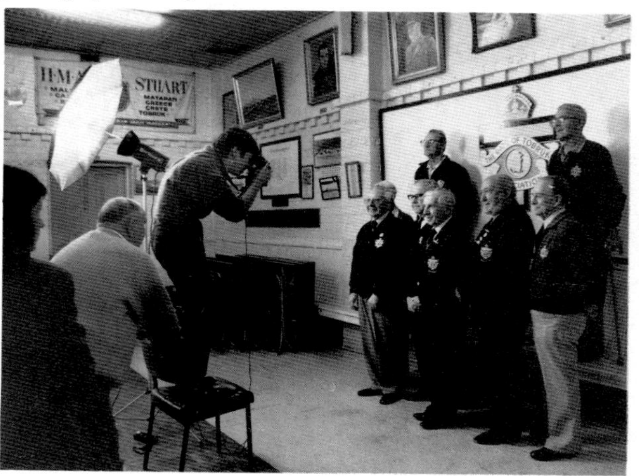

surface, often having to improvise with a piece of paper or side wall to avoid the harsh shadows of a direct flash.

Film Film quality has improved markedly over the last decade. Improvement in crystal formation has resulted in greater resolution and more definition with less grain. Even under poor light conditions, the higher ISO films still possess a clarity of image that would have been impossible ten years ago.

The most popular film is Kodak's T-Max Professional which is rated at 100, 400, and 3200 ISO. 400 ISO is the most versatile as it can be rated at 800 or 1600 ISO and developed longer. This is also true of Ilford's HP5 and Kodak's Tri-x, and some photographers prefer these films. T-Max 3200 produces a very acceptable result even in a dimly lit room or a street at night.

Colour film is processed by a Kodak Flexi-colour machine which is set up for Kodak Ektapress film rated at 100, 400, or 1600 ISO.

Changing technology

After developing a negative amd making a print, the next step is to scan the photograph into a form suitable for printing on a newspaper press. The image is broken down into a collection of dots — darker areas will have more dots than lighter areas — so that continuous tones become gradations of very small dots. In newspaper photographs these dots are far larger and more apparent than they are, say, in books, although the process is essentially the same.

But this procedure is changing, and it is now possible to dispense with negative and print entirely. Kodak have developed a system whereby a special back is attached to a Nikon 3 camera. It can store in digital form up to 600 images, either in black and white or in colour. These digitised images can be transferred by telephone to anywhere in the world and be seen on screen within seconds of being shot. The image can then be enhanced, manipulated, or cropped on screen as necessary.

What makes a photograph 'good'?

Good newspaper photography is subject to the same considerations of composition, balance and design as any other form of photography, but there are, nevertheless, several special requirements.

A black-and-white print should be slightly softer than an exhibition print because it will print in the newspaper with more contrast. Faces should appear slightly lighter than usual, as they can lose definition and darken on the printing press.

Colour prints should contain as much detail as possible and be true to the actual colour. It is important to avoid an excess of blue. When printed on newsprint, blue can be very dominant.

Characteristics of good newspaper photographs

Image Newspapers want a photograph that, because of its story content or its design, is striking and eye-catching. A front page photograph need not accompany a story if it is bold enough to attract the reader's attention. Whether an article appears on the first, third or eleventh page may be determined by the quality of the relevant photograph.

Statement This is the story or idea behind the visual image. It is what the photograph says to the reader. It is an old adage that pictures speak louder than words — they are a universal language that can wrench the emotions and evoke feelings common to us all.

Use of the camera Whether the subject is shown crying, smiling or frowning obviously influences how the viewer interprets a photograph. But there are other less obvious but equally important considerations. The choice of camera angle is one. (When photographed from below, a subject seems larger than life, strong and dominant; from above, the subject appears less threatening.) The position and intensity of the lighting is also important. (Back filtered light creates a romantic effect, harsh sunlight is more dramatic, as is early morning and late afternoon light.)

Design A well designed photograph will hold the viewer's interest. Considerations such as balance and composition are important. The photographer must be aware of the visual elements of point, line, plane, texture, shape, form, and negative space (the area around the subject). Positioning lines at different angles influences where viewers look next as their eyes follow the lines to see where they go.

Repetition is another tool to keep the viewer reading a photograph. The eye tends to jump from one white tone to another, from one circle to another.

The careful use of space is another aspect of good design. The space surrounding an image is as important as the image itself. The photographer must ask whether it is an interesting shape or whether it encloses the image too closely and makes the viewer feel uncomfortable.

The background should not be so intrusive that it detracts from the main subject. Does it contrast with the image or does it interfere?

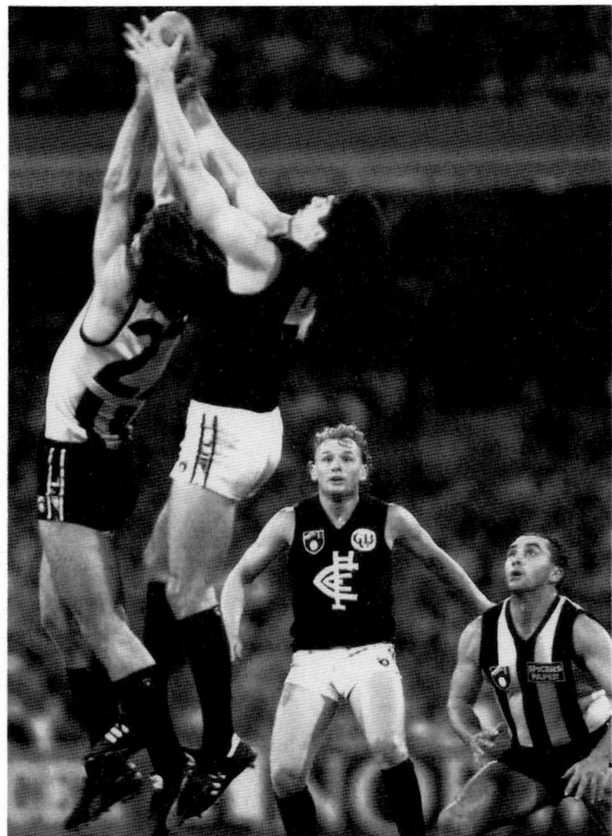

A digital photograph taken with the Kodak Professional Digital Camera System (DCS). The digital separation of tones (in a black and white photograph) or colours appears as large grain. Ray Kennedy took this photograph during the May 1992 Collingwood Centenary Match

Balance is another aspect of good design. Does the image sit on the page comfortably? Does it seem lop-sided or about to fall over? Is the main subject balanced by the use of the negative space or another object?

Image quality Is the main subject in acceptable focus? Are there details in the photograph where they are needed? Is it interesting enough to retain the viewer's attention?

Print quality A print should be clean and free from scratches and large dust particles. Most black-and-white photographs should have a variety of tones ranging from a rich black through to crisp white. Tonal range is also important in colour photography. A contrasting range of colours is usually preferred (a strong, cool colour against a bright, warm one increases the intensity of both).

A Newspaper's Timeline

Editorial		Pictorial
	7.45 am	
Chief of staff arrives and reviews the news of the day by scanning the overnight news		The Pictorial Coordinator checks news broadcasts and morning newspapers for ongoing stories and ideas which might make good pictures
Draws up news list (local, state, and national)		Gives assignments to photographers rostered on early (if not given jobs the previous day if aware of special events)
	9.30 am	
Story ideas are put forward and discussed at Morning Conference with six editors		Picture ideas are put forward and news ideas exchanged 100 prints and picturegrams are processed in the Pictorial Library
	10.00 am	
Chief of Staff assigns reporters to various jobs as they begin shifts The Roundsmen brief the Chief of Staff		Pictorial Manager assigns photographers to jobs Journalists request photographers to accompany them
	1.30 pm	
News Editor arrives and takes over and checks the wire copy and begins a ring-around of the bureaus to find out how stories are shaping up		Pictorial Editor contacts other newspapers across Australia for photographs Grams from overseas are assessed
	2.00 pm	
Assistant News Editor arrives. Journalists brief him/her on their stories		Photographers are contacted via 2-way radio or car/mobile phone to monitor their progress and send them to other jobs
	5.15 pm	
A page list is prepared for the Evening News Conference		Photographers return to complete developing and printing
	6.00 pm	
Evening News Conference begins where all the day's main news and feature stories are brought before the conference and their importance discussed The Editor decides on page 1 and 3 stories		Pictorial Editor attends the Evening News Conference
	7.00 pm	
Sub-editors work on general section and layout. They liaise through the night with the editorial and production staff		Picture Conference begins where pictures are examined and selected by six editors. Space, the strength of the articles that goes with the photographs, and the quality of photograph itself are assessed
	12.00 am	
	1st edition is off the presses. (It goes interstate and to the country areas.)	
Often the first few pages are re-jigged for the next edition to accommodate breaking news stories.		Late shift photographers continue until 2.30 am
	1.30 am	
	2nd edition is printed	
	3.15 am	
	Final edition is completed	

CHAPTER 3

THE PRESS PHOTOGRAPHERS' WORK

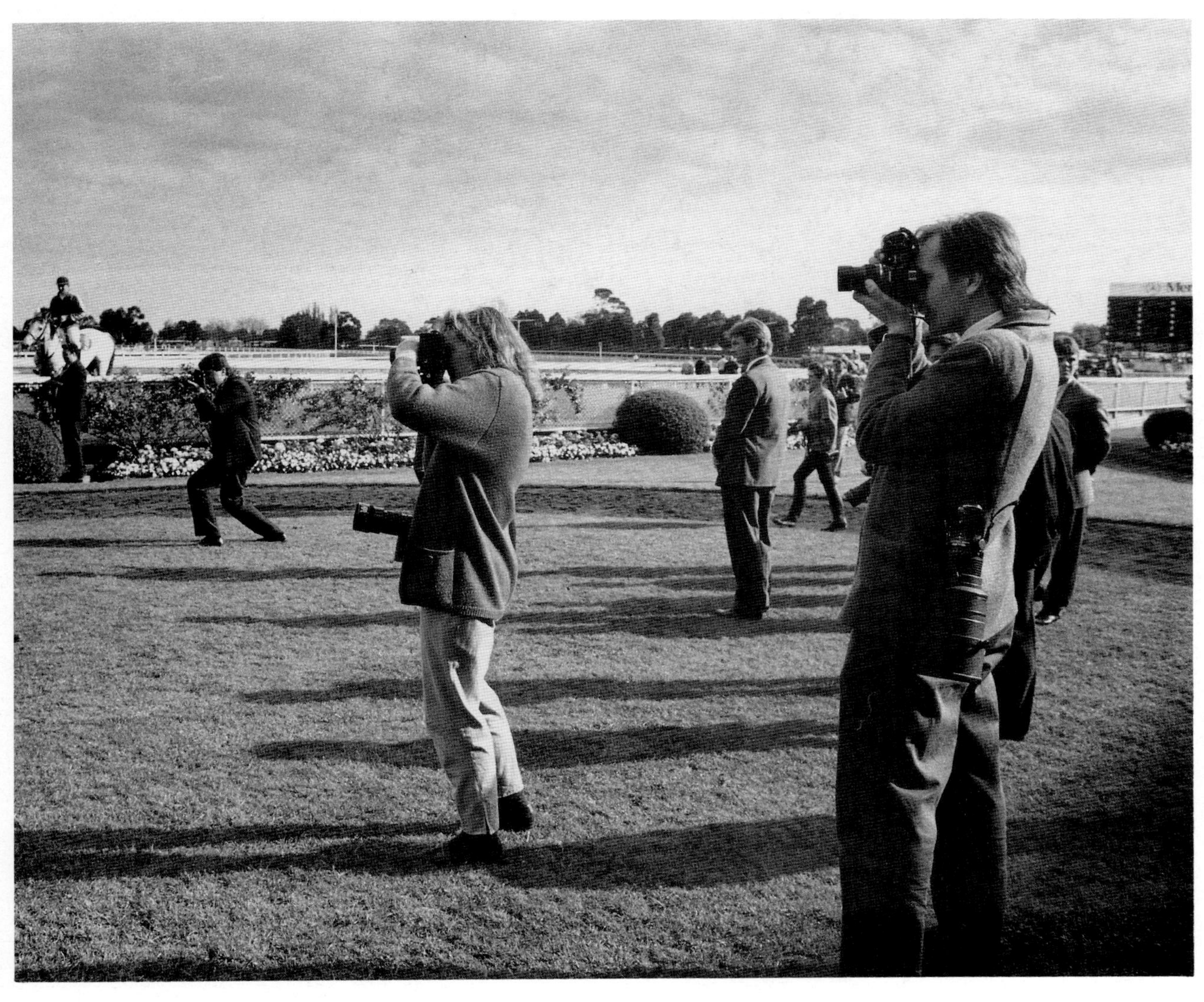

Craig Abraham

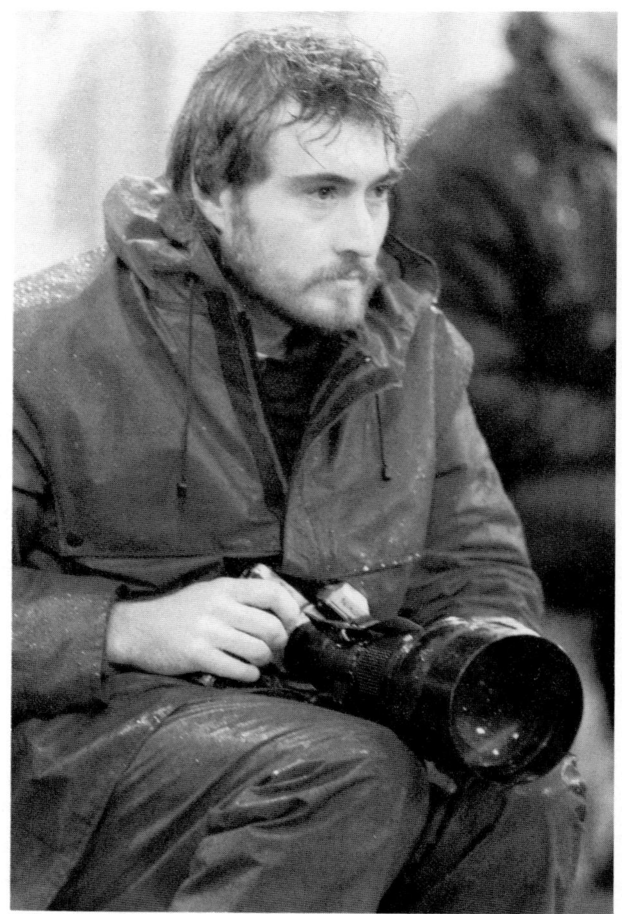

'I have no basic rules about the game, but I believe that photos should be taken as they happen. I don't feel the compulsion to make something exciting if it's not.

'I might move people to where the background and the light are good, but then I let them do their own thing. I try to get candidness into the photograph. It's my aim to capture people as they are. If people do not cross their arms, I will not ask them to.

'My preference is for the classic portrait, where I am one-to-one with the subject. Ideally, I like to sit in on an interview to find something about that person that would make a wonderful picture.

'Approaching a job without preconceived ideas allows me to assess people as I meet them. Each photograph is fresh. I don't think that I have the right to contrive pictures and give the reader a false illustration.'

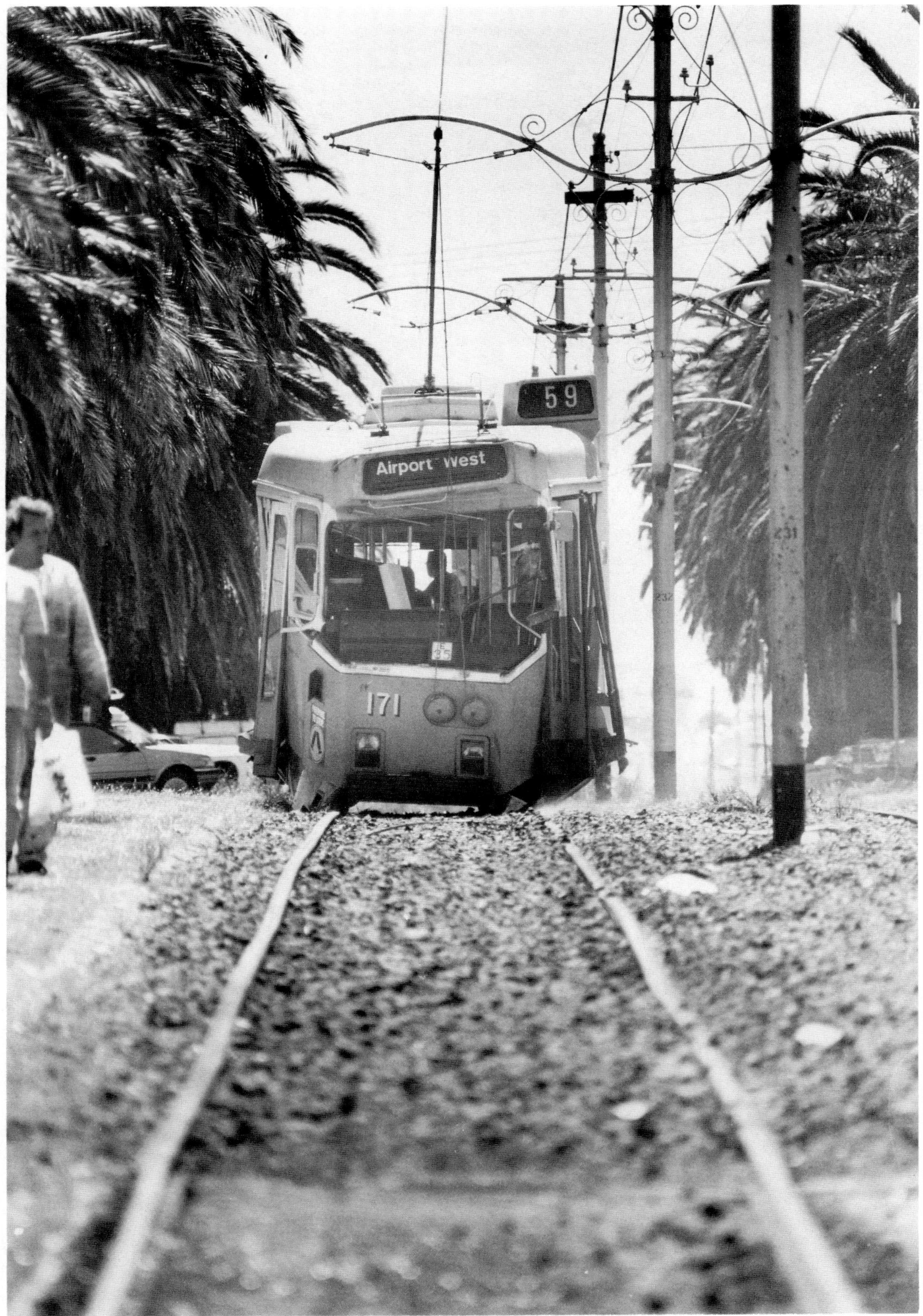

I was heading into work when I was told that two trams had been involved in a collision. I took pictures of injured people and the interlocked trams, but it was when the trams were separated that I realised that not only was the tram bent, but the tracks were also. What caught my eye was the absence of straight lines. (Nikon F3)

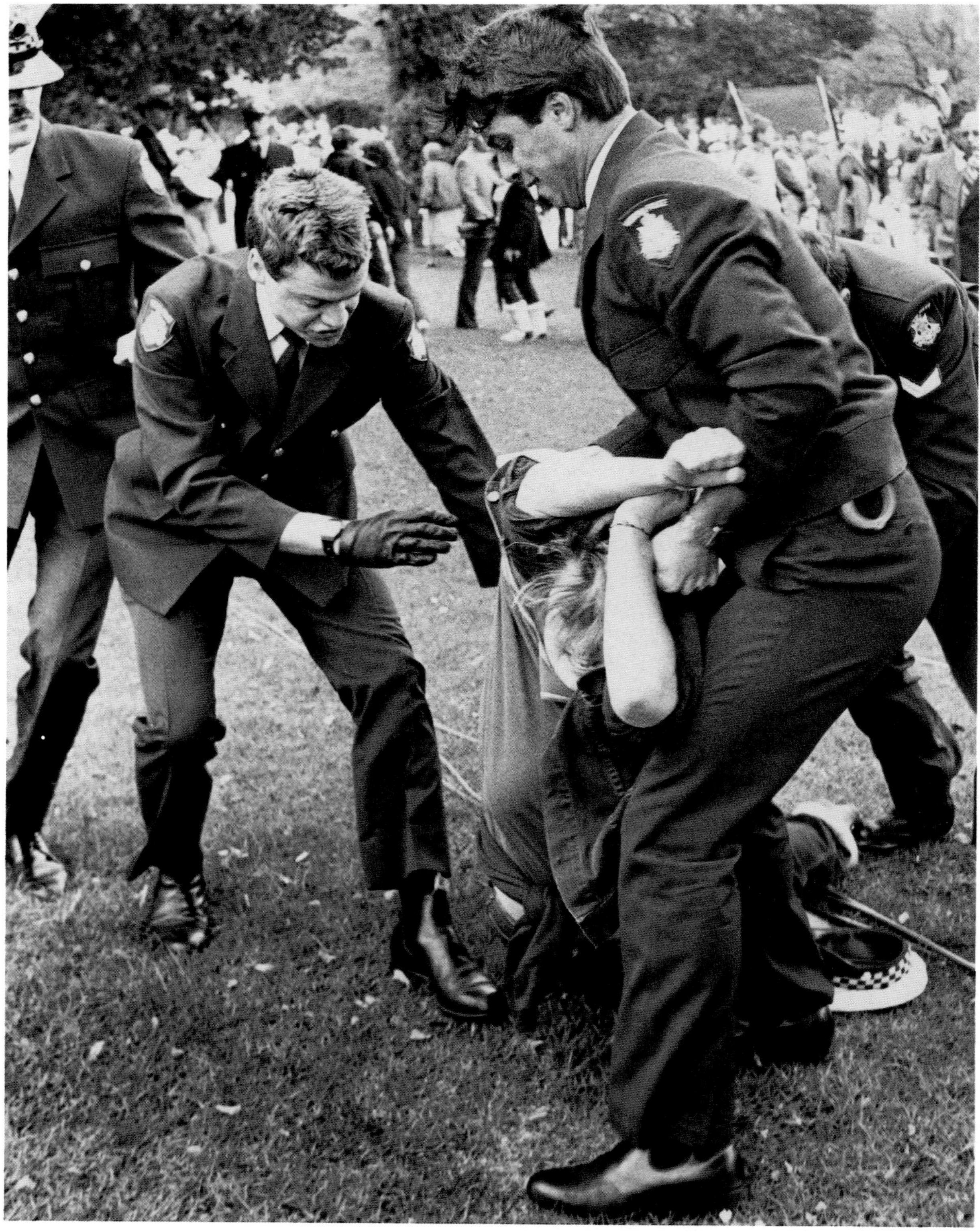

ANZAC Day. As usual there were protests. This person's views about rape in war were not taken lightly by the police. (Nikon F2)

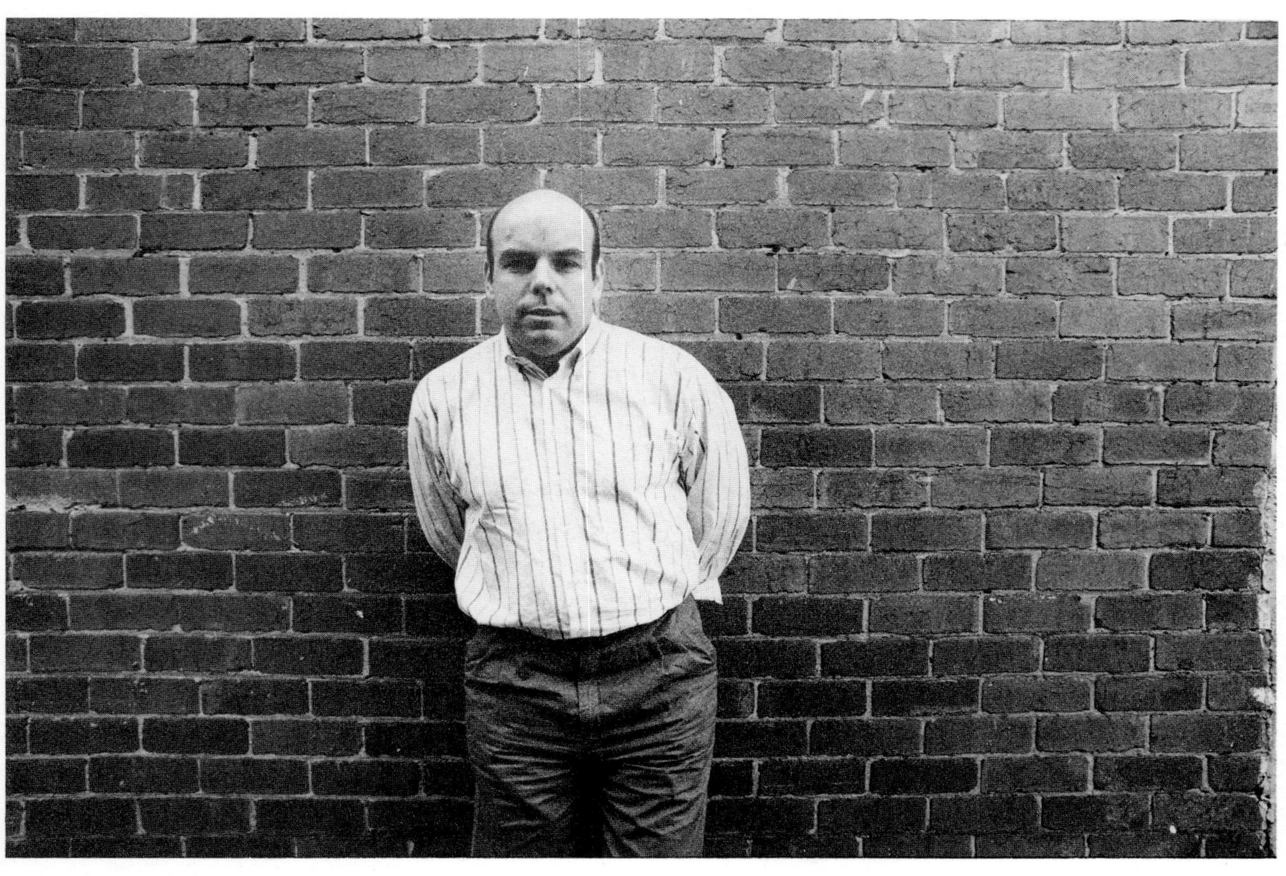

John Friedrich, former head of the NSCA. I had only one opportunity for this shot, so I lifted up the camera and fired. I thought I had taken three frames, but Friedrich said, 'Four is enough'. He was right. He impressed me with his reply as my camera can take five frames per second. The brick wall was there as I had encountered him in an alley way. (Nikon F4)

Geoff Ampt

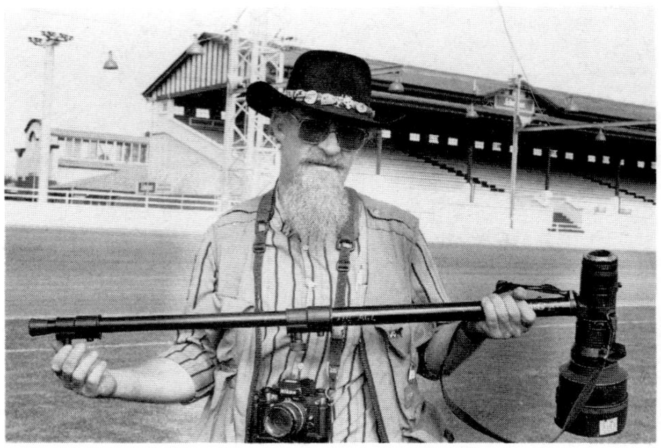

Photo: Linda Lees

Geoff Ampt started with the *Age* in 1972 and since 1985 has been the principal racing photographer.

'You must always keep your eyes open for an interesting shot. Mostly, you are photographing horses, yet there are lots of possible ways to do that.

'During the Spring Carnival — the 6-8 weeks from football to the Melbourne Cup — I usually go to the track at 5 am, seven days a week. I need to know all of the important horses, trainers and jockeys. There is no point taking a photo if you cannot identify the horses when you get back to the darkroom. Knowing the jockey's colours can be the only identifying mark that you have to work from. During the trackwork, you don't even have that.

'In 1989, with the start of the *Sunday Age*, the Sports Editor, Pat Smith, changed from wanting just the finish of the race. It left it open for me to try other ways of seeing racing. I'm not restricted to the finish line alone.

'I enjoy the work for the thoroughbred breeding column. It allows me to visit stud farms and see the newly born foals.

'I most often use a 600mm lens as it is difficult to get too close to your subject. I've recently gone back to Tri-x after finding T-Max a bit too contrasty.'

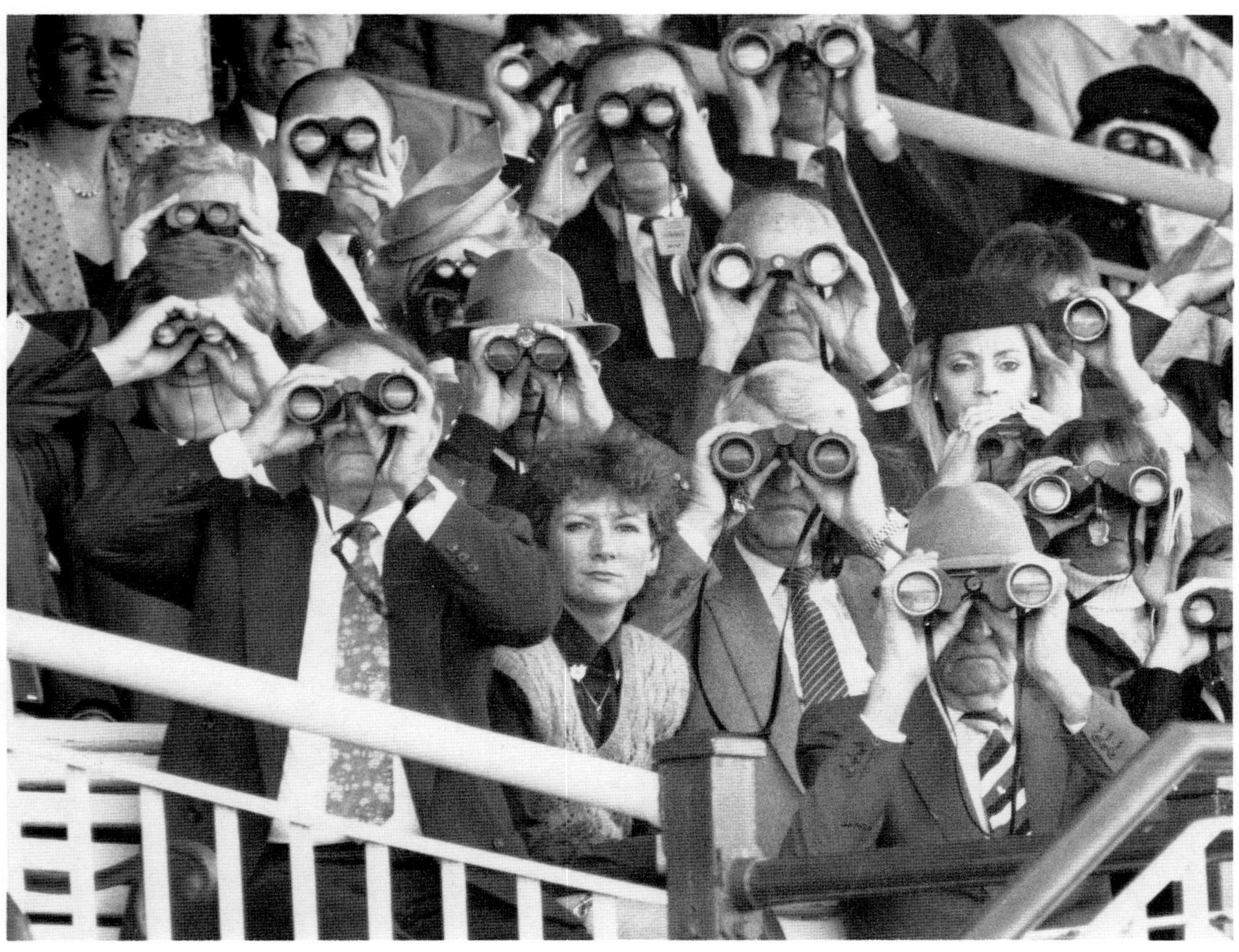

Flo Kennedy, strapper of Almanrad, watches the Underwood Stakes. (Tri-x film, 600mm lens, 500th/second, f5.6 aperture)

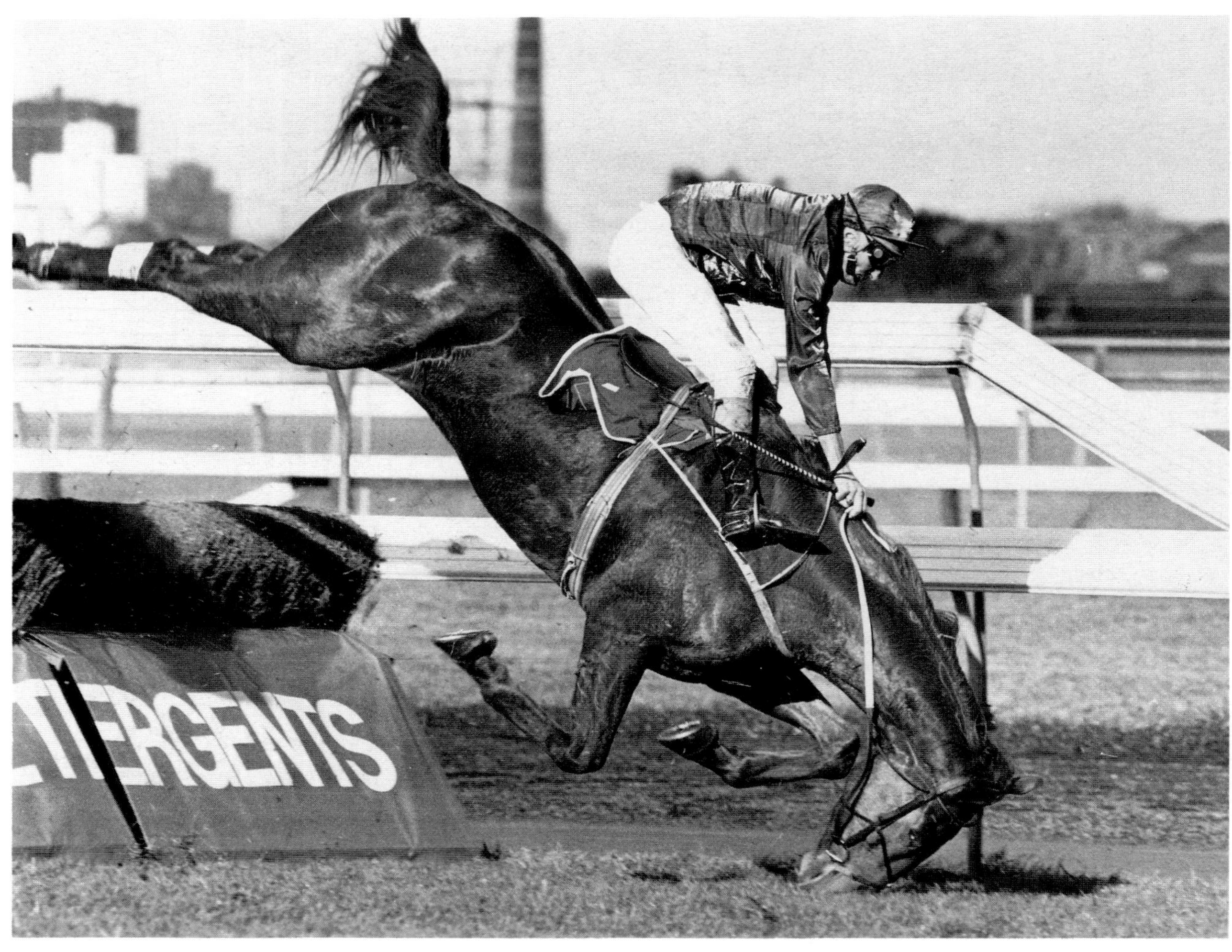

Bill Londregan falls with Just Return at the last fence during the 1988 Grand National Steeplechase at Flemington

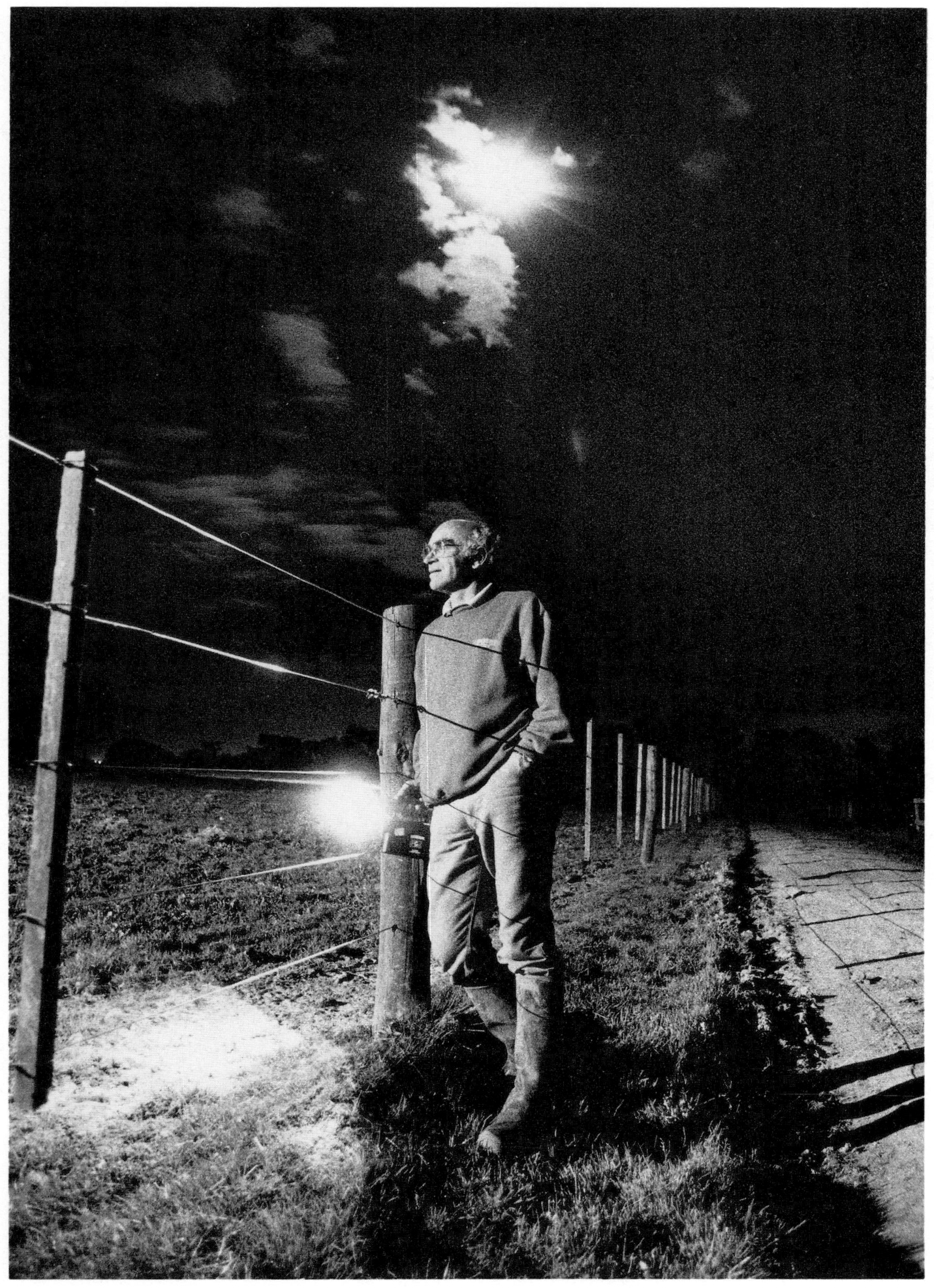

Studmaster and vet Bill Riches watches for mares about to foal on his property at Berwick.
(Tripod, T-max film, 800 ASA 1/4 second at f4 aperture)

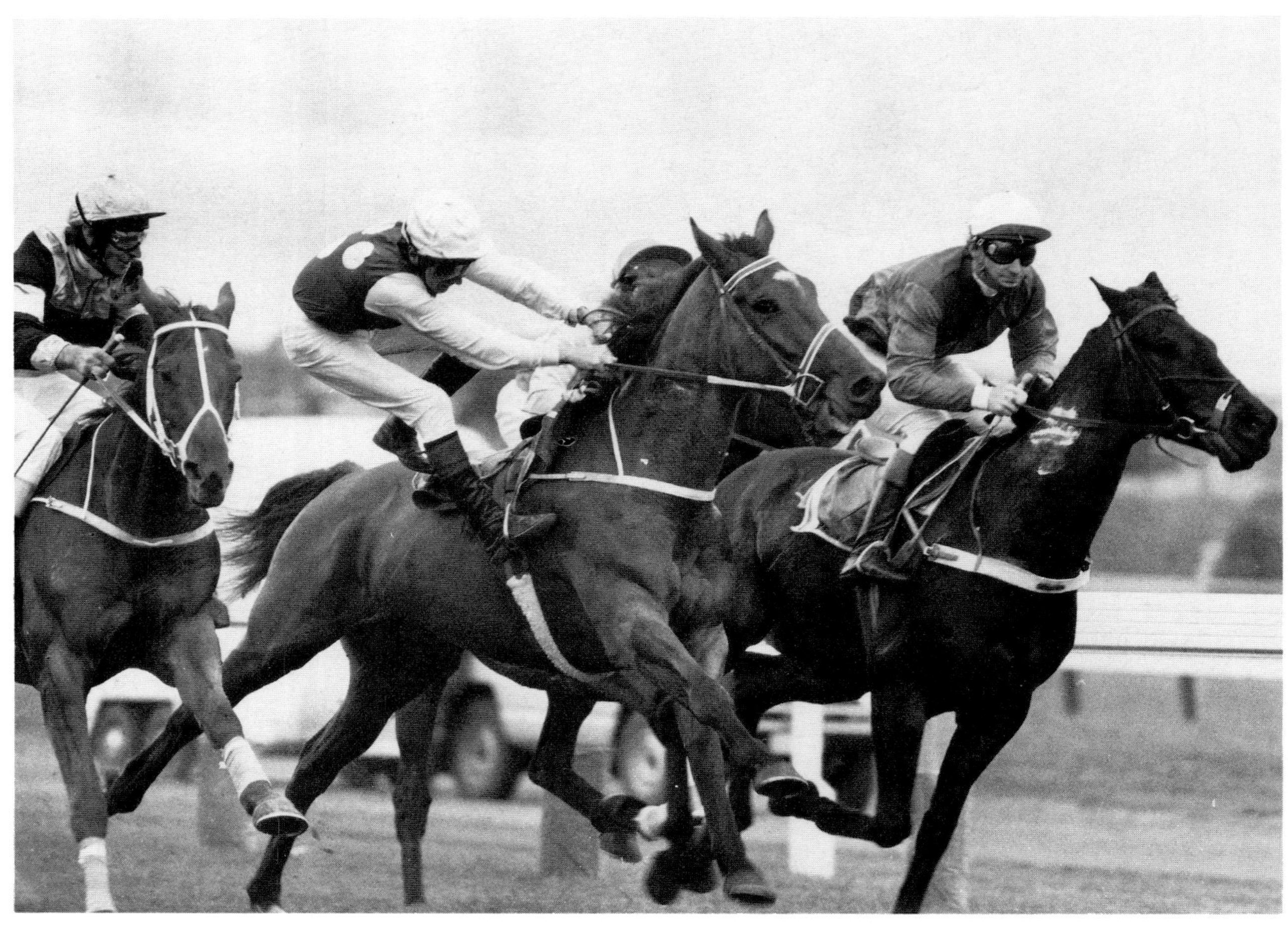

David Johnson nearly falls from the saddle of Chancellor Lad at Flemington during the Eudunda Hurdle — they recovered to finish the race. (Ilford HP5 film, 300mm lens, 100th/second)

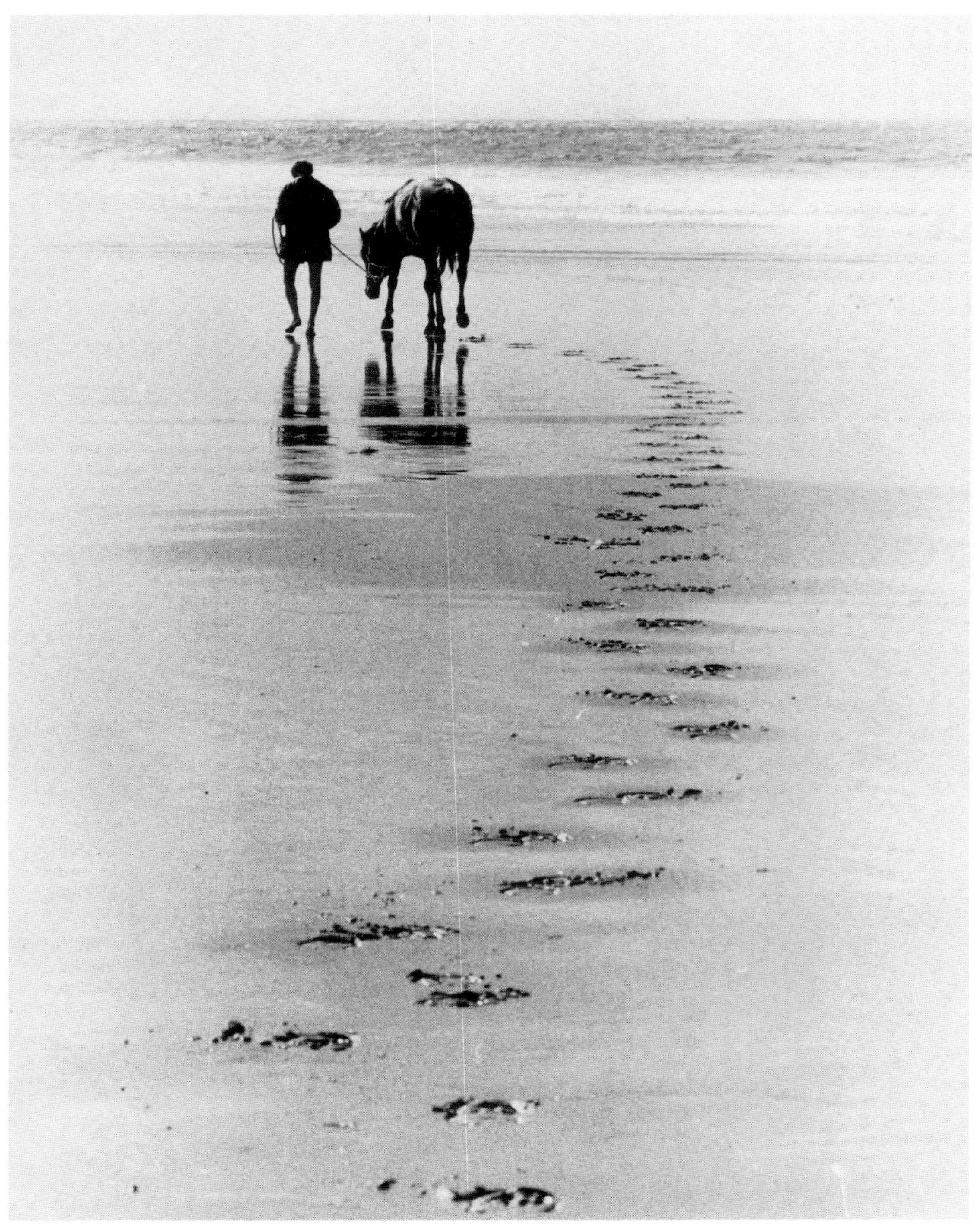

Western Australian trainer/driver Barry Perkins takes his champion pacer Preux Chevalier for a walk along the beach at Torquay after working for the Interdominion final, which they won

Philip Castle

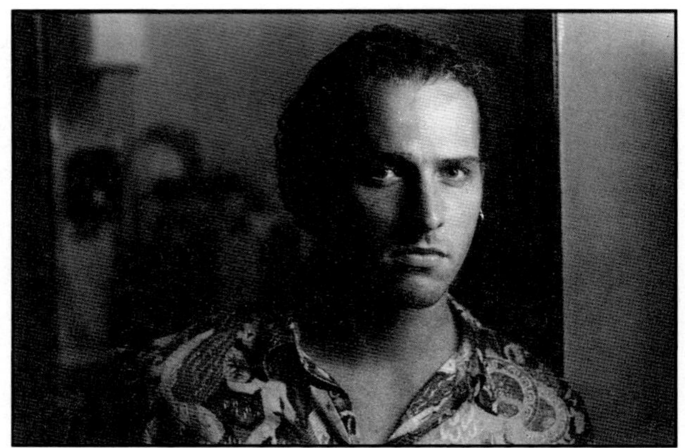

'I was always interested in art in High School. Photography attracted me by the way it enabled one to give created images the appearance of reality with all its consequences. These pictures could even seduce their audiences with elements of true reality.

'By my HSC year I knew that I would pursue a career in photography. Having done work experience at the *Age* and the *Australian* newspapers, I decided that photographic journalism would be a practical and meaningful way to earn money when I left school (even if a little more artistically restricting than I had hoped would be my theatre of operation).

'Soon after finishing my last exams I applied for a cadetship with the *Age* and was accepted. I spent two years performing traditional cadet functions and attending Photographic Studies College at night before being let loose with a camera. I figured out that photography for a newspaper, even if its prime function is journalism, can allow the artist much opportunity for expression.

'It's true that photographic journalism does not to a great extent allow the artist freedom of expression by the way it dictates that the subject must be shown so as to reflect as much of the truth as possible and nothing but the truth. But the content of the photograph is only half of the artist's medium; the other half is technique of presentation. As long as the above criteria for content is met, the artist can proceed with any manner of composition and camera technique to give flavour to his image.

'I find the amount of input I give to my images very satisfying and the unpredictability of subject matter is good mental exercise.

'Press photography, I'm glad to find, has turned out to be pretty much as I hoped. I'm glad I took the job four years ago.'

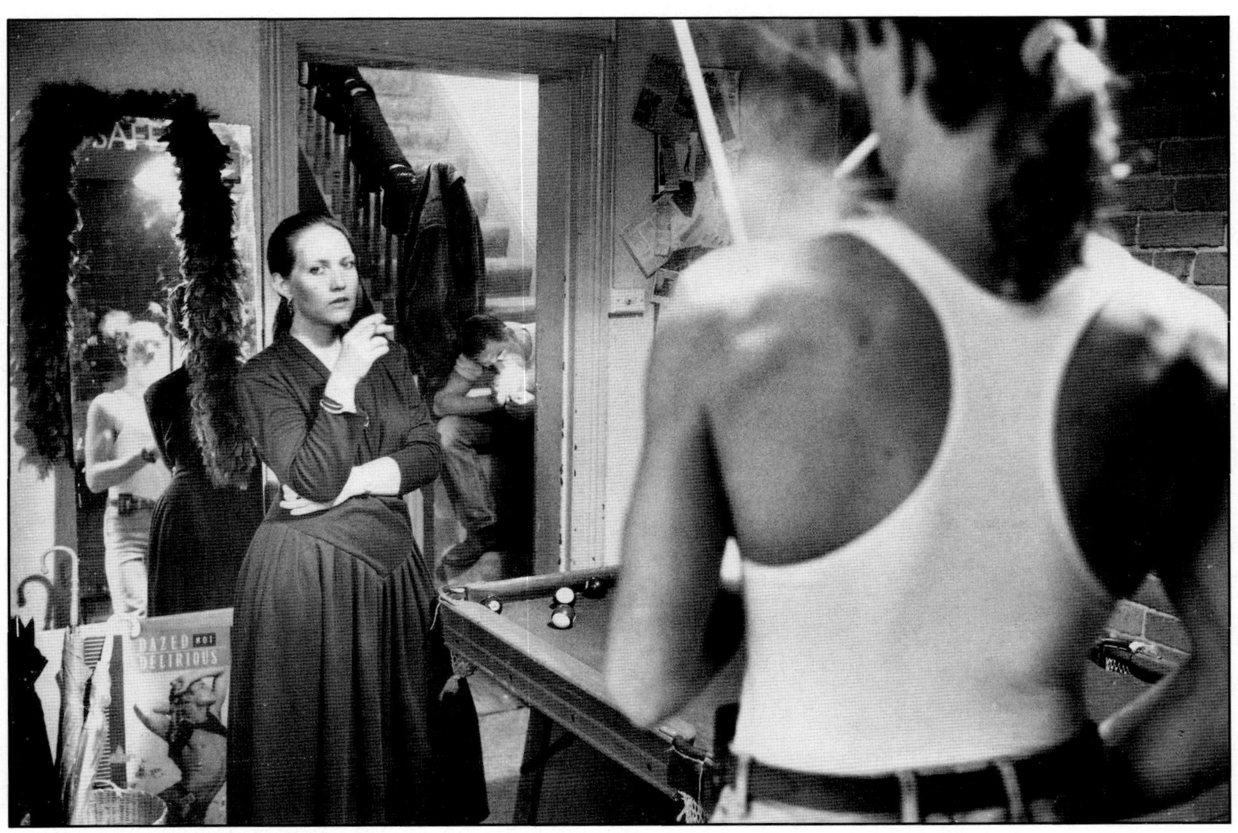

Illegal brothel owner Helen Dods with prostitutes in her former all-male brothel.
(T-Max 400 film, Nikon F3 camera, 35mm lens, 15th/second, f5.6 aperture)

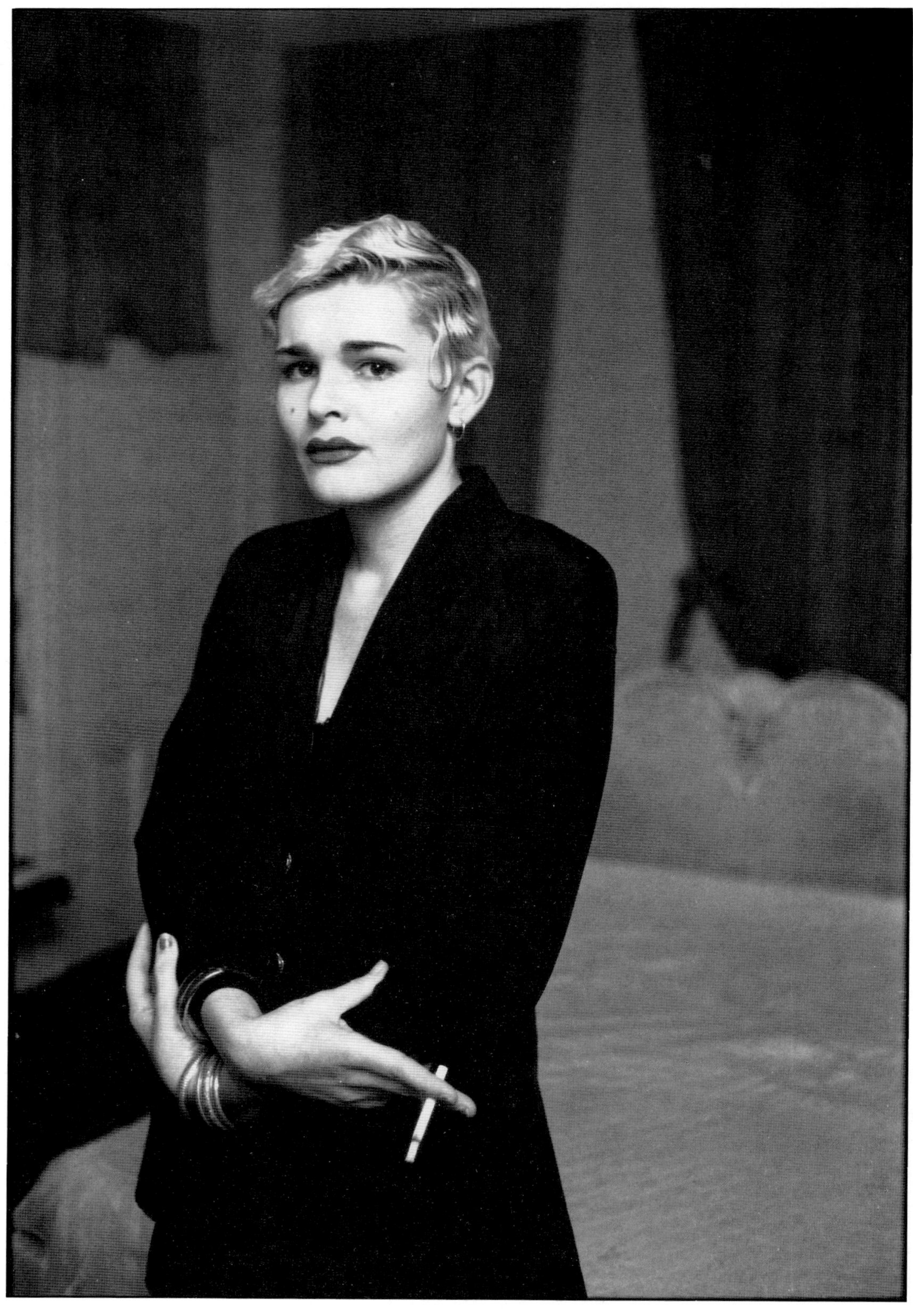

'Paris', a trans-sexual prostitute in a Fitzroy brothel, January 1992

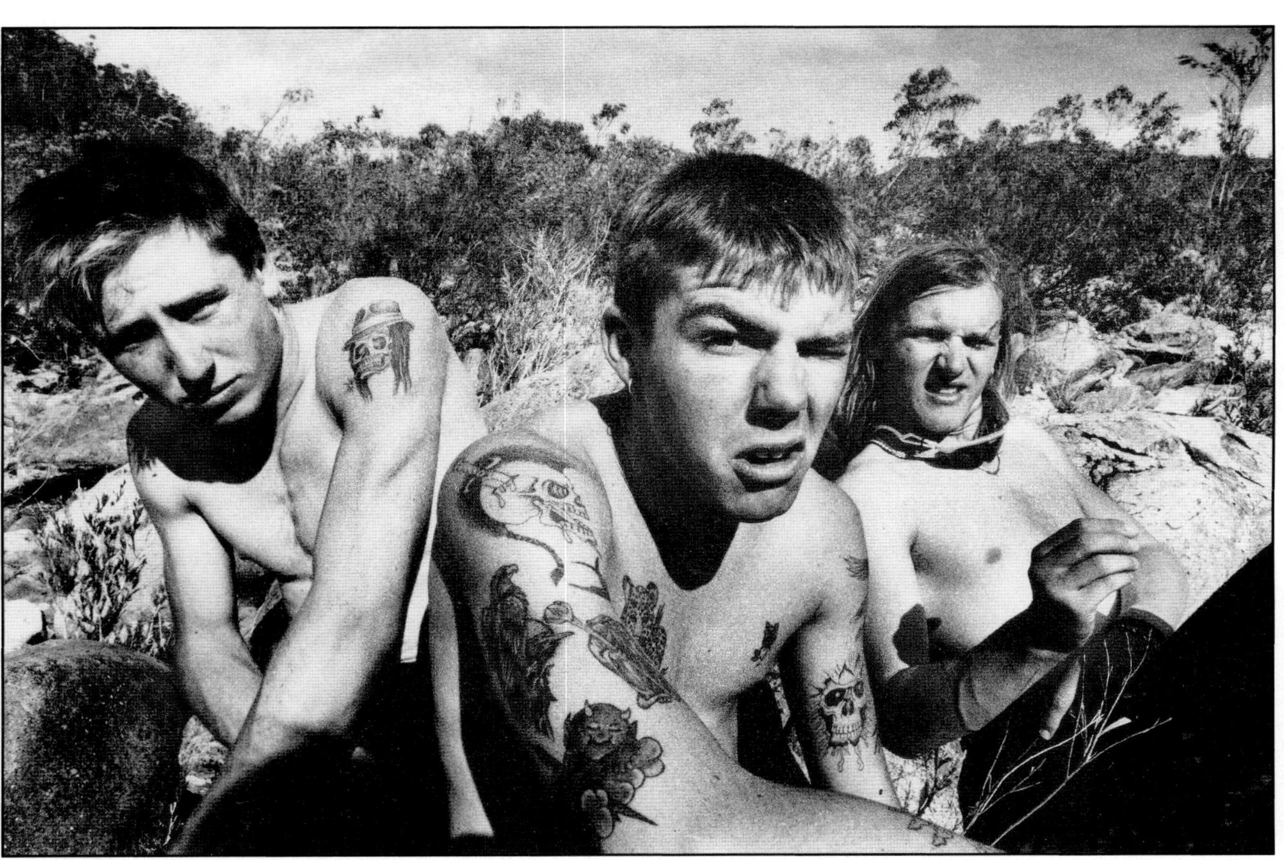

Boys from the Grassmere Youth Training Centre on a police-organised, 'outdoor experience' program, Snowy River

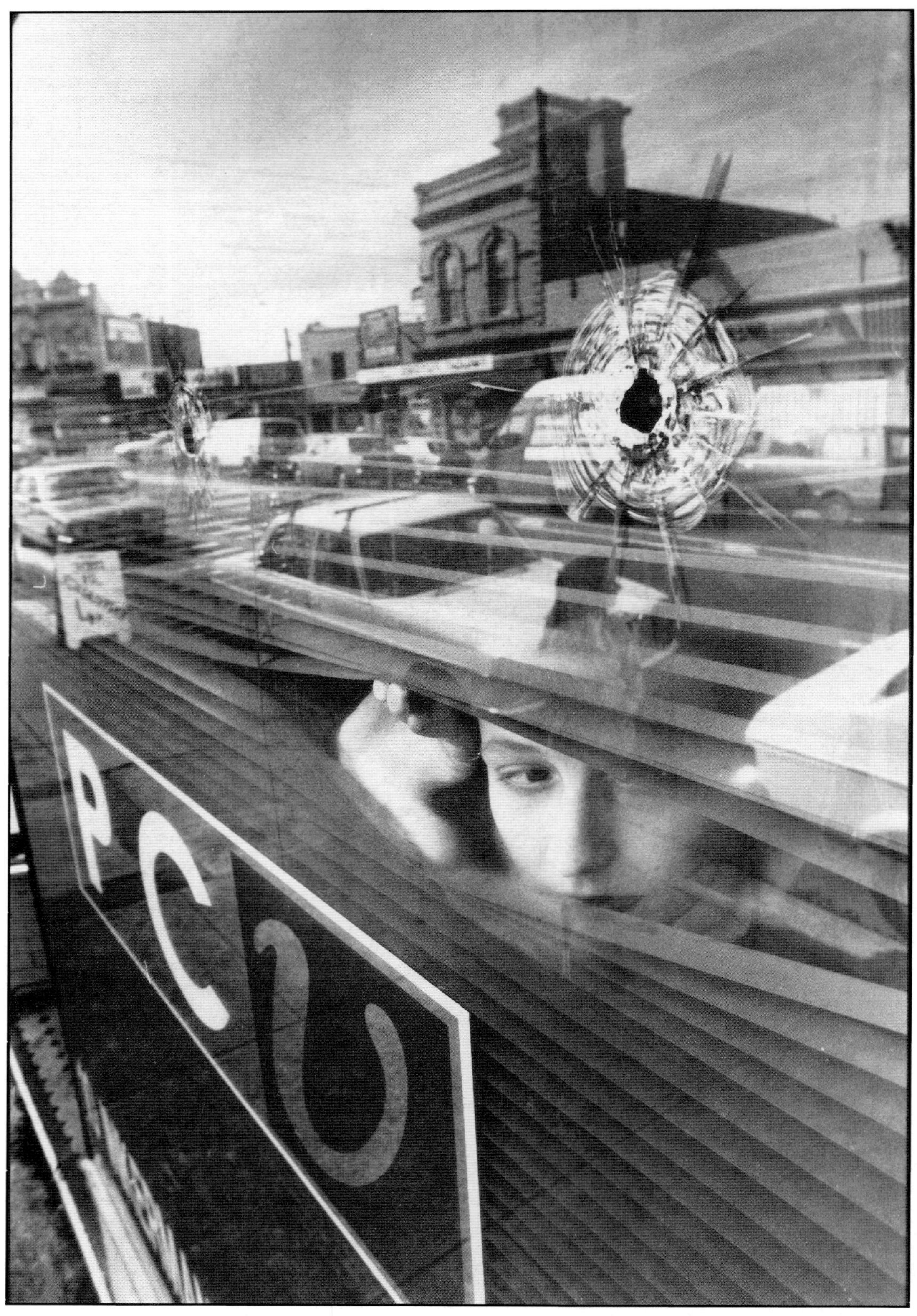

'Business as usual': Sarah Fair, the women's project officer at the Prostitutes Collective Office

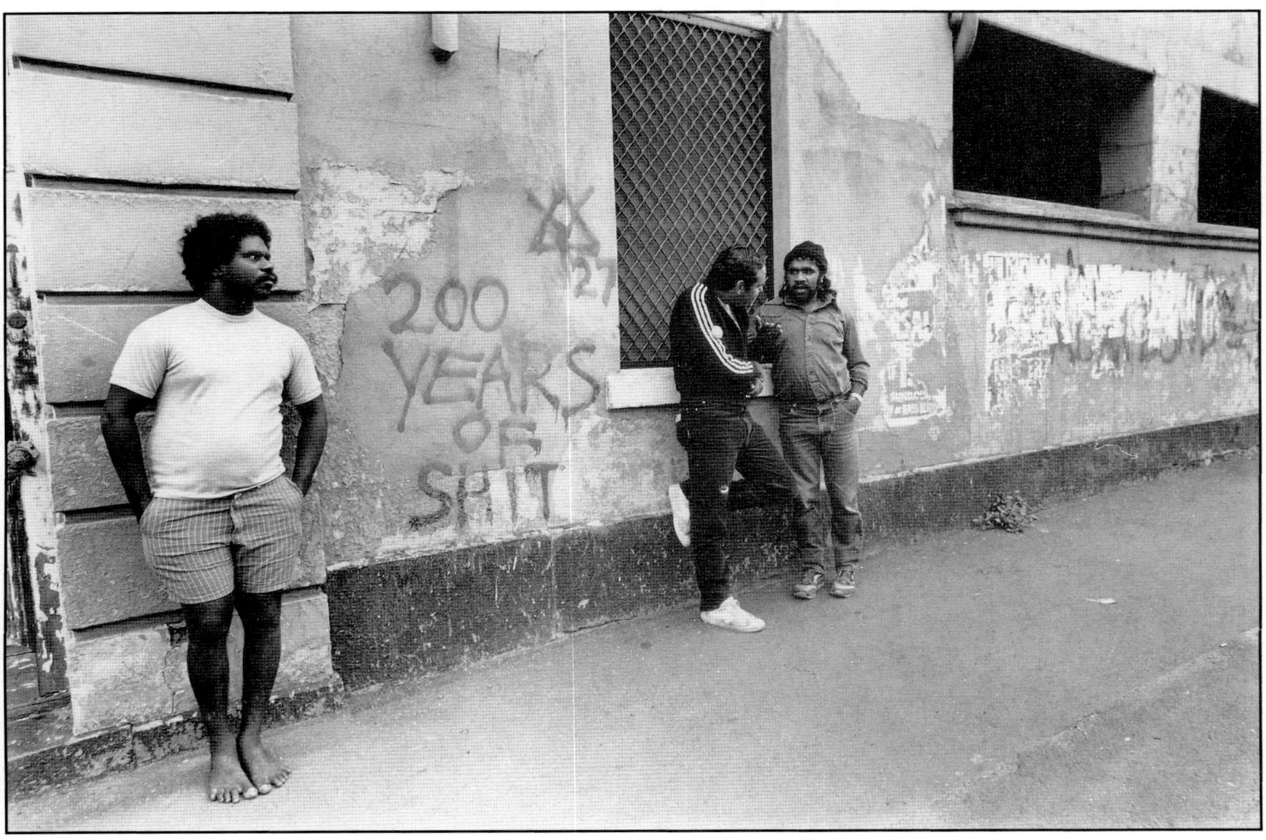

Uncaptioned

Jason Childs

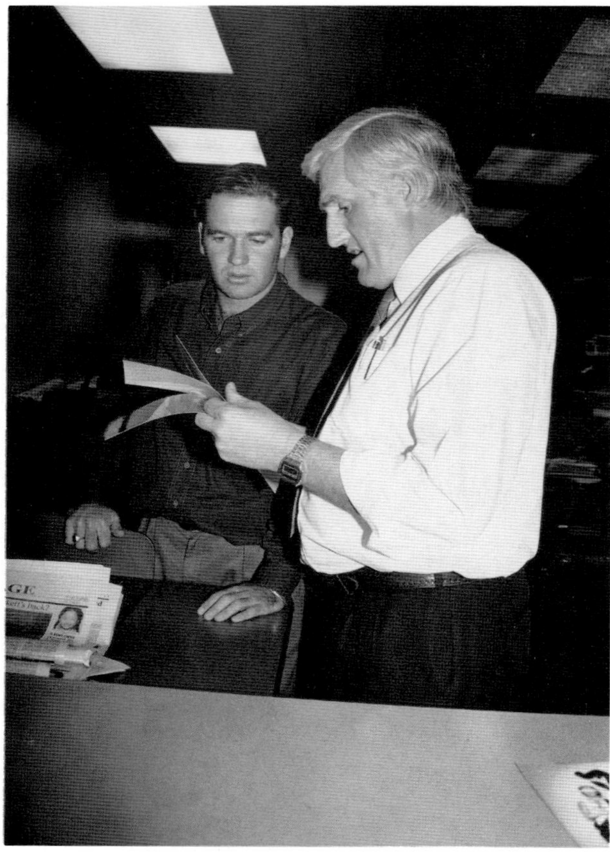

Jason Childs, left, and John French (photo: Kristine Beach)

'I began at the *Age* in 1986 as a cadet after finding the degree course at the Melbourne Institute of Technology more directed at advertising than sport. My interest has always been in photographing those sports that require control of speed and body movement. My friends were skateboarders, skiers, and surfers, and I find it a real challenge to capture the movement and the excitement. [Jason contributes regularly to surfing magazines in Australia and overseas.]

'Photographing surfing is very frustrating. You are at the mercy of nature. It takes a lot of dedication and time waiting for the waves and the right conditions. As a surfer, I have to choose between taking a camera or a board. To take the ultimate shot is every surfing photographer's aim: a wave that hasn't been photographed before, or that timeless shot of great surfers that reveals their style, or that perfect moment when the surfer is encased in a tube. Every surfer surfs for that moment.

'You have two basic choices with equipment. You can use a long lens of 600mm with a 1.4 converter or an 800mm lens and stand on the beach, or you can use a water-housing for your camera and get into the water yourself. It is only in the water that you can truly show the surfer in the tube. You have only one or two seconds to capture the moment that is so special that you will never forget it for the rest of your life.

'Being right in there is very exciting. There are very few sports that can be photographed so closely. But you have to watch out for droplets on the lens which can destroy a good photograph. You can use a wide-angle lens of 20mm when you are two metres from the surfer, but at that distance it can be very dangerous.'

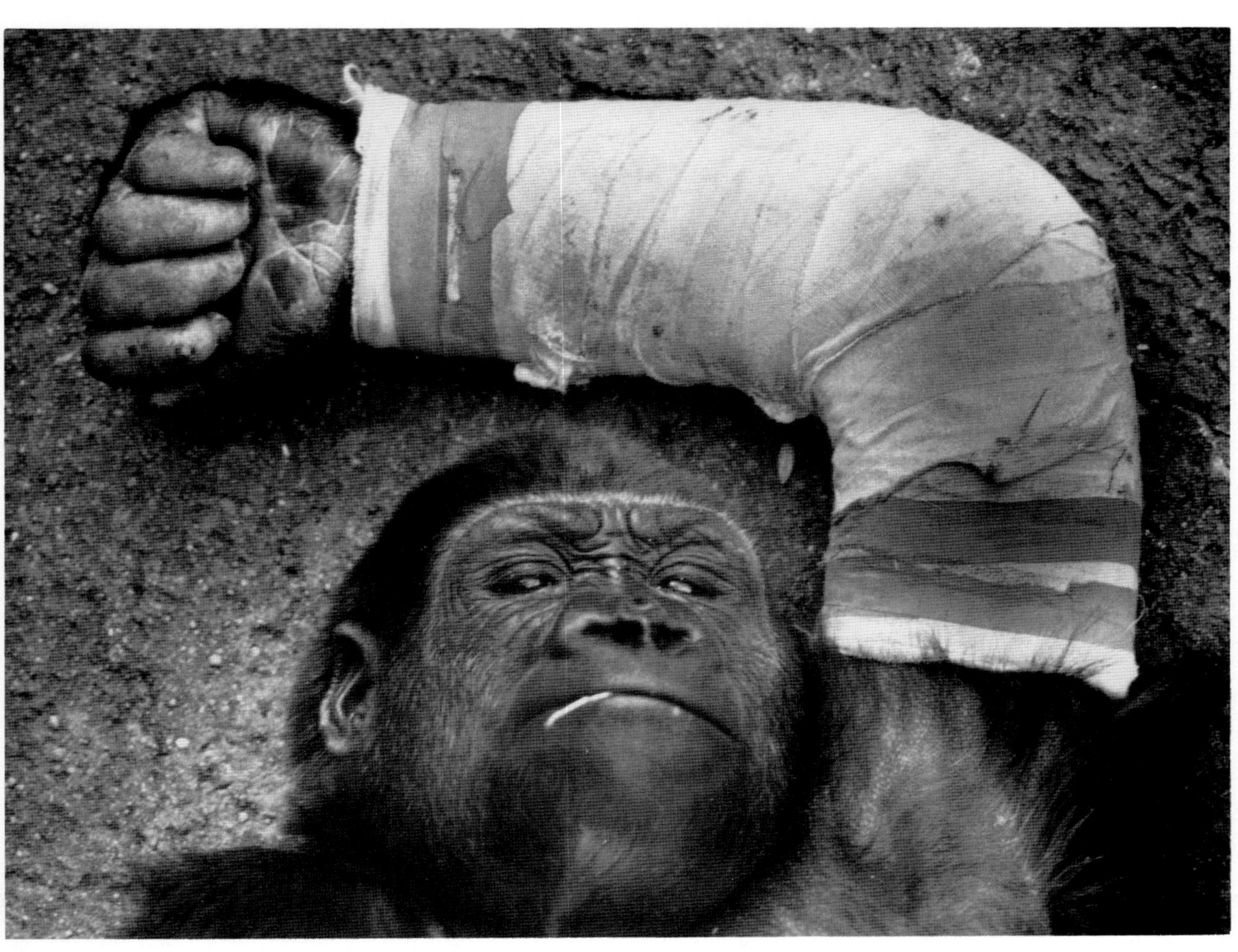

Gorilla Muruzi at the Royal Melbourne Zoo after breaking his arm while playing. I took the shot looking down on him, after waiting for two hours to capture this pose and expression. (800 ISO film, 300mm lens, 250th/second, f5.6)

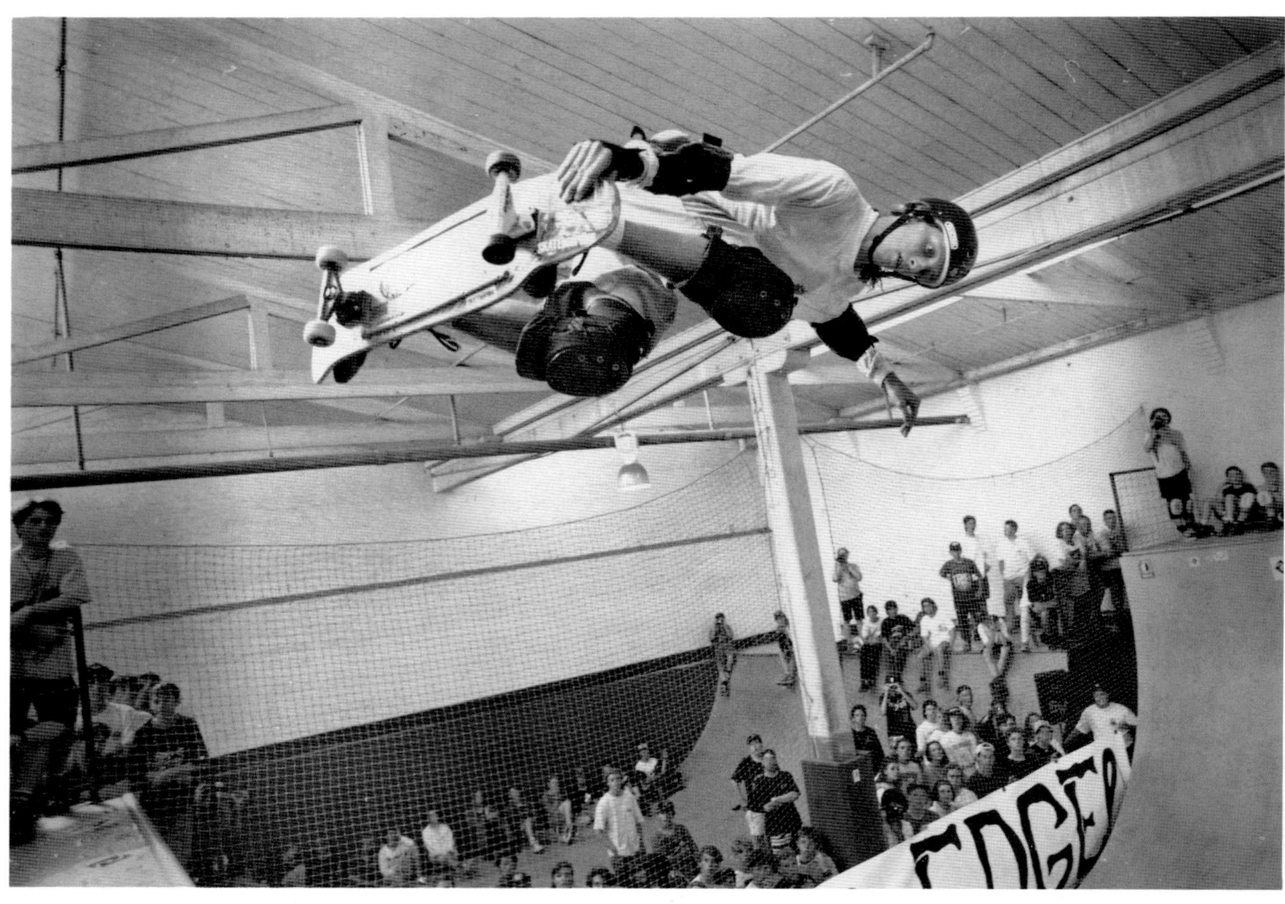

Eight-times world champion skater Tony Hawk from California demonstrates his skills while in Australia. A picture taken on a day off, the Age *was short of pictures that night and ran this one on the front page the next day*

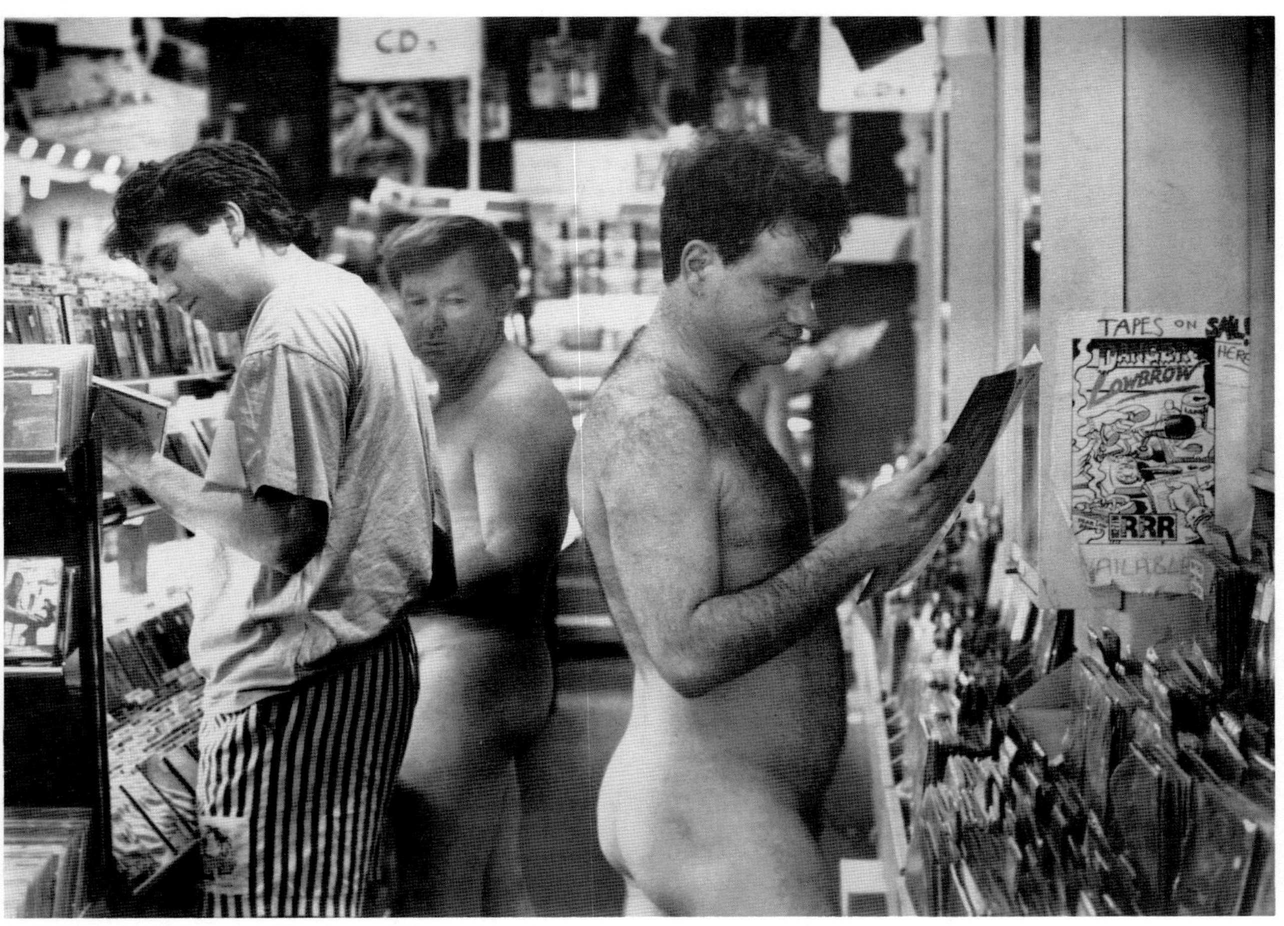

I was sent to Gaslight Records to photograph a publicity stunt. The shop was giving away free records to any person who stripped off and then looked for their record. The shot was a candid one. (1600 ISO film, 85mm lens, 125th/second, f5.6)

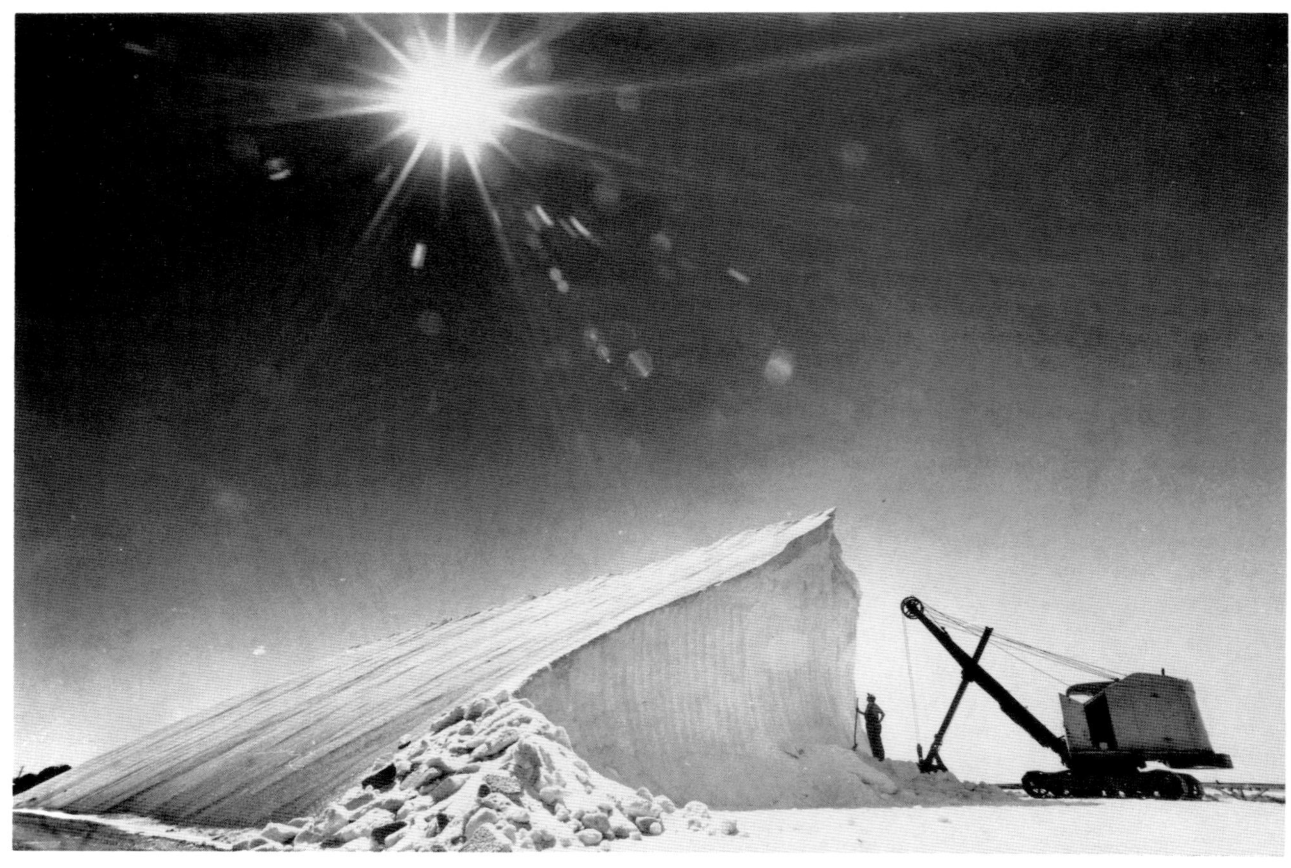

Salt mine. This shot was taken while returning from a country trip for the Age. *The mound looked like snow in the middle of summer, so we went in and organised a man to stand in the photograph to give it size definition. (400 ISO film, 300mm lens, 500th/second, f8)*

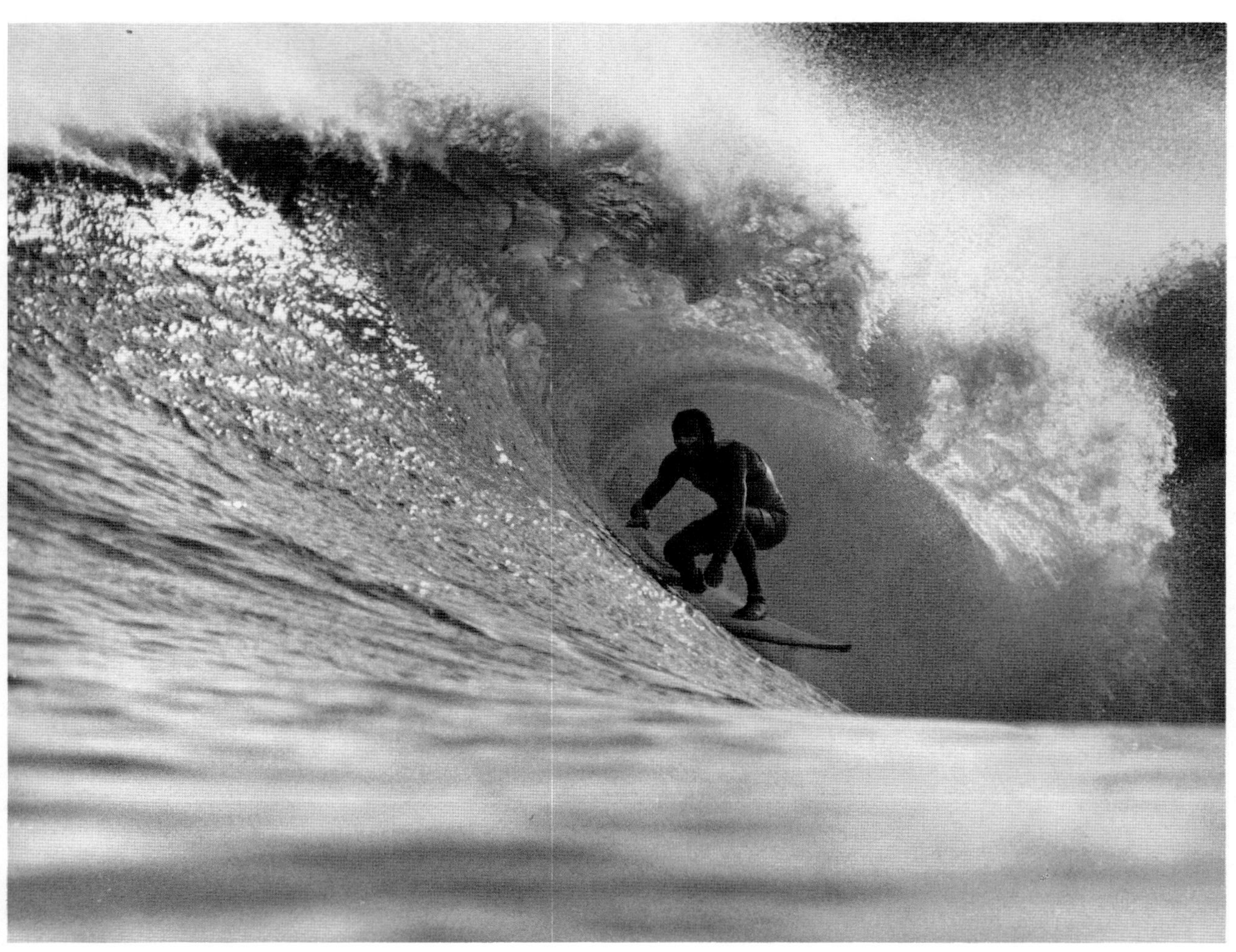

Bradley Crowe surfing at the island of Nias, Indonesia, 1989. Taken from a canoe.
(300mm lens, 1000th/second, f5.6)

Peter Cox

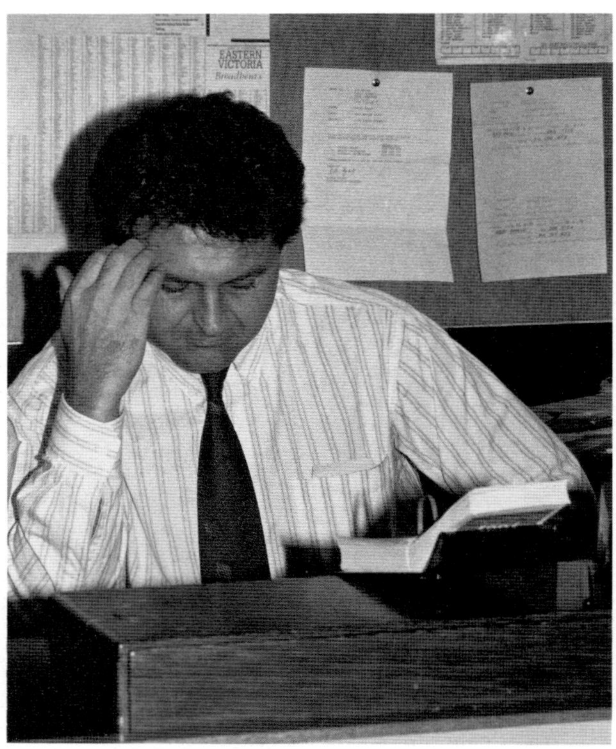

Photo: Kristine Beach

Peter Cox began his photographic career as a cadet at the *Age* in 1972 and worked there until 1979. He then moved to the *Sun News Pictorial* until 1988, when he returned to the *Age* as Assistant Pictorial Editor. He is still found occasionally on the road with his camera in hand.

His role consists of allocating jobs to photographers, most often on the night shift, as well as attending news conferences with the Chief of Staff and the foreign, business, and sports editors, and presenting the photographs for the day. He also helps with the final cropping and sizing of photographs for the next day's paper.

'Acting as a team coach, balancing and assessing each photographer on the day is difficult. You must choose the best person for the job, the one who can cover it adequately and sensitively. The best photographers are those who can make a good photograph from an ordinary job. John Lamb is unsurpassed in this area.

'Often press photography is over glamorised. A photographer may wait in the cold for hours and have only a few seconds to catch a picture. The thrill of press photography is when you are caught up in the events where you feel a part of the action. As with my photograph of Nelson Mandela, you have a chance to meet the man who is part of history.

'Sport is a very involving and important part of Australian newspaper photography. We push sport to the front page more than most countries, as it is rare that we have "earth-shattering" events in Australia. As a result, we do excel in sports photography. The likes of Terry Phelan and Clive McKinnon from the *Sun*, Stuart Hannagan and Bruce Postle at the *Age* inspire others to reach these heights.'

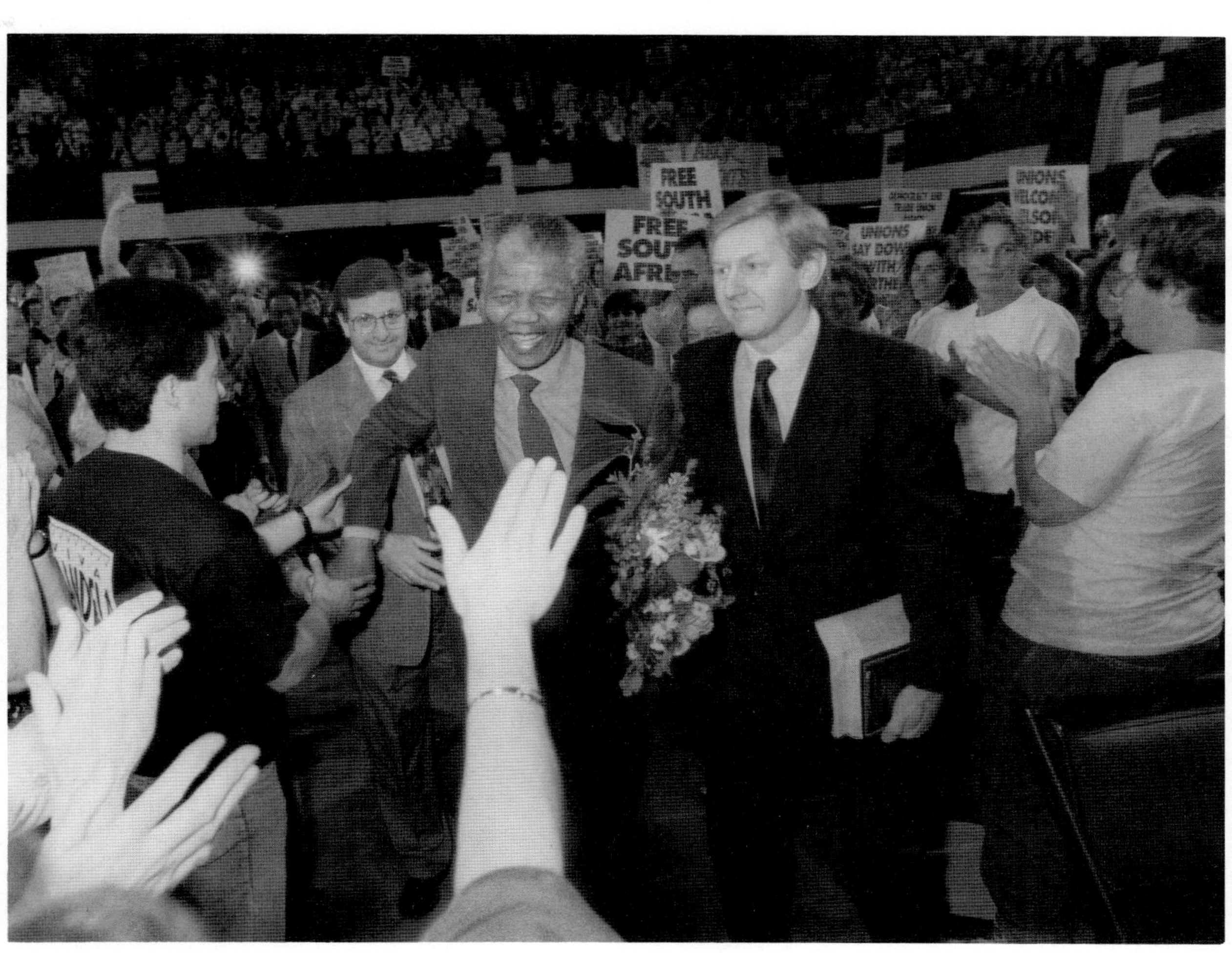

Union leaders John Halfpenny and Martin Ferguson greet Nelson Mandela at the Melbourne Town Hall, 25 October 1990. Support for the South African black leader and calls for the abolition of apartheid were overwhelming

John French

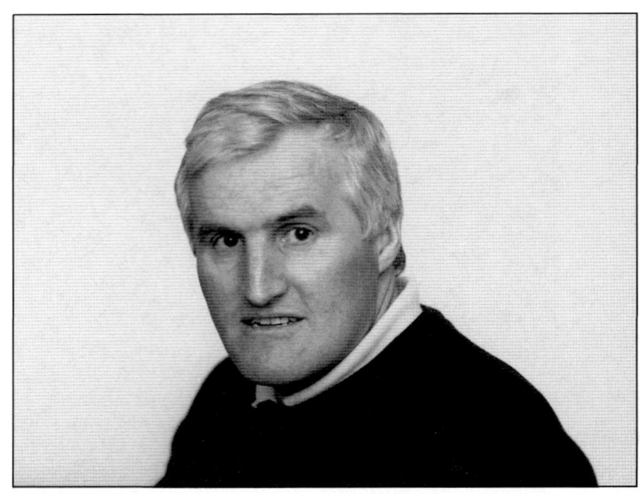

John French joined the *Age* as a cadet in 1969 after leaving school.

'After 21 years as a press photographer and the last five years permanently behind the picture desk, I get little chance to do press work. But, you never know what might come up. So, I always carry my equipment with me. If I'm not in my car, which can carry all the gear, then I at least have a little auto focus in my pocket which will give me a coverage.

'Press photography is a life, not just a profession. Those photographers who like to work their eight-hour days and leave the office will never really succeed in this game, nor satisfy themselves.

'A press photographer is the photographer who can take any sort of picture better, faster, and make it interesting for page one. They are a commercial, portrait, industrial, wedding, sport, news, magazine, and every other type of photographer. Above all, they want the best picture every time.

'In 1976, I became an assistant to the Pictorial Editor, making me half managerial and half hands-on. I was able to develop my sports photography skills at this time.

'The most satisfying sports pictures that I have taken have always come from Australian Rules Football. It is an unpredictable sport which shows aggression with sensational expression.

'In 1985, I became Pictorial Co-ordinator and, in 1989, Pictorial Manager. I'm still a press photographer, just a bit rusty.'

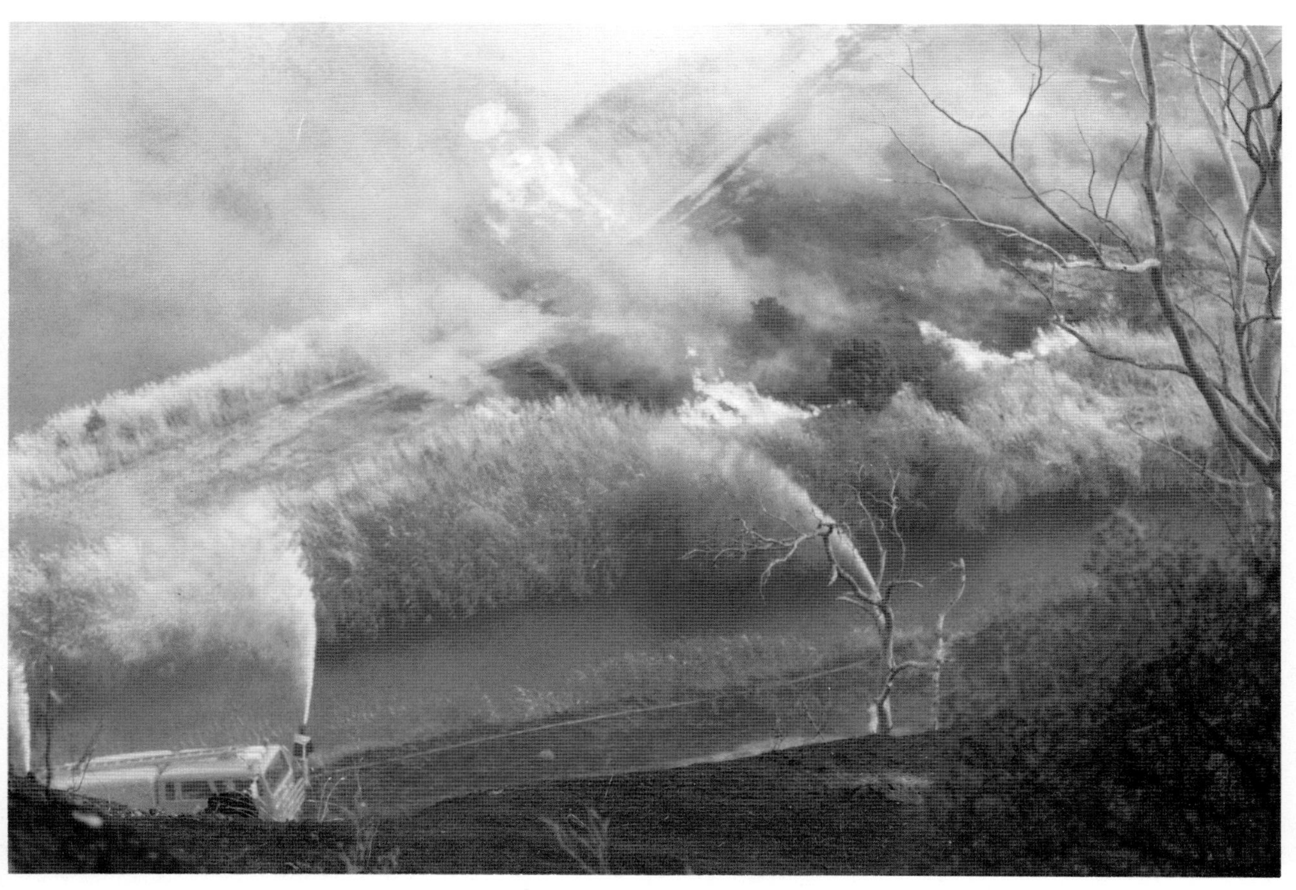

This grass fire threatened suburban Melbourne. I was on my way to work, driving along the freeway on a very hot January afternoon, and noticed smoke. To locate the origin of the smoke took a few minutes and by then the fire was nearly out. Fortunately for the picture, a stiff breeze fanned it and it started up again. (Avondale Heights, 4 January 1991. 100 ISO Kodak Gold film, Nikon F4S camera, 85mm lens, 250th/second, f8)

Stuart Hannagan

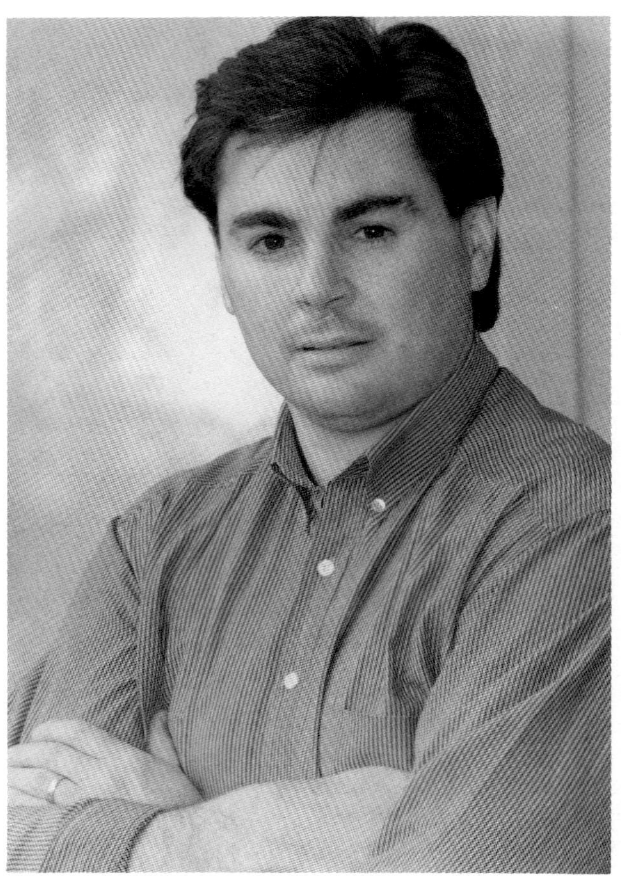

Stuart has been involved with press work for ten years, working at the Adelaide *Advertiser*, the *Herald Sun*, and the *Age*. For the past five years he has been a full-time sports photographer and has covered such events as the 1990 Commonwealth Games, the 1992 Olympics in Barcelona, the World Swimming Championships, cricket tests, tennis and golf finals, and thousands of football games.

'There are a few rules to follow when photographing sport.

1. Try to travel as light as possible (which is usually still very heavy).
2. Before an event it is important to plan and analyse the play. A photographer needs to know as much about the players and the game as a journalist does.
3. Choose your spot from which to photograph very carefully. That can make or break a picture.

'The main priority is to sum up the whole event in one image. Often that is very hard to do; sometimes impossible. I usually print four or five pictures and then discuss them with the sports editor, who has a very good photographic eye. We then get down to one or two images.

'To get the highest quality photograph, I try to use the lowest ISO film possible to minimise the grain. Print quality must be as near perfect as possible — 60 per cent of a photograph is made in the darkroom.

'I bring two important things to sports photography: my understanding, knowing, and loving of sport; and my reflexes and concentration. You must focus quickly as you move with the play, and you need to be able to anticipate where the play will go next. A metre can make all the difference to the sharpness of your image.

'The great thing about photographing sport is that you don't have to set it up — the action is all around you.'

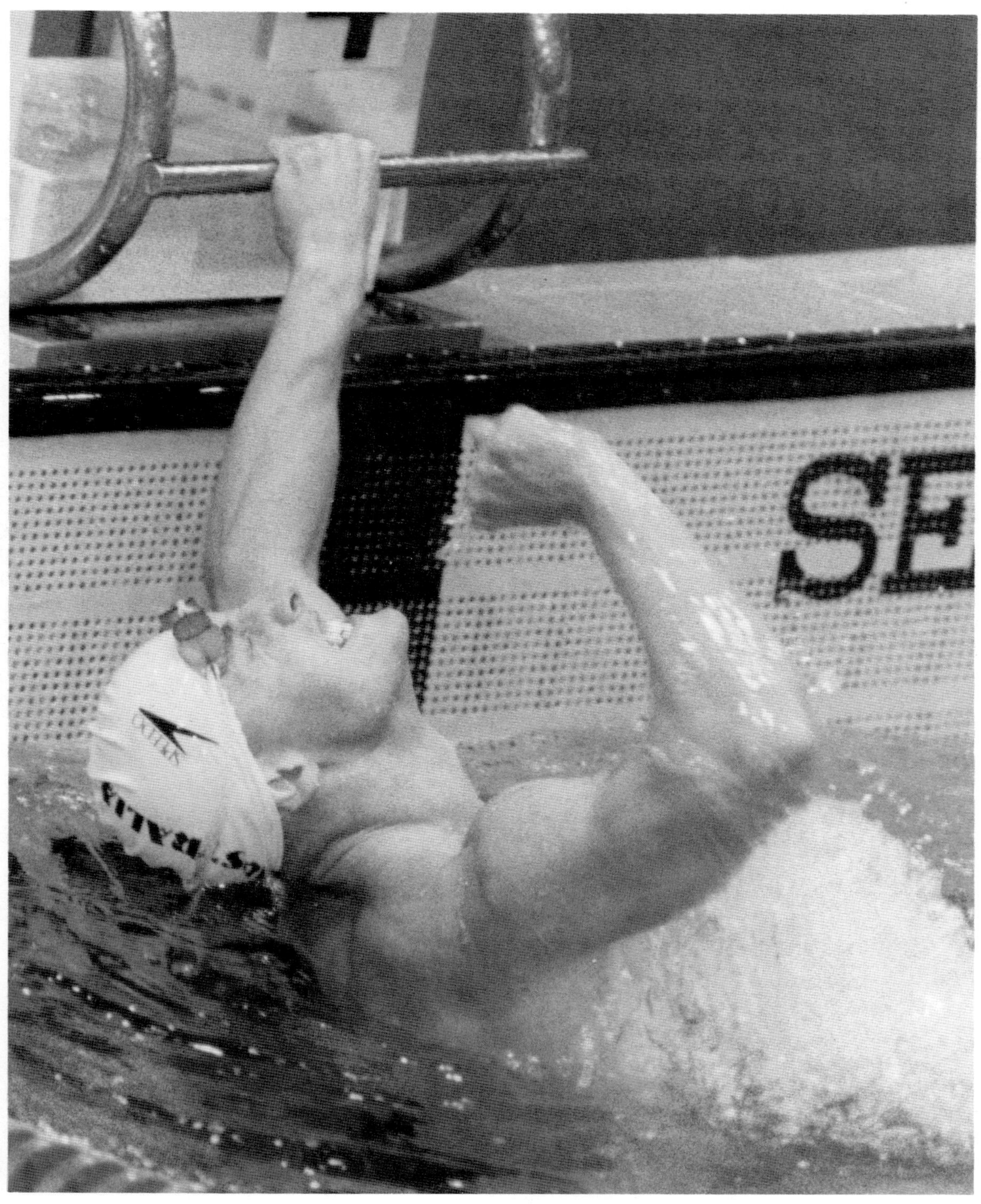

Andrew Baildon wins at the 1900 Auckland Commonwealth Games. (1600 Ektapress film, 600mm lens, 500th/second, f4 aperture)

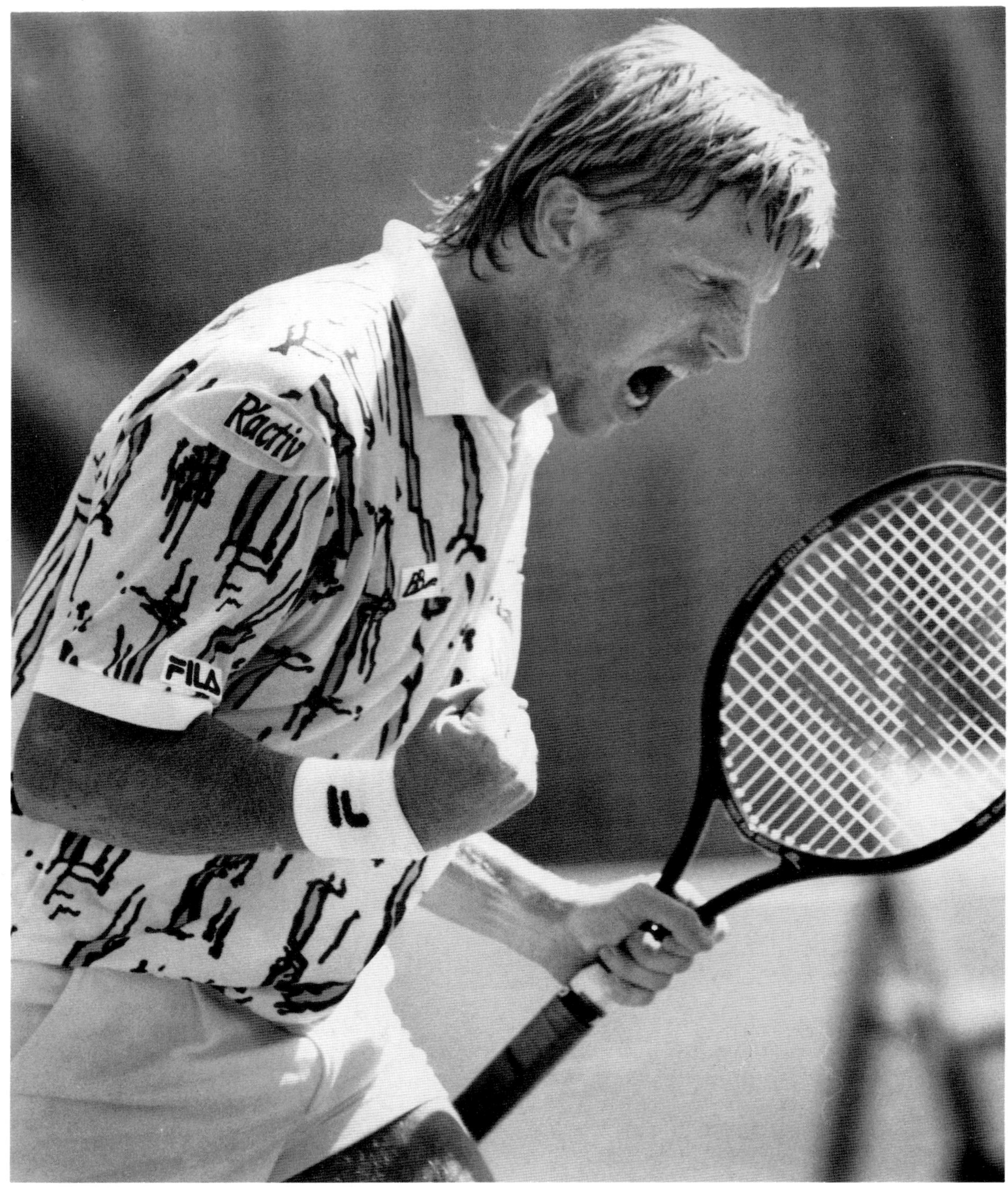

Boris Becker during the Ford Australia Open. (400 ASA film, 400mm lens, 500th/second, f5.6 aperture)

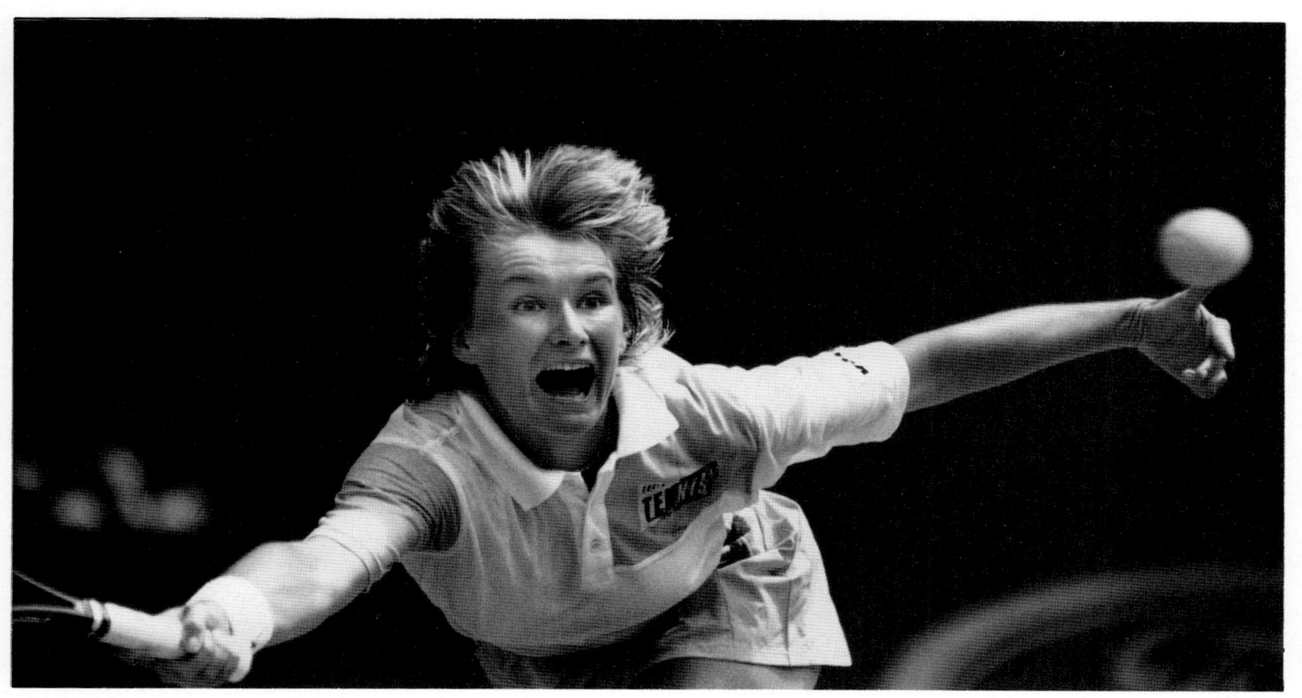

Jana Novotna at the 1990 Ford Australia Open. (400 ASA film, 400mm lens, 1000th/second, f5.6 aperture)

Tina Haynes

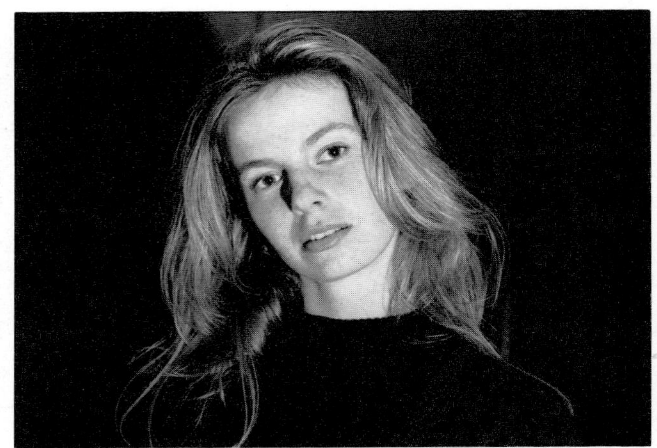

'It wasn't until I was 15 that I was inspired by photography. Then it became available to Year 10 students at Mooroolbark High. Before this I had wanted to be involved in Graphics, but the more I took photographs, the more exciting the whole process became. I went on to complete TOP studying photography at Brighton Technical School. This led to two weeks' work experience at the *Age* which gave me a wonderful insight into press photography.

'In February 1988 my cadetship came about. I was to spend two long years of it in the darkroom, and I've been photographing ever since.

'The *Age* has a range of sections which enables you to shoot anything from straight press-type work through to Magazine art style. I like the combination. The type of work that I prefer is best described as documentary style with an art edge.

'It's great being exposed to so many events and meeting so many people and then being able to record it all.'

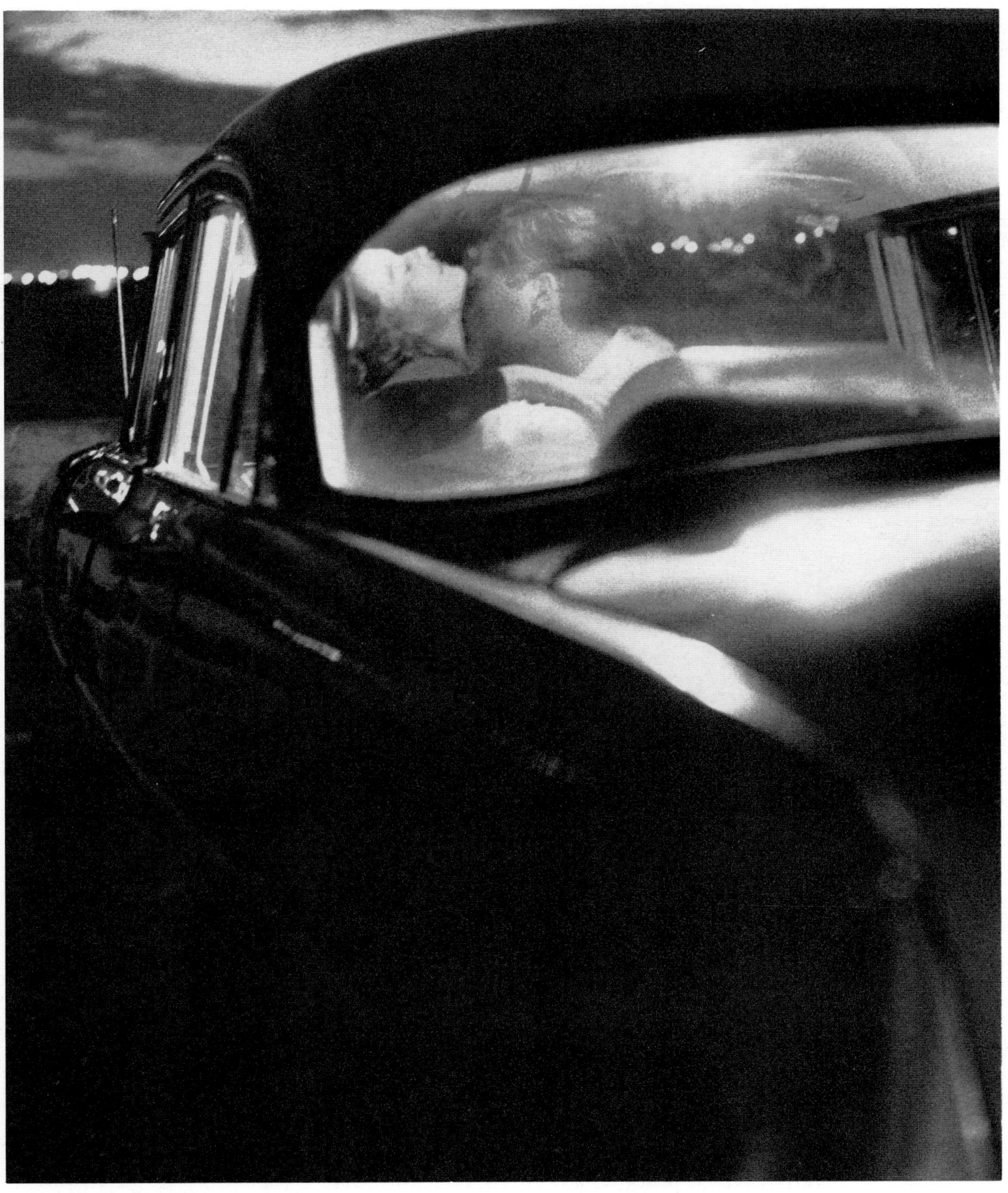

This photograph, taken at Half-Moon Bay in 1992, was used on the front of the Age *Entertainment Guide to illustrate 'Auto Erotica', a story that looked at the best necking spots in Melbourne*

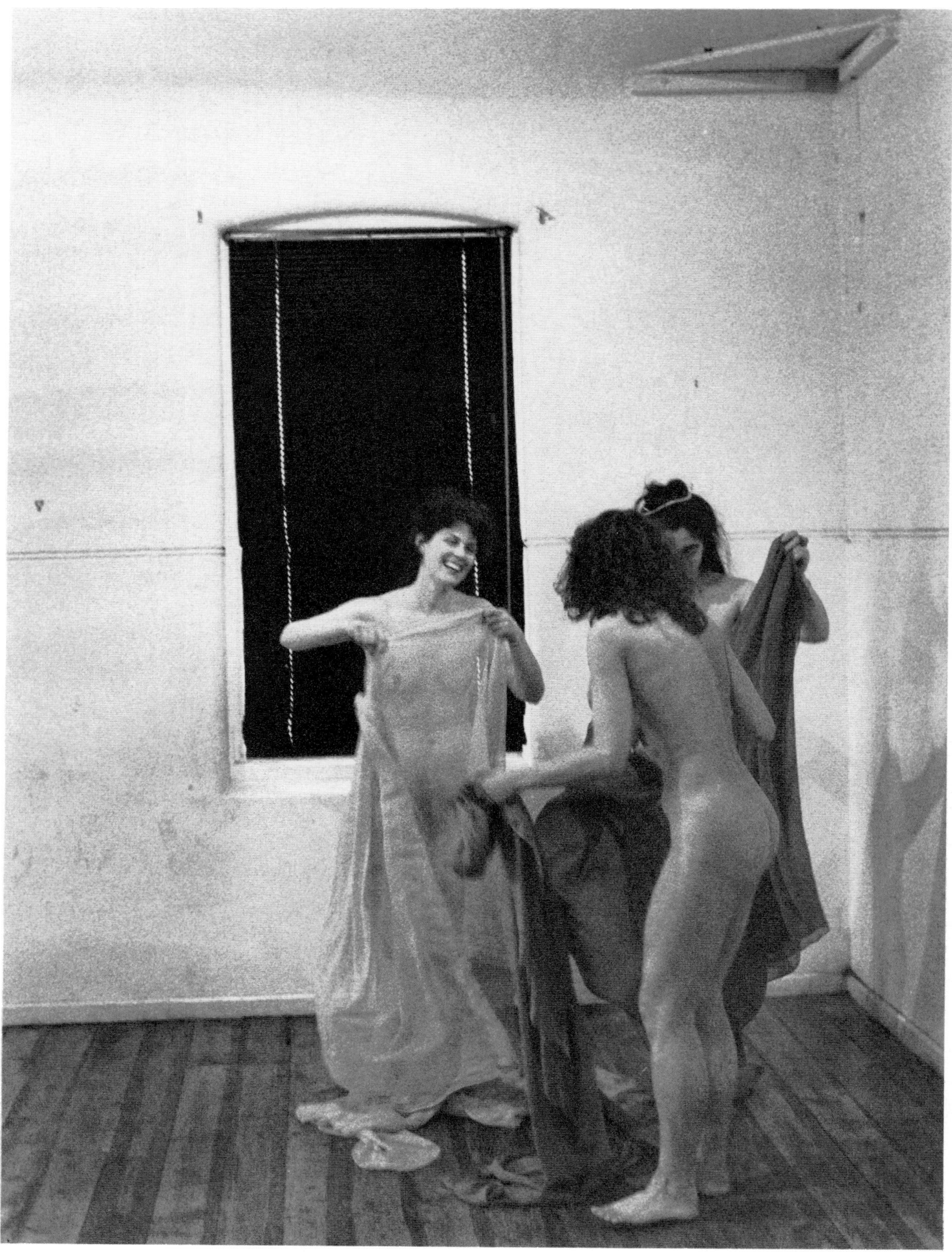

This photograph was used on an Entertainment Guide cover to illustrate a story investigating the work of life-drawing models

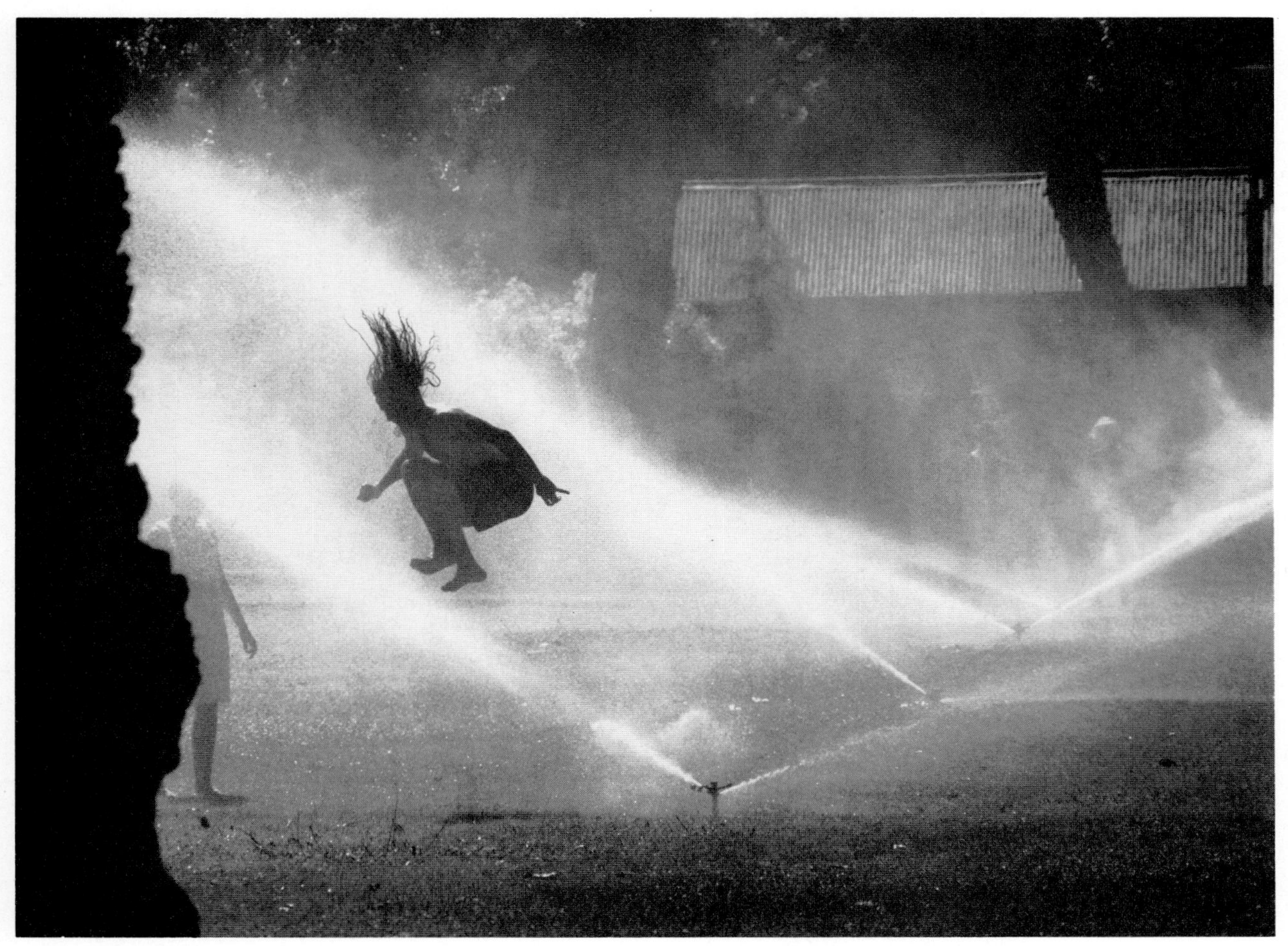

I was asked to find a general hot-weather picture for the first 40-degree day of the summer season in January 1993

Ray Kennedy

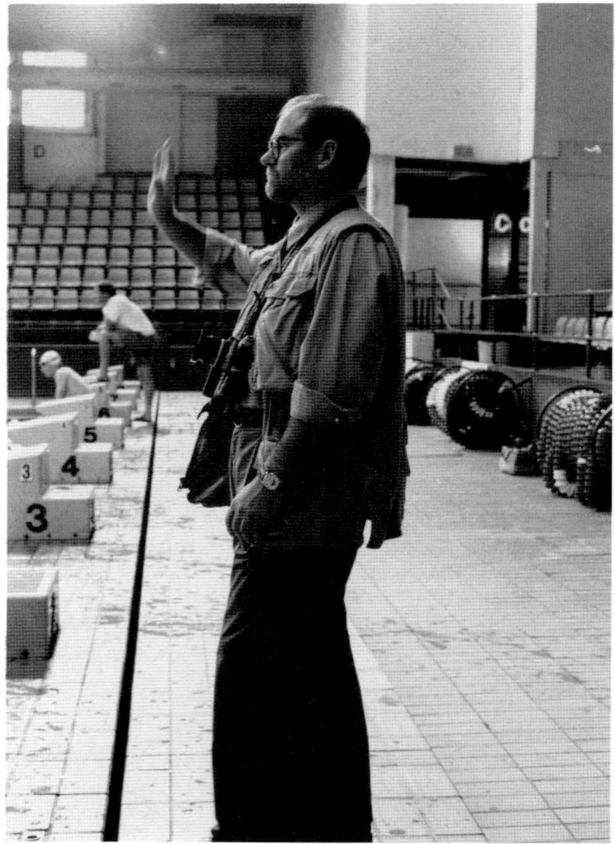

Photo: Linda Lees

'My interest in photography goes back to my school days. In 1966, I began work as a darkroom assistant in a studio in Melbourne. After about 18 months, I realised that I was not learning much. I met a photographer with the RAAF who told me the airforce had one of the best photographic courses in Australia. I joined up and spent six years with the RAAF as a photographer and completed a basic and post-graduate course in photography.

'When I left the RAAF in 1974 I became a colour printer cum photographer until I got a job in the darkroom at the *Age* in 1976. With my background, I was soon able to show my ability with the camera and found myself doing more and more work outside. I steadily progressed to become a senior photographer with the paper.

'The big difference that I noticed when I began taking photos for the paper was the speed at which I had to work. Most times you have only one chance to get your photo. Newspaper photographers have to be on their toes all the time. This leads to some mistakes, but quality is always important.

'To me, the story is important. I like to know the journalist's train of thought, their angle. But, regardless of the story, I aim to make every photograph good enough for the front page.

'My main ability lies in being an all-rounder. I prefer to change specialties — it's more of a challenge. I specialised in sport for years. Each sport has particular problems — the speed of the players, the size of the playing field. With news photographs, I deal more directly with people and try to get a better photograph by making them feel relaxed.

'I try to look at the composition of a photograph carefully. I have more time to do that with features than with sport shots and news jobs. I look at the overall rectangle and the shapes within it. I like to lead the eye into the picture with clean lines.'

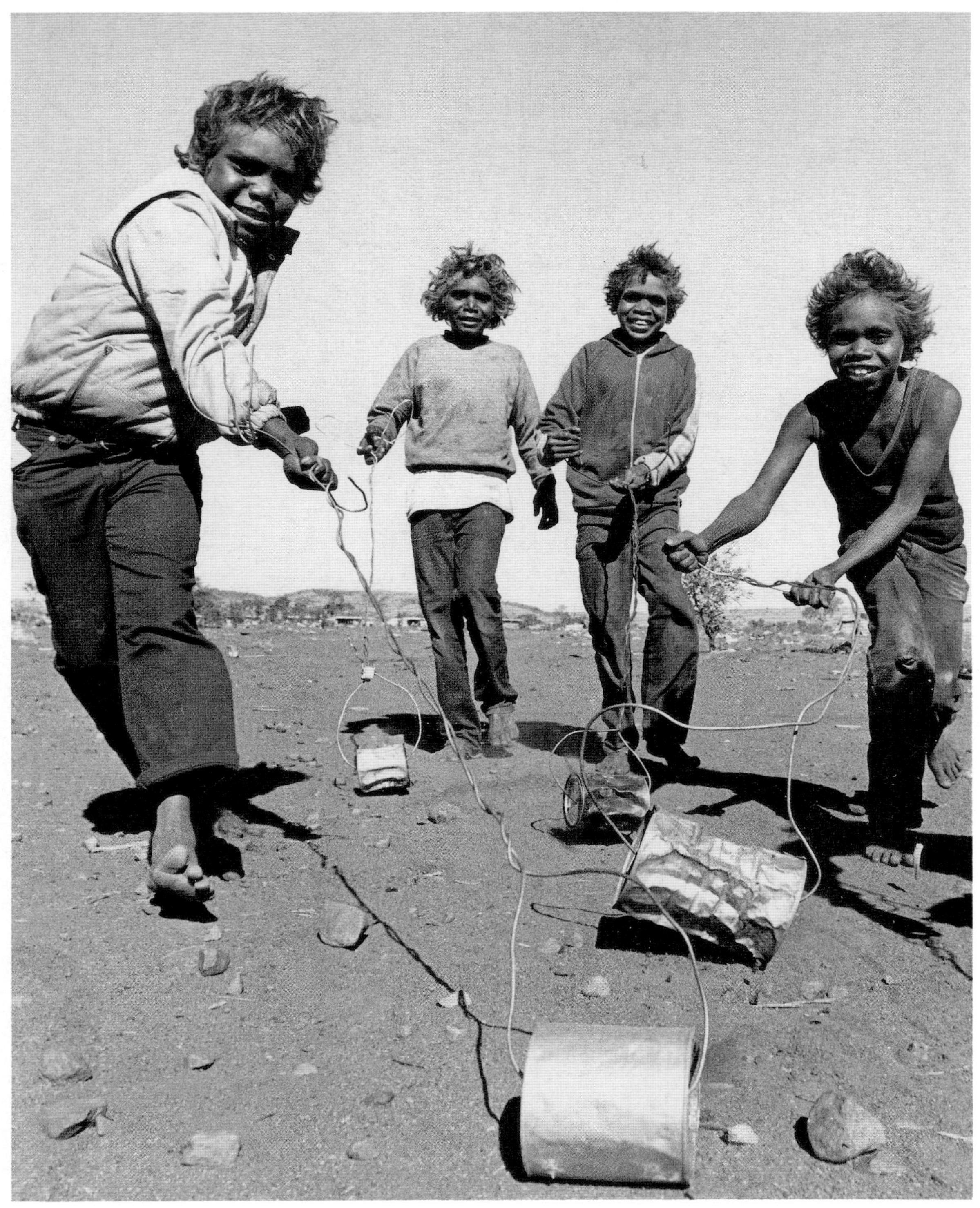

Aboriginal children race cars at Kintare, N.T.

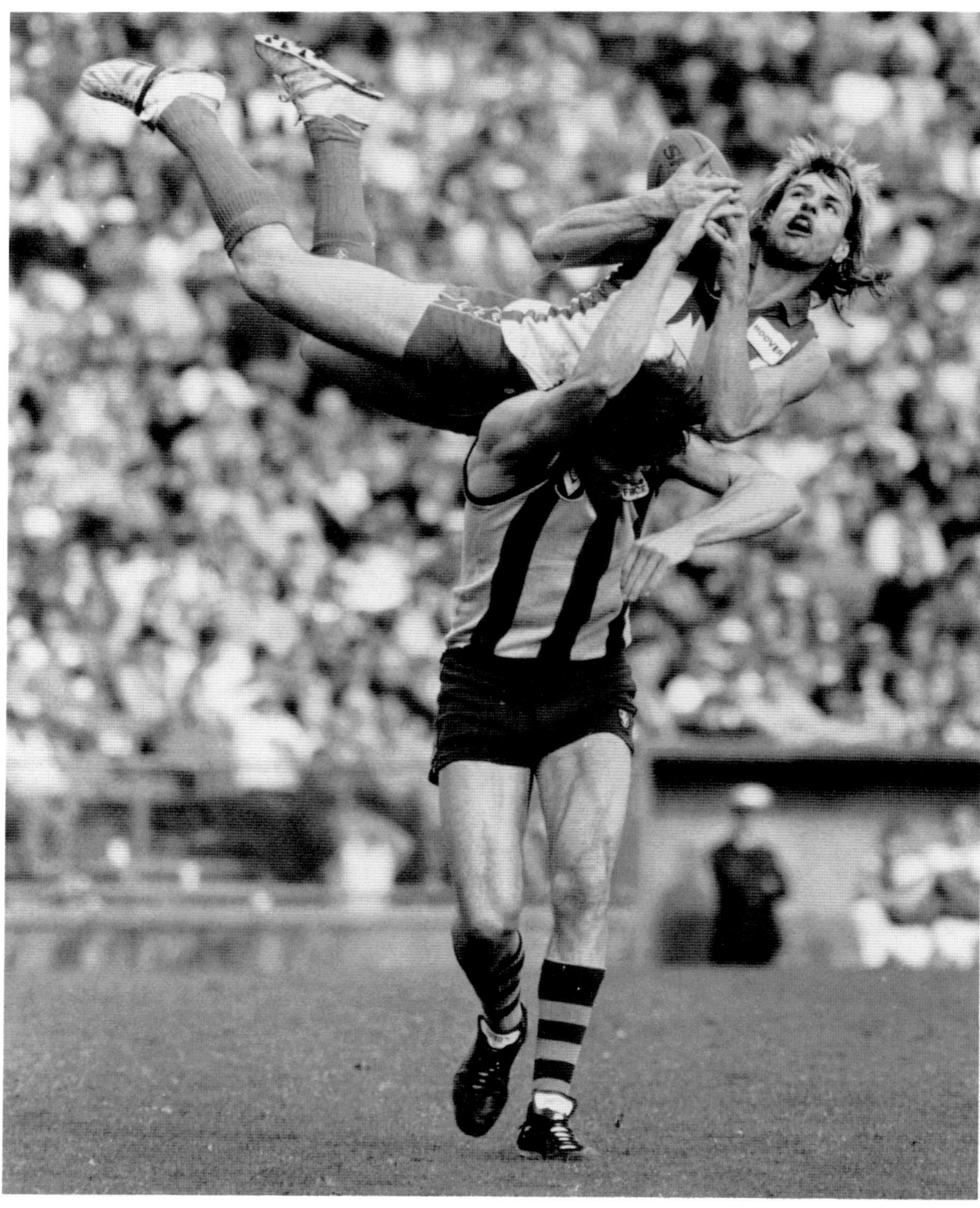

Warwick Capper marks over Chris Langdon. 1987

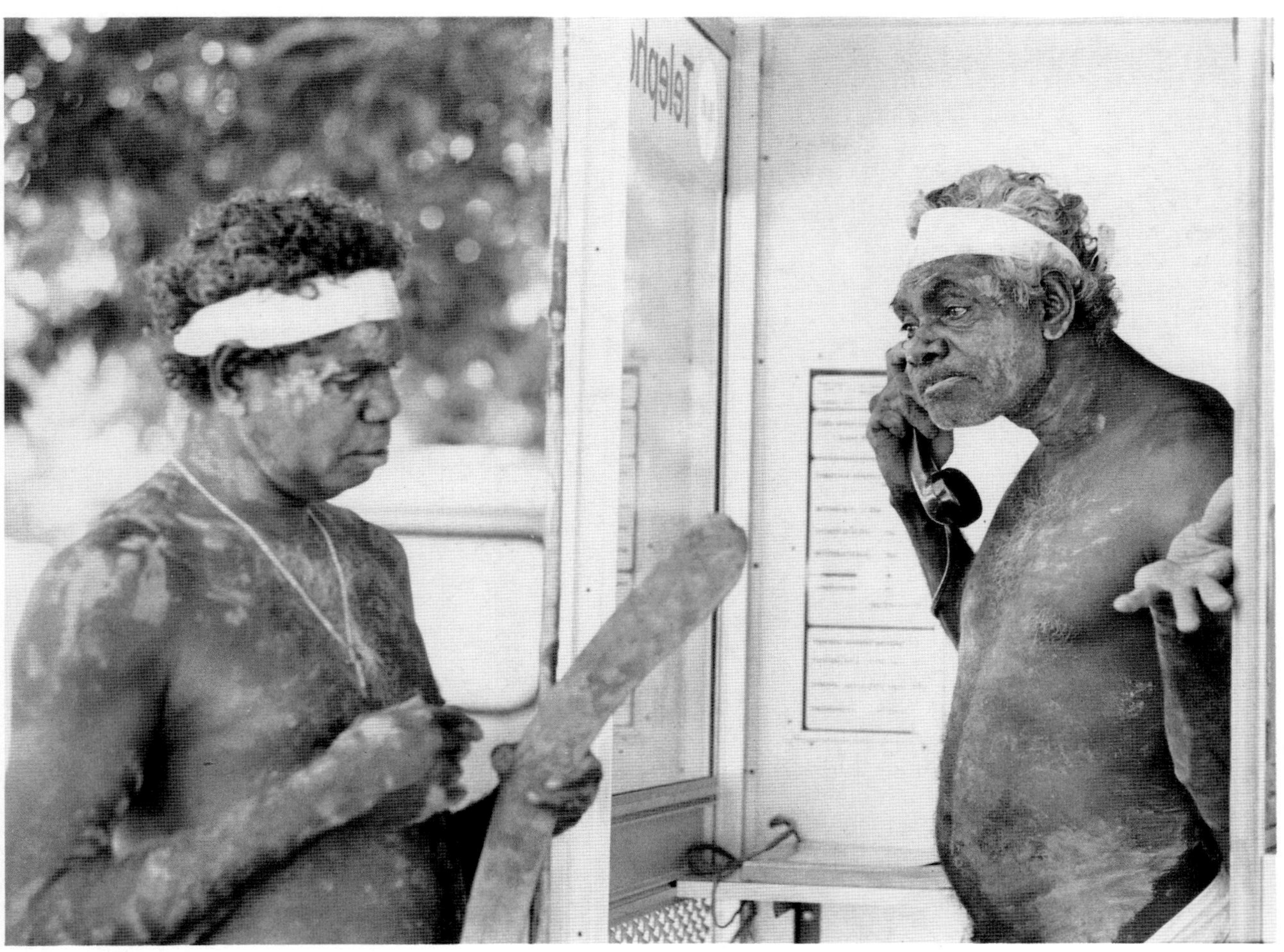

Jimmy Numbato, watched by Jacob Miler, uses the new phone at Daly River Crossing, N.T.

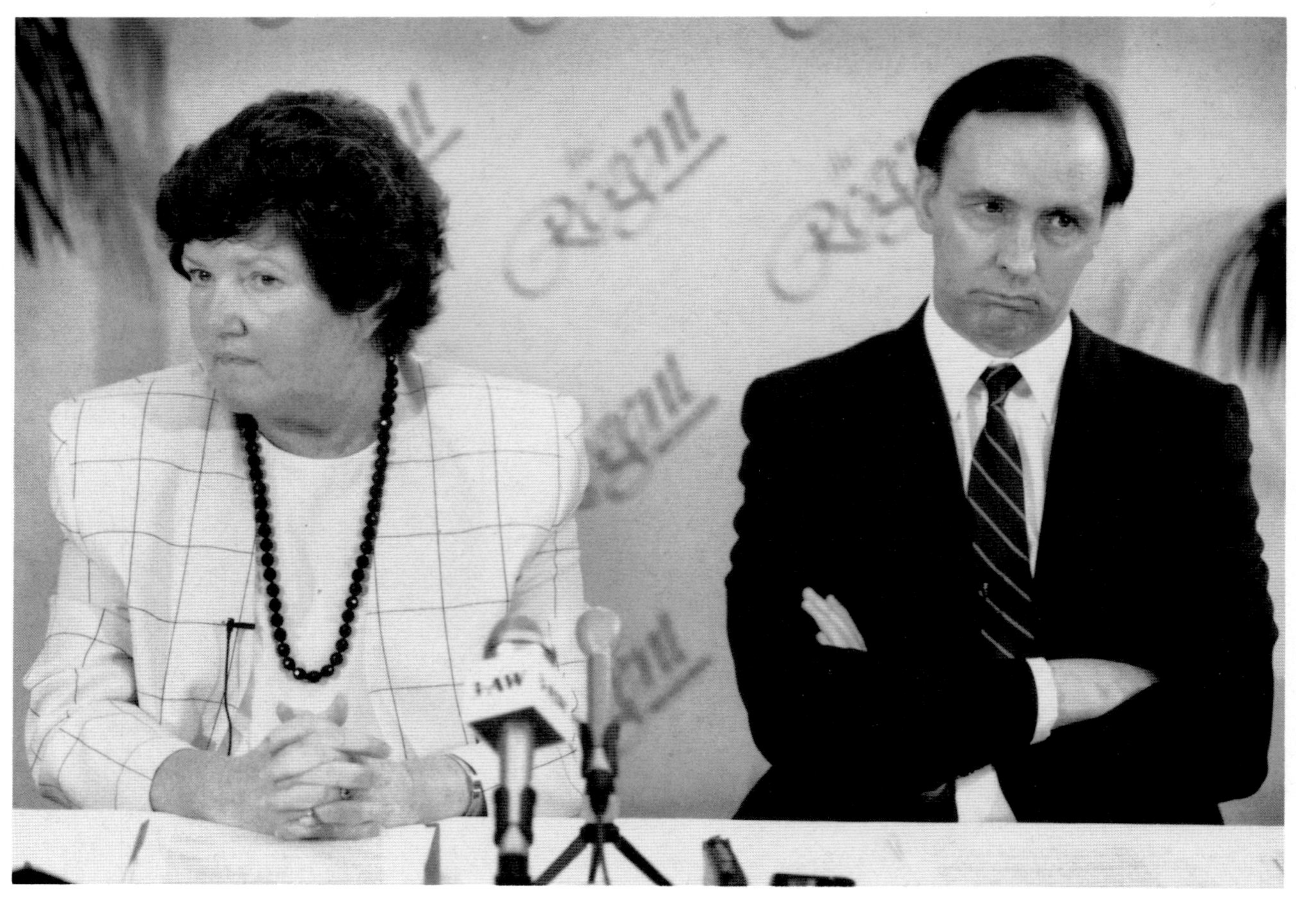

Joan Kirner and Paul Keating at a press conference to announce the sale of the State Savings Bank

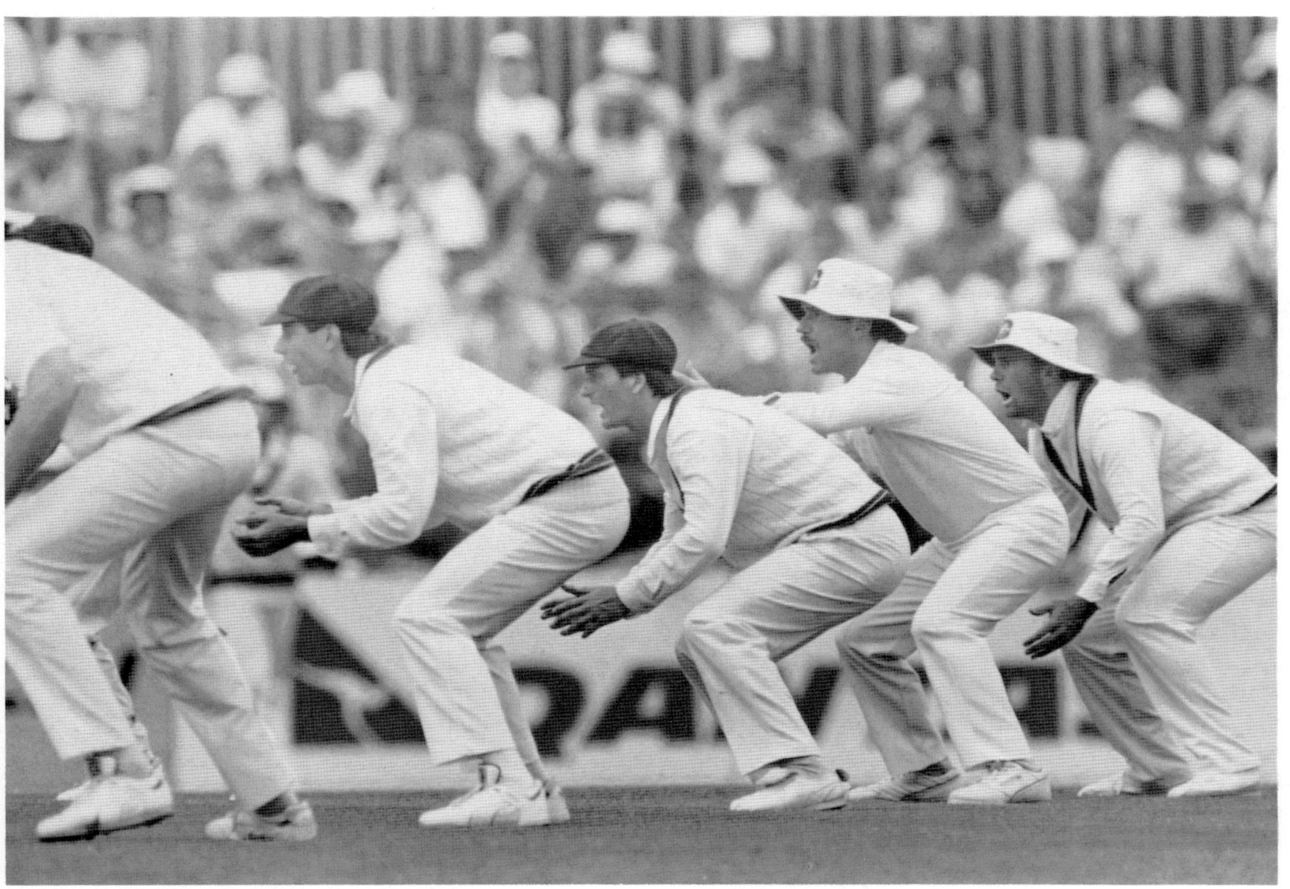

Australian slip fielders appeal in unison against Sri Lanka

John Lamb

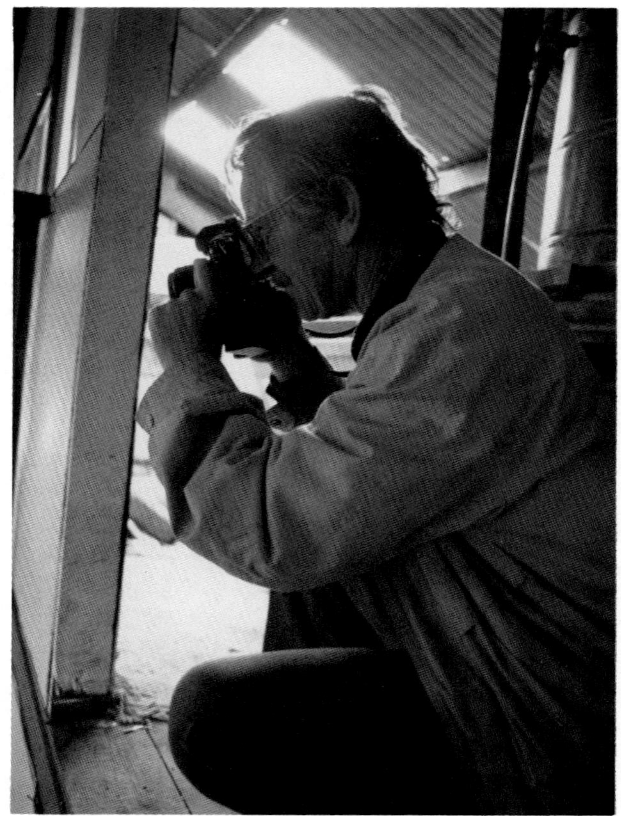
Photo: Kathleen Whelan

John Lamb has worked at the *Age* for 38 years and is one of Australia's most respected press photographers. His forte is unearthing stories and finding his own pictures independently of journalists or the Pictorial Editor.

When he first began as a photographer at 16, he was told to 'go and find something'. Now, he literally walks out of the door and chooses a direction. He might try the hospital and talk to the first person he sees. He asks questions, always looking for the humorous or the emotional.

His small build and laughing eyes do not intimidate people. Part of the secret of his success is that he is a very good listener.

'Press photography can be heartbreaking. It's a lot of work for very little reward. Often your best work will not be published or, if it is, will be printed so small that the image is lost. I also wonder if the readers of newspapers even notice the photographs. So much work goes into producing a daily newspaper — it's a real bargain at 70 cents.

'On the job, you have to give 110 per cent. There's always a picture to be found. Often, you have to create it. When I go to do a job, I decide what picture I want. Sometimes, I might have 12 ideas and have to choose the best of them. You have to assess the situation, look for all the angles and possibilities.

'There's a lot of competition. The opposition (other news photographers) want to knock me off — want to get a better picture. They are aware of me. That gives me the edge — while they're watching me, I'm concentrating on the photo.

'Often the Pictorial Editor will ask me to find my own jobs. Occasionally, I spot something as I drive along, but that's rare. I usually look for the human-interest angle. People are what newspapers are about. I often look for the humorous side of a subject, if appropriate.

'You've got to put your heart into your photos. If you have no feeling for what you are taking, your picture shows it.

'I'm not a great talker mostly, the more creative photographers aren't. They see, think and feel instead. That comes through in their work.'

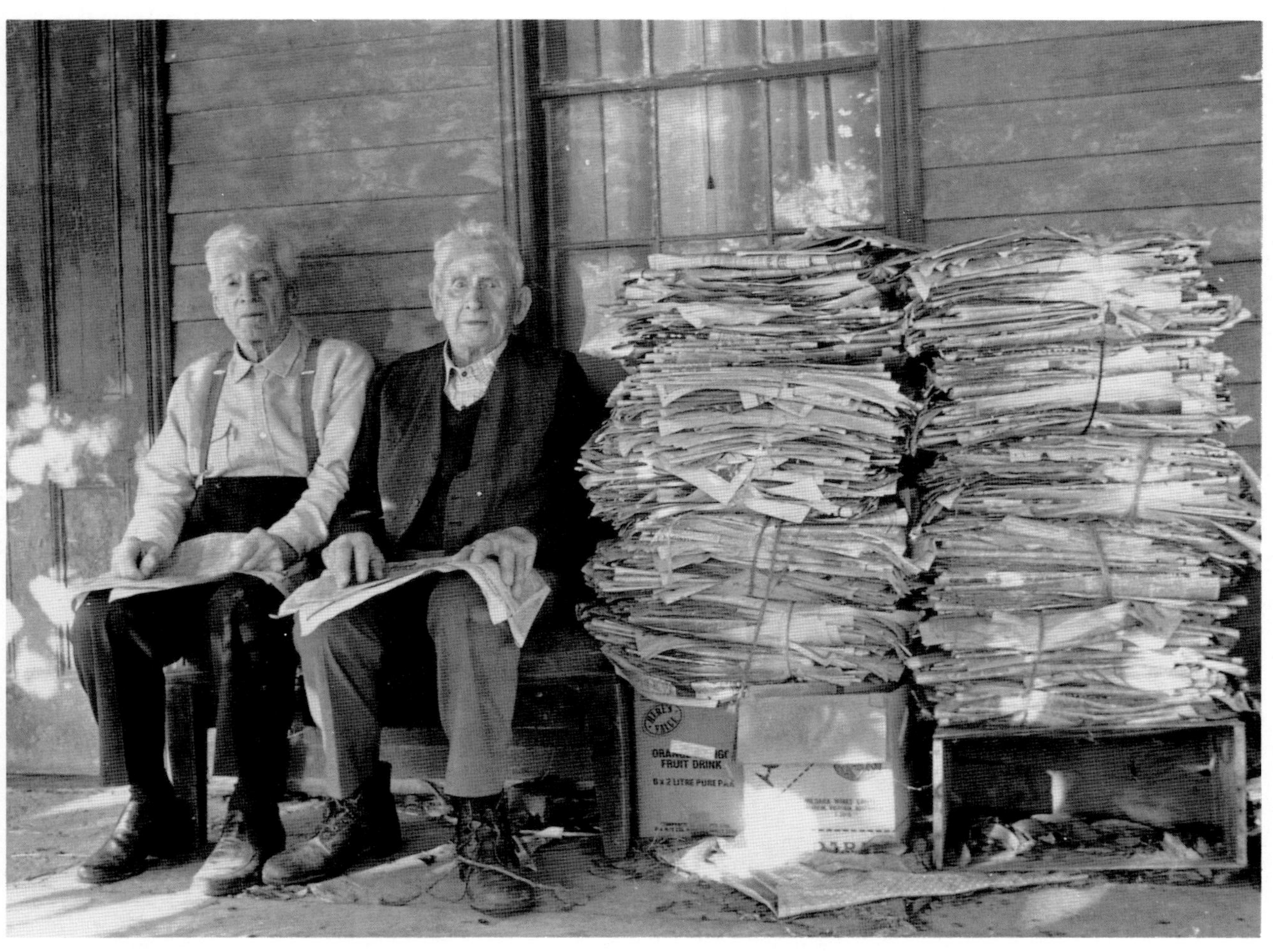

Two brothers, one 98 years old and the other 92, photographed in 1985 at the home where they were raised

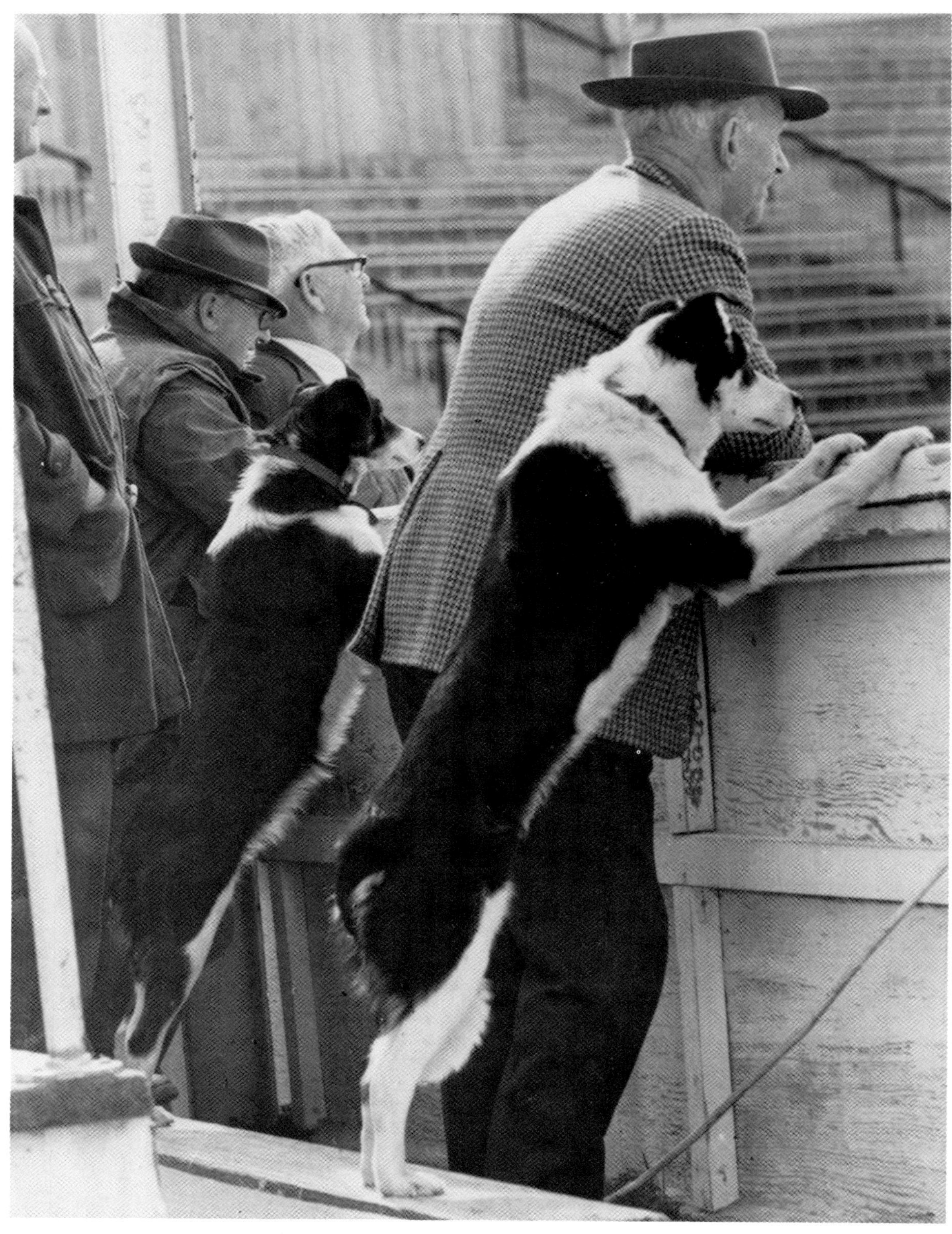

Alex Coutts and his two dogs, Lyster Maggie and Mossbank Moss, watch the sheep dog trials. 1980

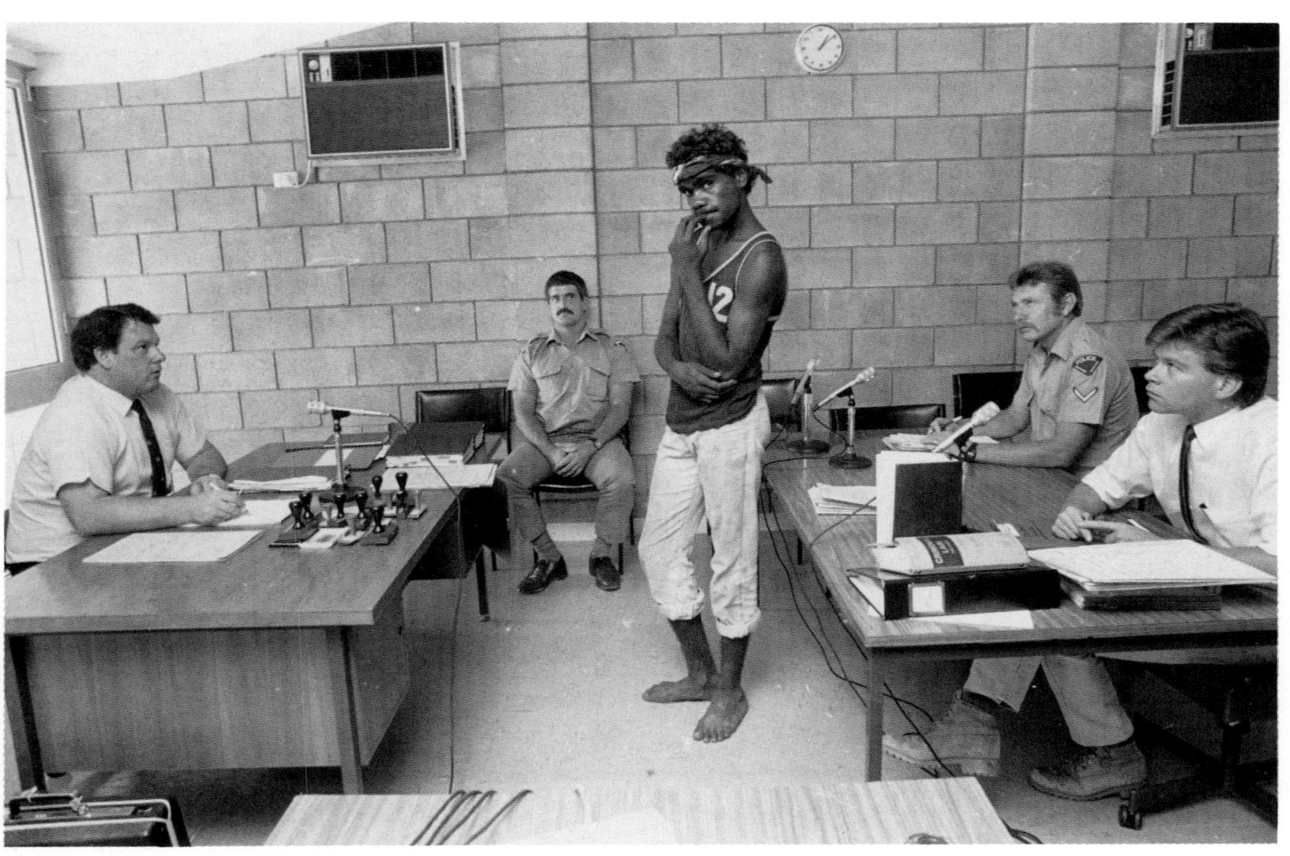

Robney Herbert, of the Walpiri tribe of Lajamanu, being questioned by Tim Hinchliffe, a magistrate who travels by plane throughout the Northern Territory, 1985

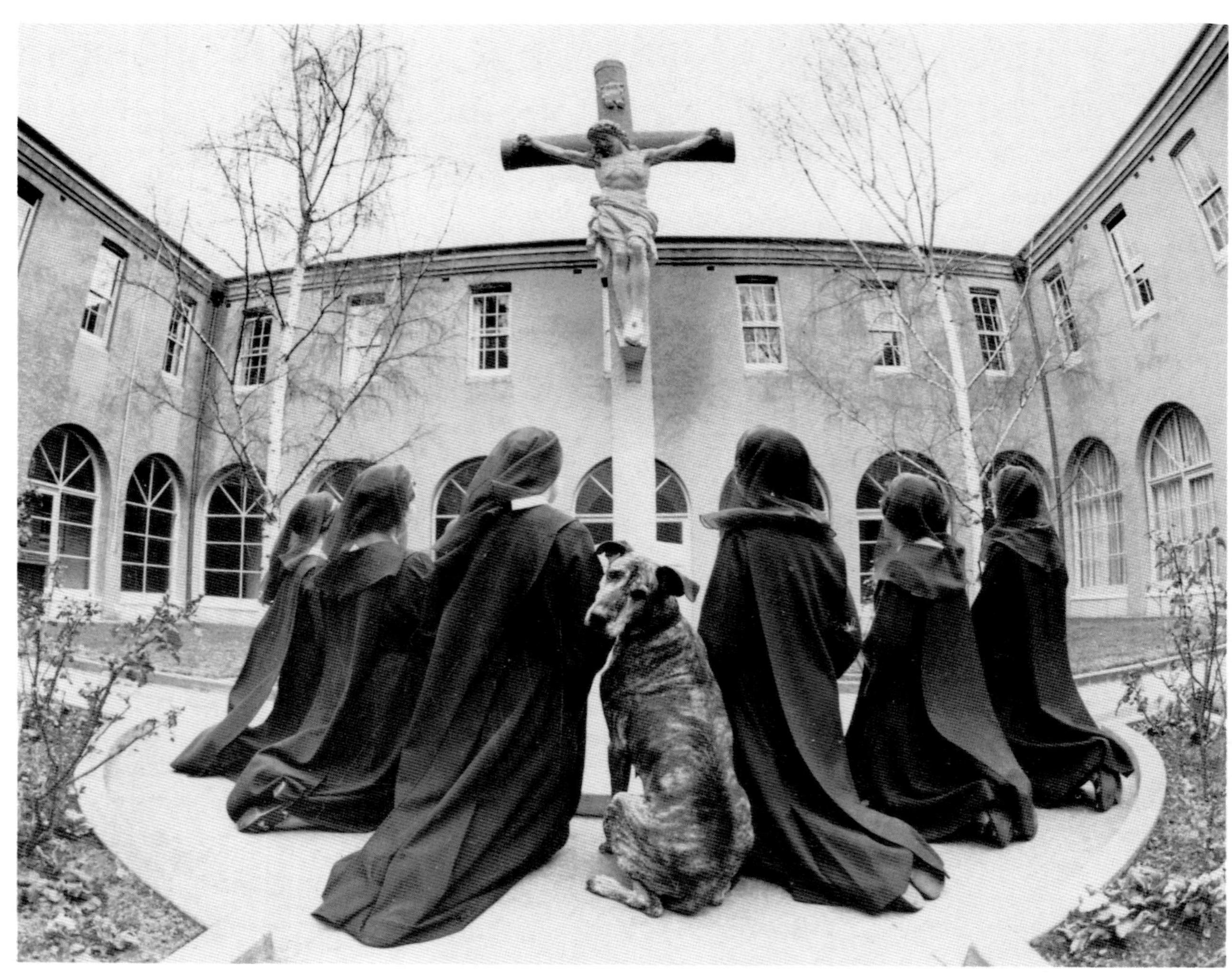

Carmelite nuns with one of their Great Danes. Kew, Victoria. August 1980

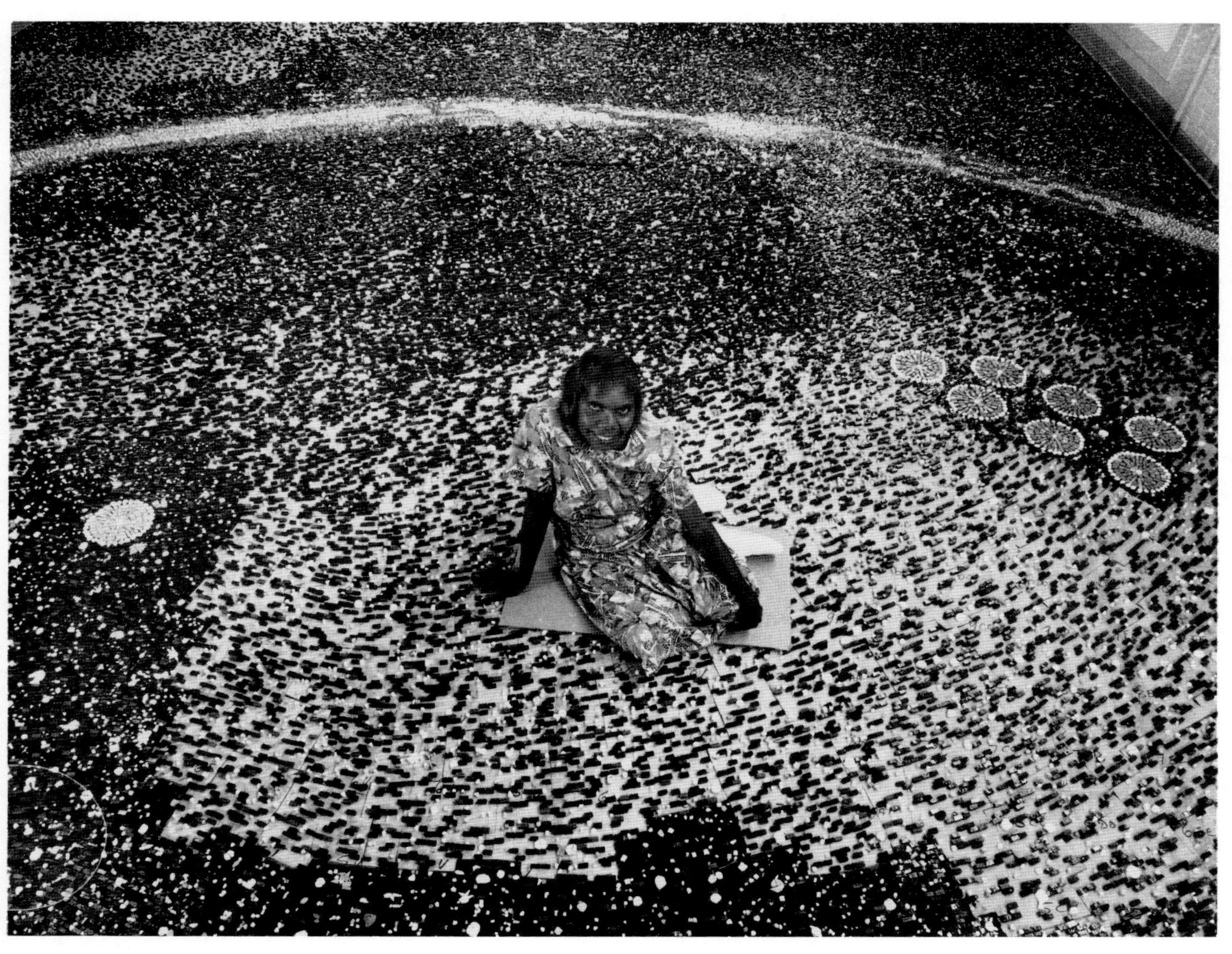

Nora Napaljarri Nelson with 'Milky Way Dreaming'. The mosaic, commissioned for Darwin's new law courts, was designed from her painting. December 1990

Mike Martin

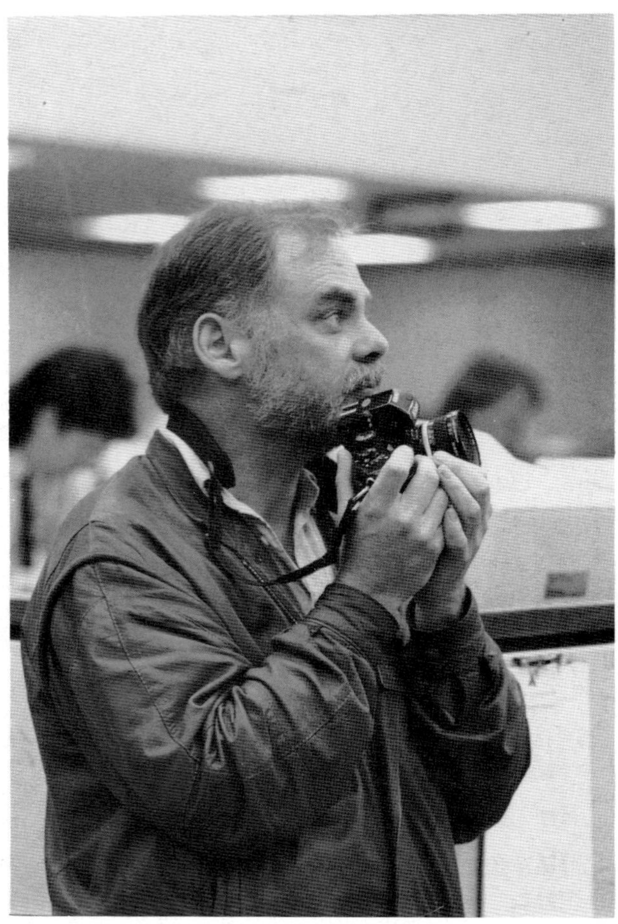

Photo: Kathleen Whelan

Mike Martin started as a press photographer with Albury *Border Morning Mail* in 1967 and with the *Age* in 1978. He specialises in skiing and winter sports and covered the first World Cup to be held in Australia at Thredbo in 1989.

He is very conscious of how he prints his negatives and talks of putting in tones and taking out the background, by burning in to darken it until it blackens. He uses his hands to manipulate those tones, to prevent the light from hitting certain areas. He selects a contrast grade of printing paper according to what he wants from the final print.

'The interesting part of press photography is never knowing where you will be each day. I prefer moving around the city and state rather than working in an office. The drawback is the working hours. The news happens all day and night. It makes family life very difficult.

'A knowledge of "important" faces and names is essential. You need to know every politician, sportsperson, and prominent personality.

'And keeping up with sportspeople in action is physically and mentally demanding. You have to follow focus as skiers come down the slope. You cannot pre-focus. They are at their fastest when they're moving head on towards you. You need a very fast shutter speed (500th or 1000th of a second), which often requires you to have your aperture wide open. Your depth of field, therefore, is limited to a few metres. Your focus has to be precise.

'At an angle of ¾, you can pan your camera with the movement using a 125th or 250th of a second shutter speed, giving you greater depth of field. Often you're not sure of what you've got until you get into the darkroom.

'Choosing a good spot to photograph from is important. With speed sports you usually pick a danger spot or hazard. 'But printing is where you make the picture. It is there where I choose the framing of the photograph. Each negative is different and deserves its own style and use of tones.'

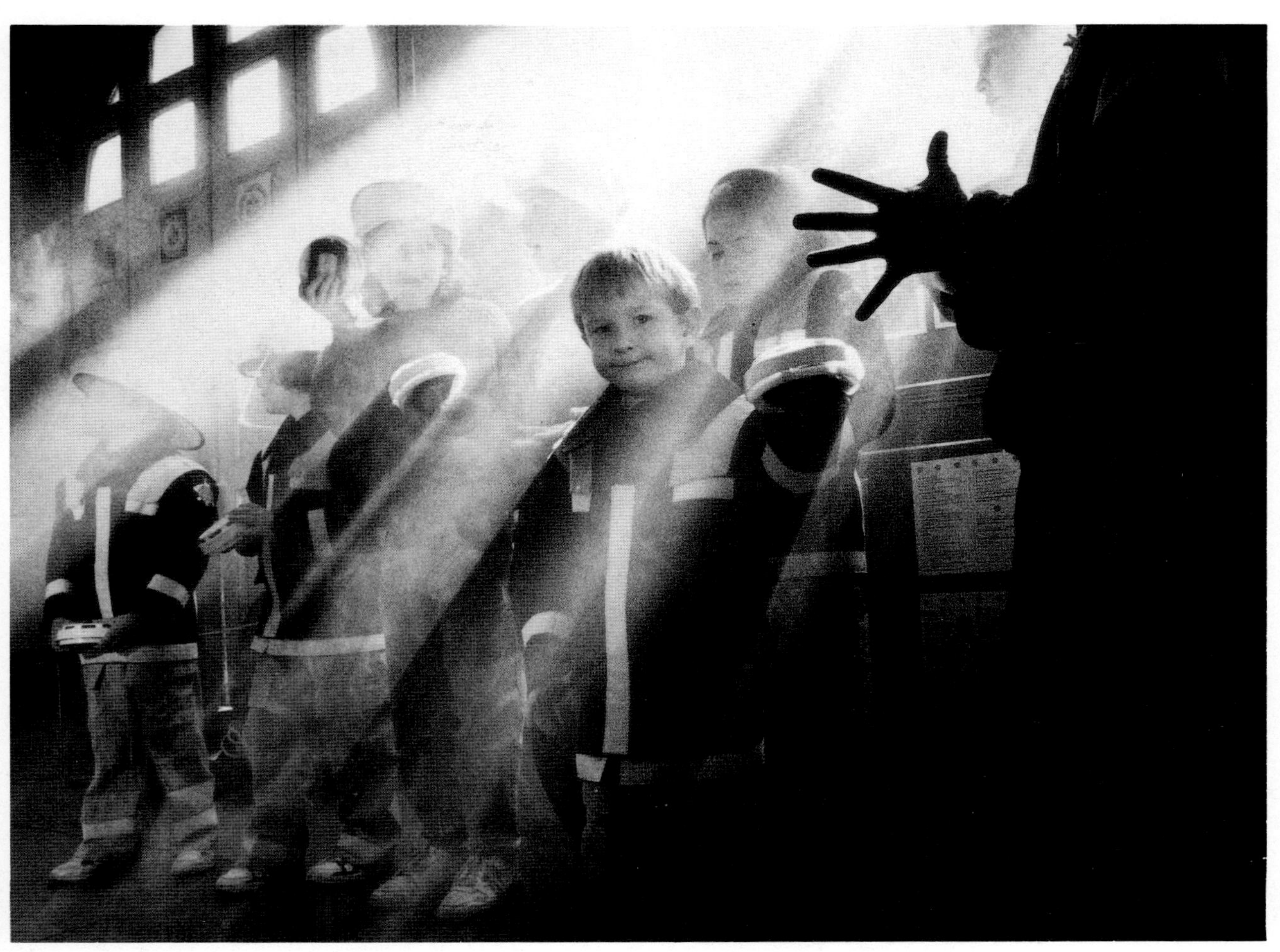

Richard Waterson, age 5, at the launch of a public awareness campaign on fire and smoke detectors at Eastern Hill Fire Station

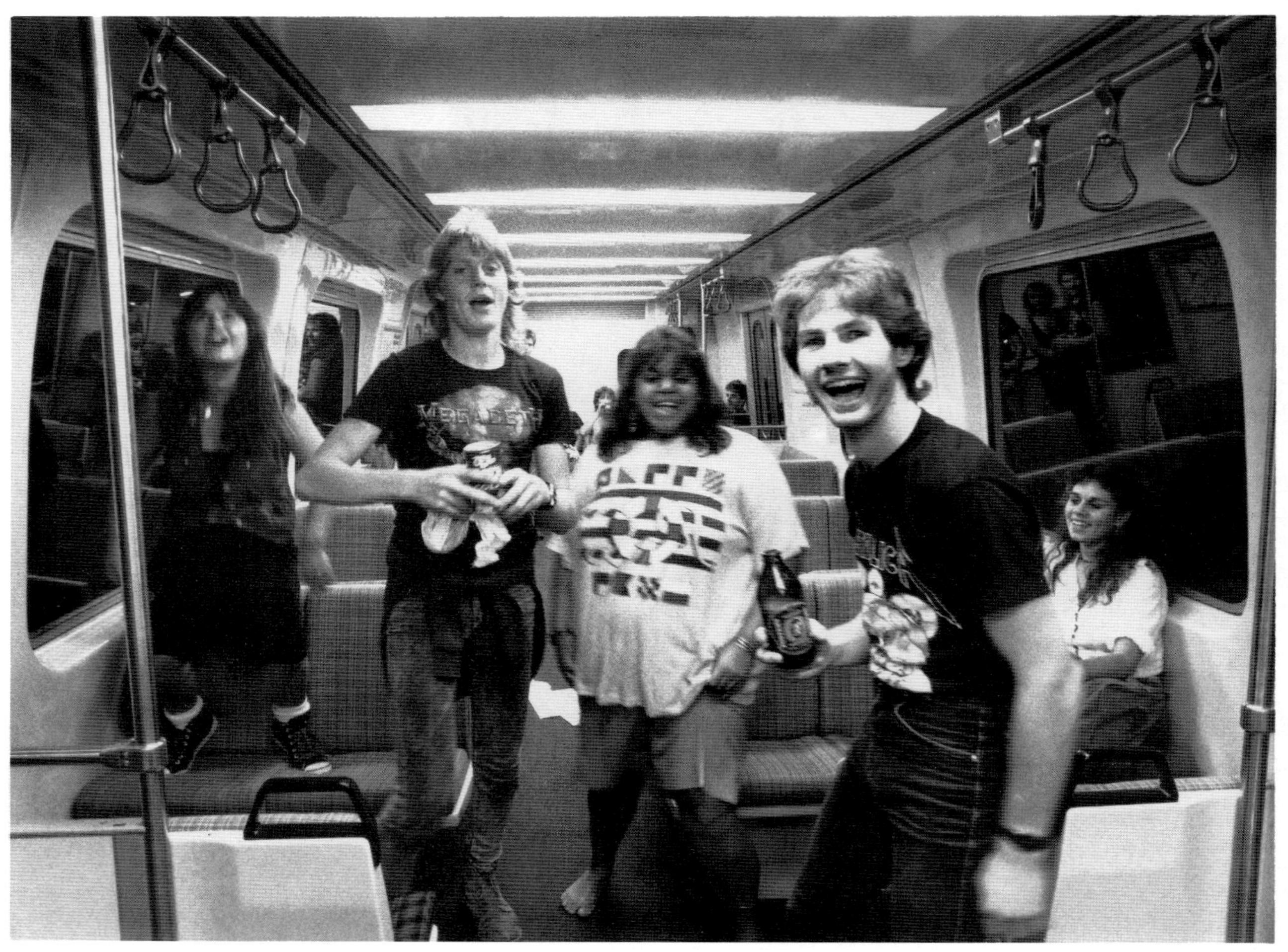

Train kids at Ringwood, 1989. (1600 ASA, 30th/second, aperture f8)

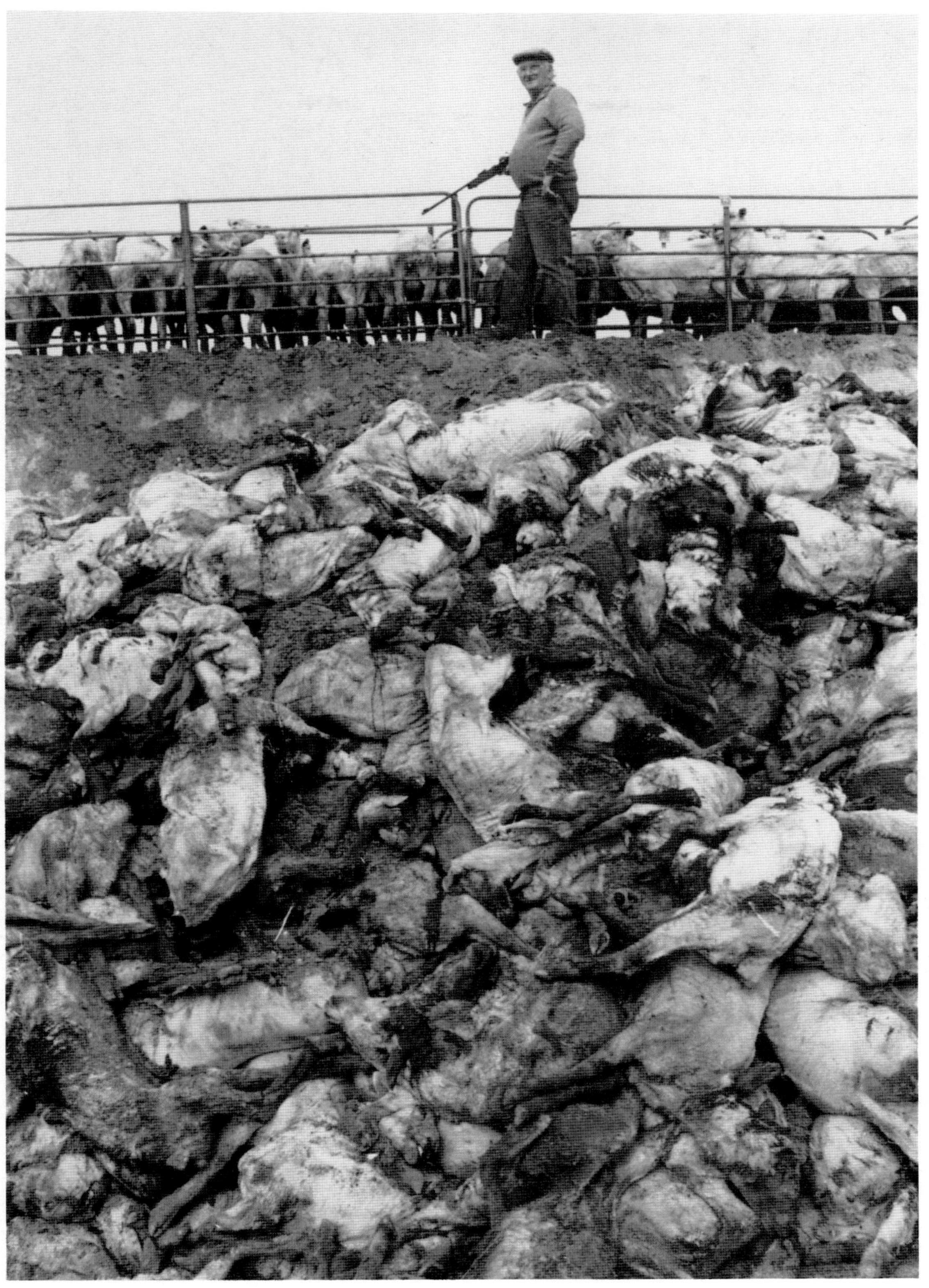

September 1990: it was cheaper to shoot sheep than to sell them

Neil Newitt

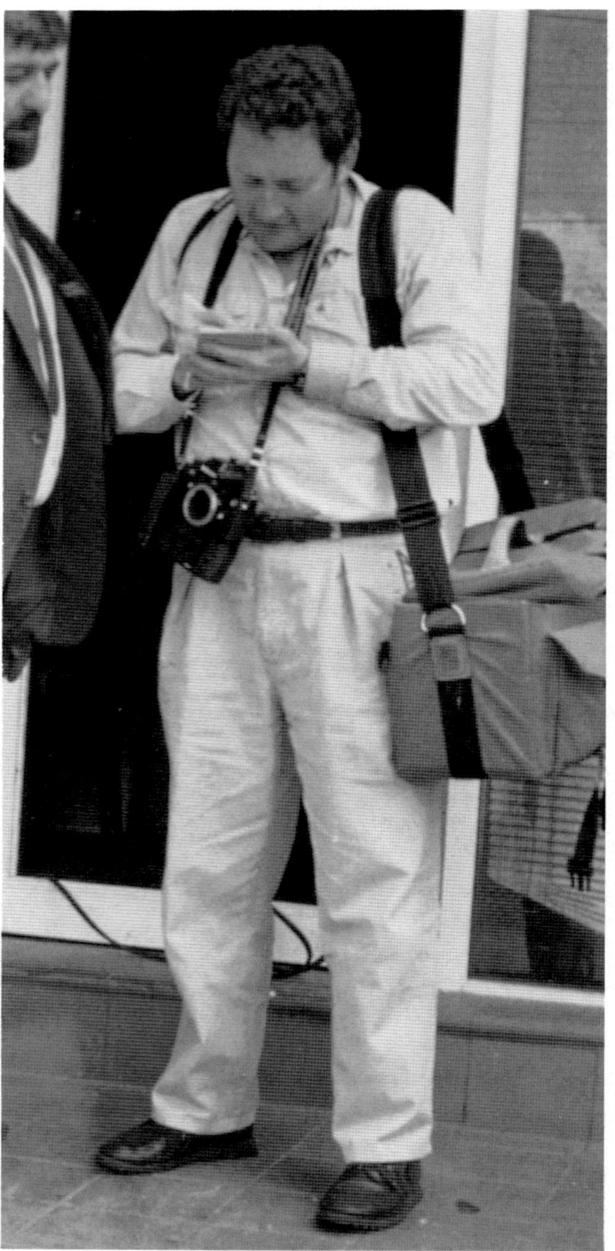

Photo: Kathleen Whelan

Neil Newitt has been a press photographer for 10 years. He began by freelancing with the Warwick *Daily News* in Queensland, where he grew up. After completing a Certificate of Photography course at the Queensland College of the Arts, he moved to the Toowoomba *Chronicle* and then to the Warrnambool *Standard*. He joined the *Age* in 1987. At one stage he spent most of his non-working hours photographing motor sports, and is one of Australia's best motor racing photographers.

'Being able to tap into the psyche of others is part of the challenge of photography, and that demands a keen interest in people. It is the human element that makes a press picture. One of the tests is knowing enough about your subject while still being able to keep an open mind so as not to cloud the story with your own bias or stereotyped imagery.

'There is also the challenge of keeping your eyes open for the obvious picture (such as a winning runner crossing the finishing line), while also being on the look out for a one-off combination of elements that will produce a memorable image. Although the basic rules of photography (composition, lighting and background) must be considered, the press photographer has little time to wait for the elements to come together and has to work on the run.

'Motor racing is one of the most difficult and dangerous sports to photograph. For track work, you can use any lens between 200mm and 800mm. (Motor bikes need a longer lens [800mm] to get adequate magnification.) With a 600mm lens, you have only a 6-degree angle of view in your viewfinder, but you have to be aware of what is going on outside that viewfinder. You need to know where the next car is and if it's coming in your direction. It's essential to keep your equipment to a bare minimum so that you can move out of the way quickly. Your reflexes must be good.

'Motor racing is not a daily occurrence in this job, but photographing people is. I always look forward to the challenge of the portrait. I try to capture the subject's situation through their surroundings or through their expression.

'With Pat Cash, the identifiable headband and the sweat tells you that he is a sportsman. John Elliot's upfront character can be suggested even at a press conference by catching him as he looks over his glasses or by including the defiant cigarette which today most of would find unacceptable. Even a small detail can reveal a lot.'

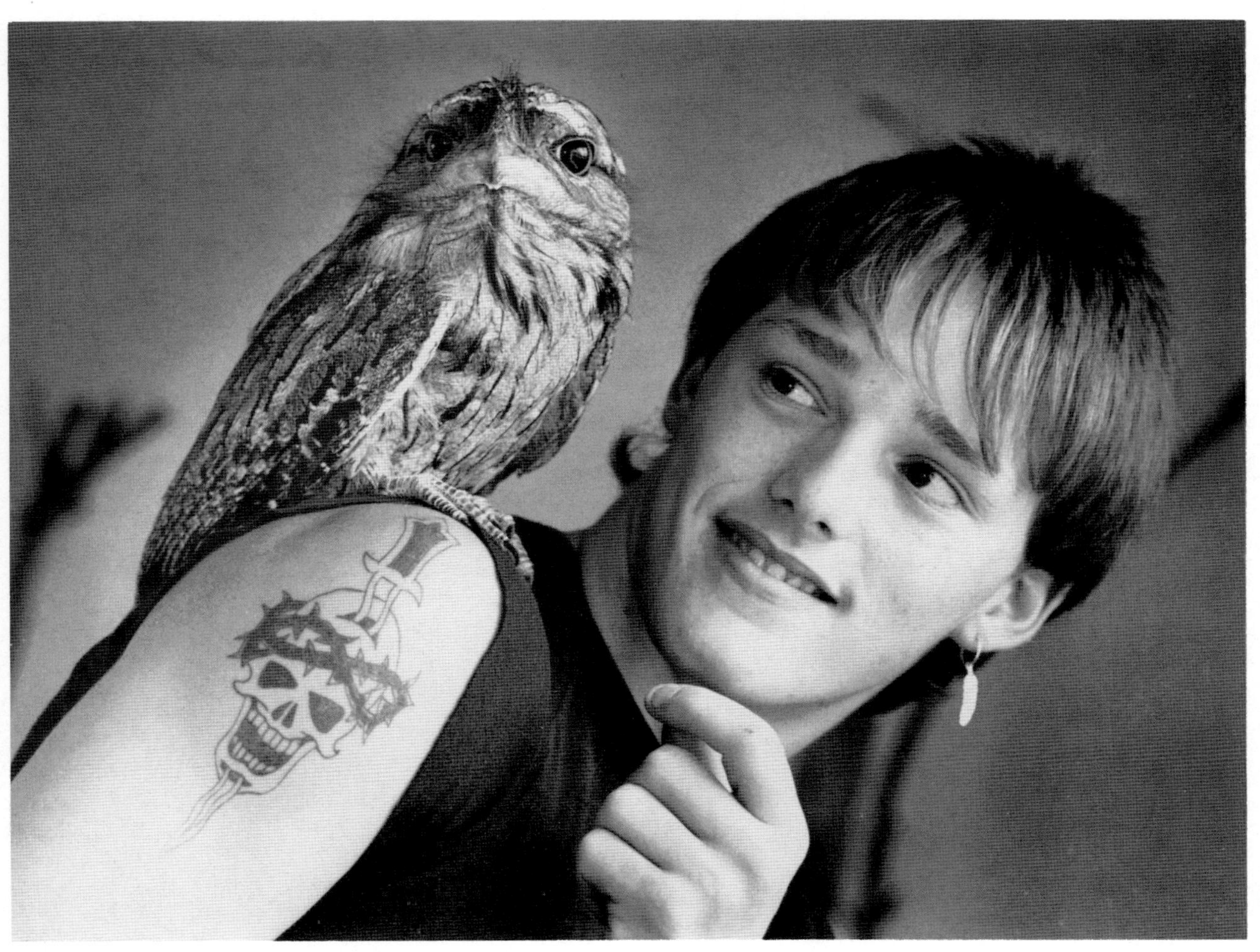

Brian Creevy, an inmate at the Langi Kal Kal Youth Training Centre near Ballarat, with a tawny frogmouth owl that was to be returned to the bush after 'rehabilitation' at the wildlife centre built by young offenders. It was photographed inside the shelter using soft window light and a fast shutter speed to 'spot' any movement by the frogmouth

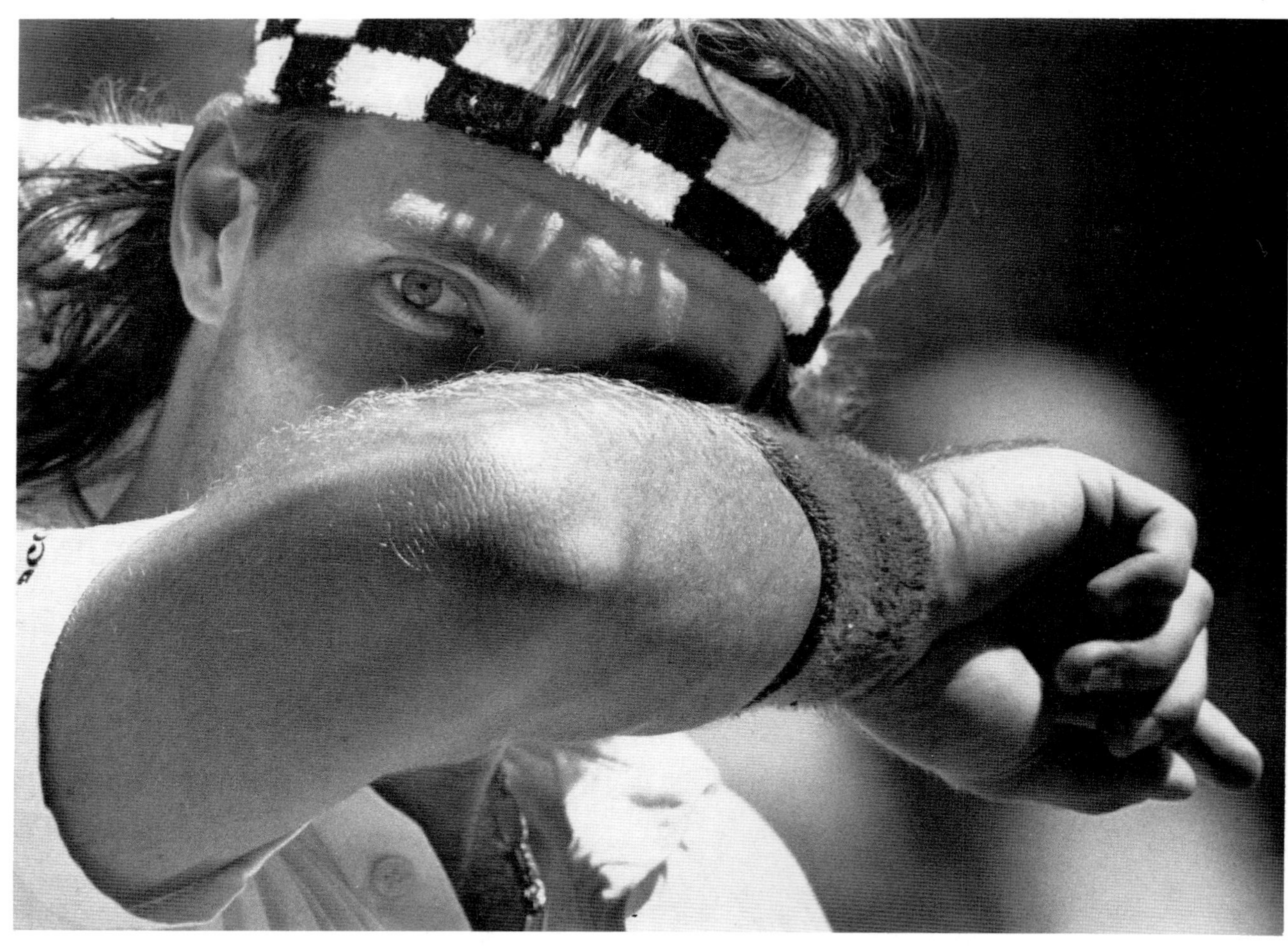

Pat Cash sweats it out during the 1988 Men's Final at the National Tennis Centre, Melbourne. By using a long telephoto lens (800mm) the background is eliminated, producing a striking portrait of a sportsman 'at work'

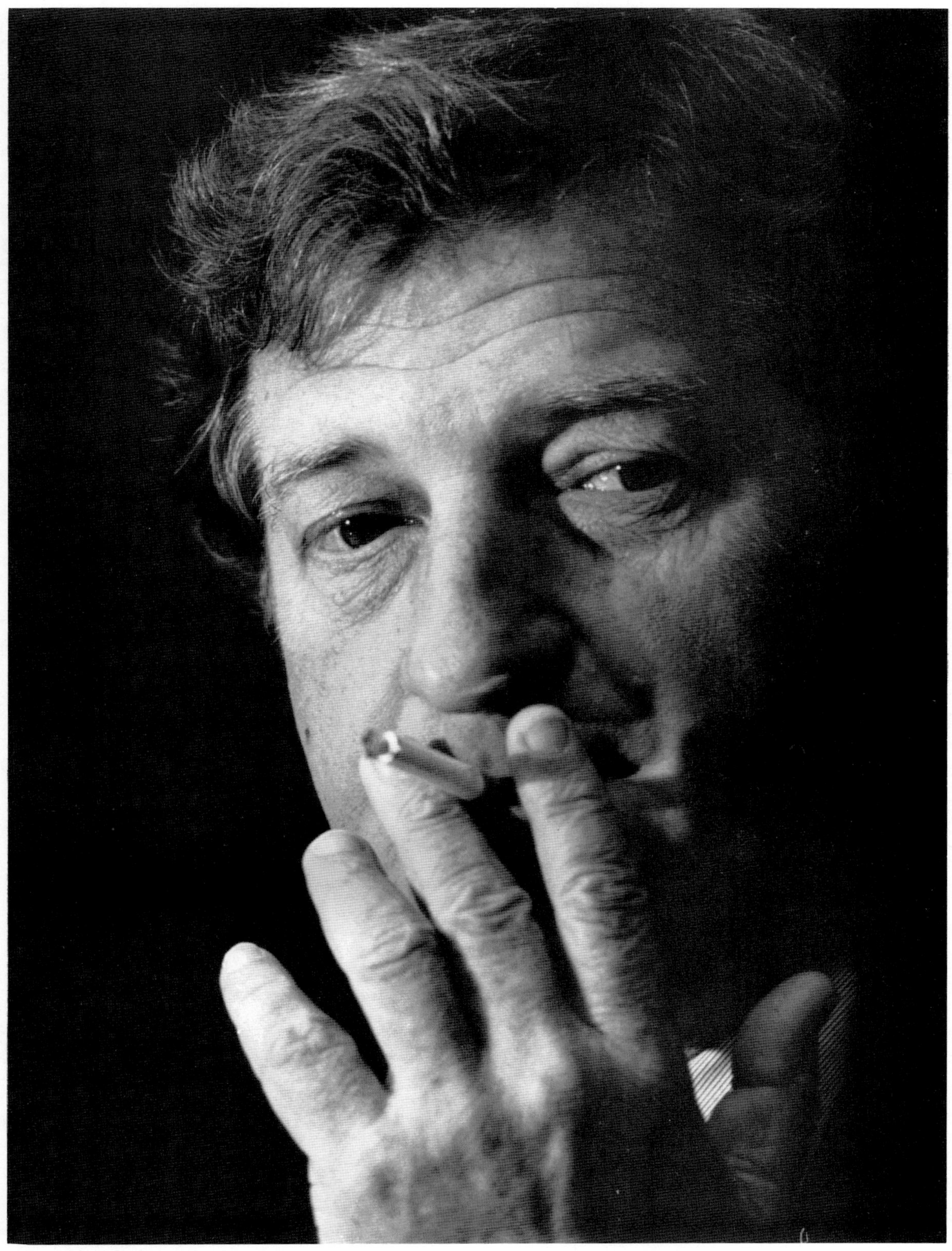

Even though it was a typical press conference, this dramatic portrait of businessman John Elliott was achieved by observing the direction of the light and then watching for the elements to come together

Bruce Postle

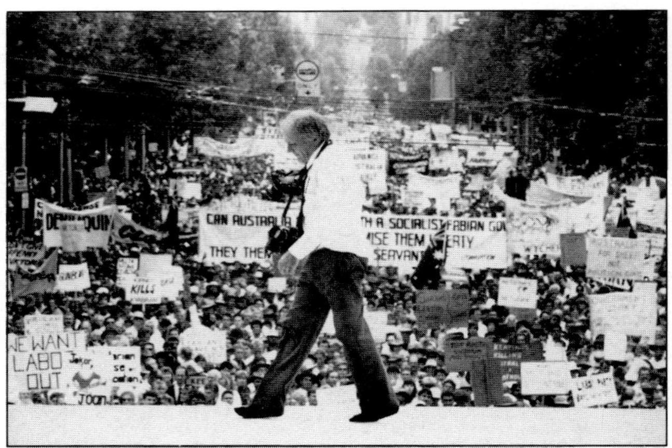

Bruce Postle is one of the few press photographers who actually prefers to organise and create pictures. If the situation permits, he will try time exposures, double exposures, all kinds of unusual 'tricks'. By using a tripod and a slow shutter speed, he can show the reader what the crowd at the Arts Festival Opening looks like over three seconds. He will even pre-plan double-, triple- or seven-fold exposures by photographing something on part of the frame before he goes to a job and then photographing the subject later on another part of the frame. Twenty years ago he was using this technique with Speed Graphic 5″ x 4″ cameras, by placing a black card over part of the lens. He would draw on the film sheath so as to know where to put the second exposure.

His preference is for black and white as it gives the viewer a different perspective to colour.

'It's an art that you acquire — being able to look at something and visualise the best shot, to think beyond the obvious, to make my own pictures. Candid shots can be dull. You can make a photograph a thousand times better by taking people to a different spot. But you must know what you are doing. People lose confidence if you shift them more than once.

'The theatre is good because you can control the lighting. If you are prepared to wait until other photographers leave, you can organise the actors without worrying that the others will copy your idea.'

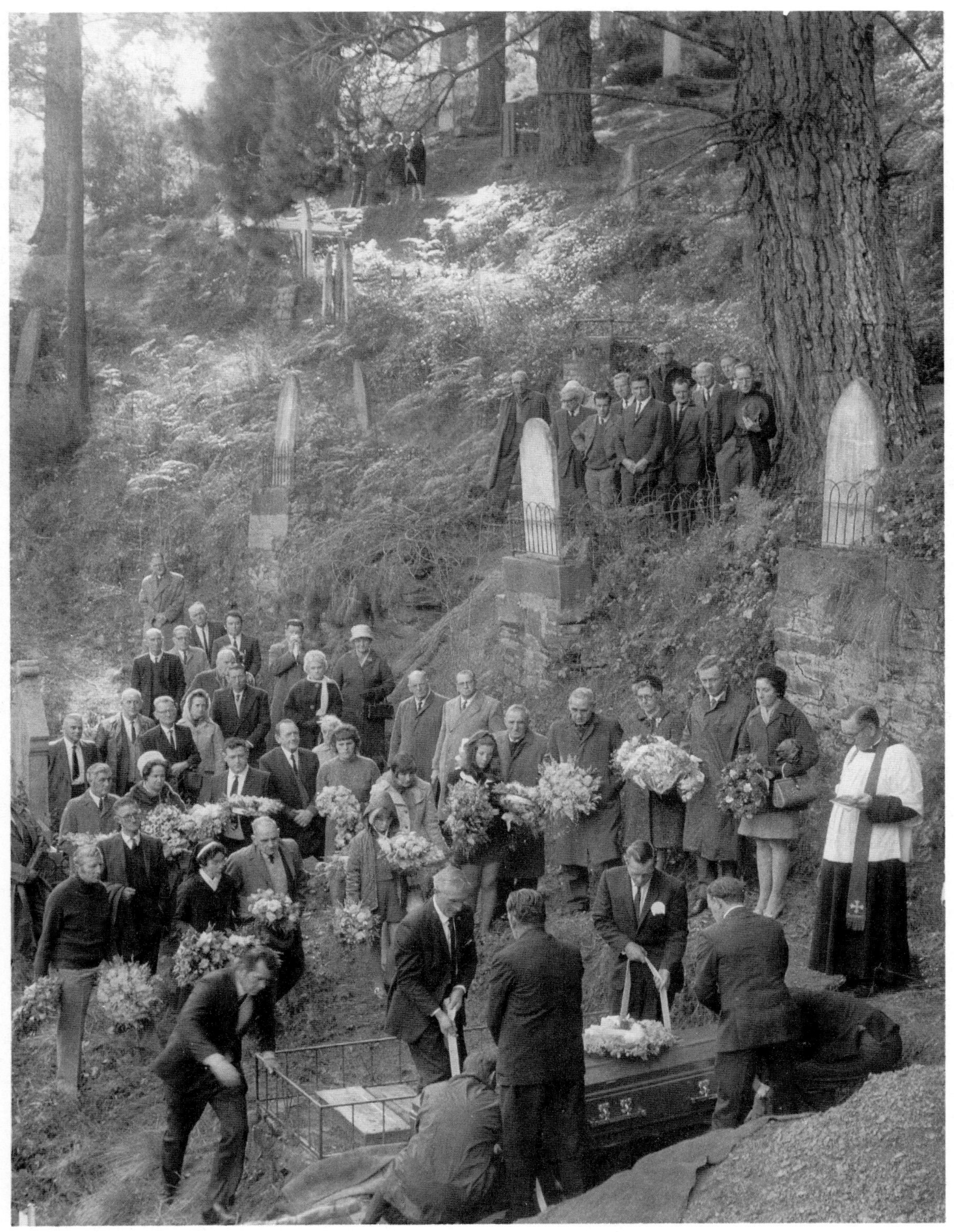

The last gold miner to be buried in Walhalla Cemetery. (400 ASA film, 35mm lens, 125th/second, aperture f8)

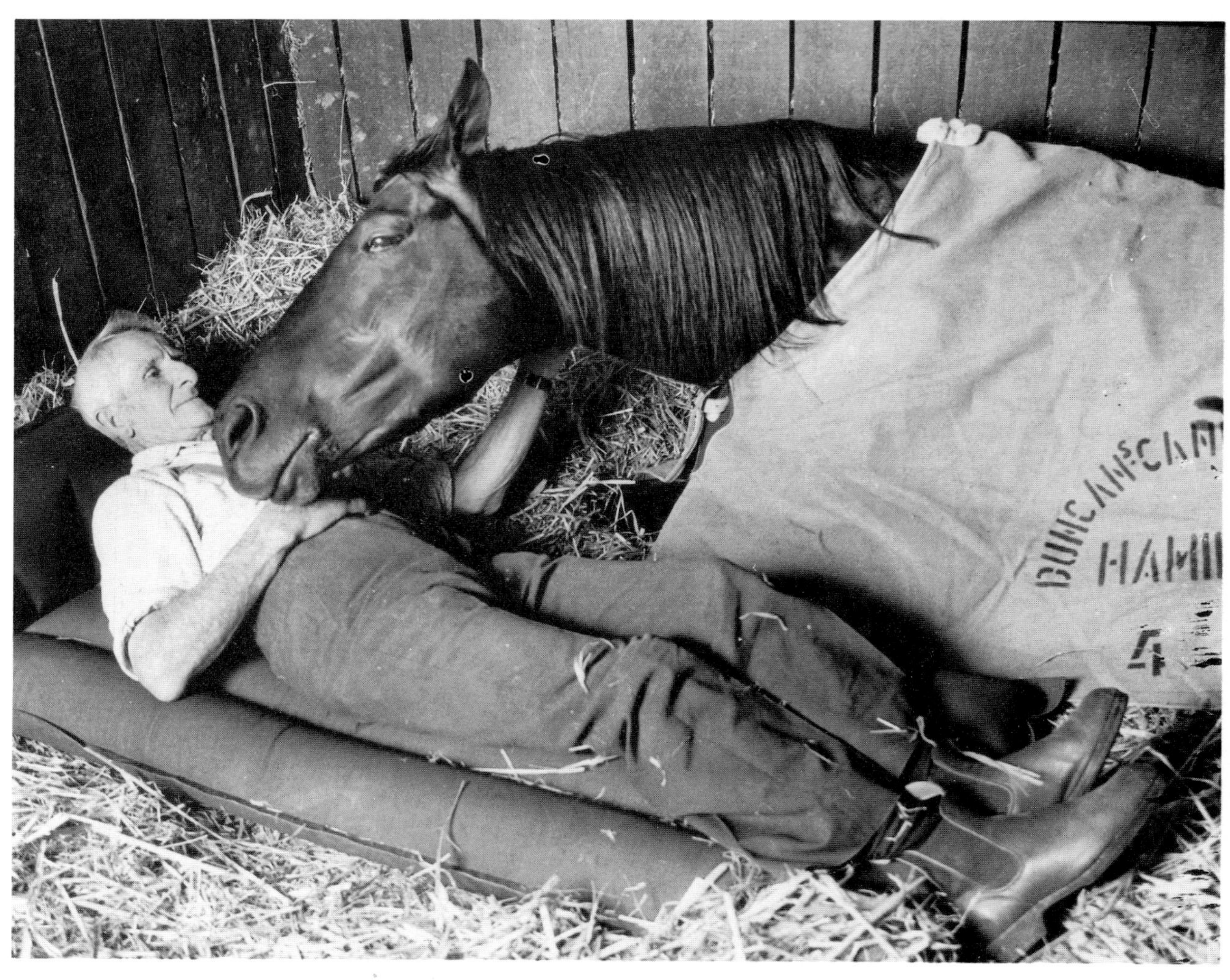

Tommy Woodcock and Reckless the night before the Melbourne Cup, 1977. 73-year-old Tommy often slept in the stables with Reckless prior to a big race to keep him calm. Tommy Woodcock had also trained Phar Lap in the 1930s

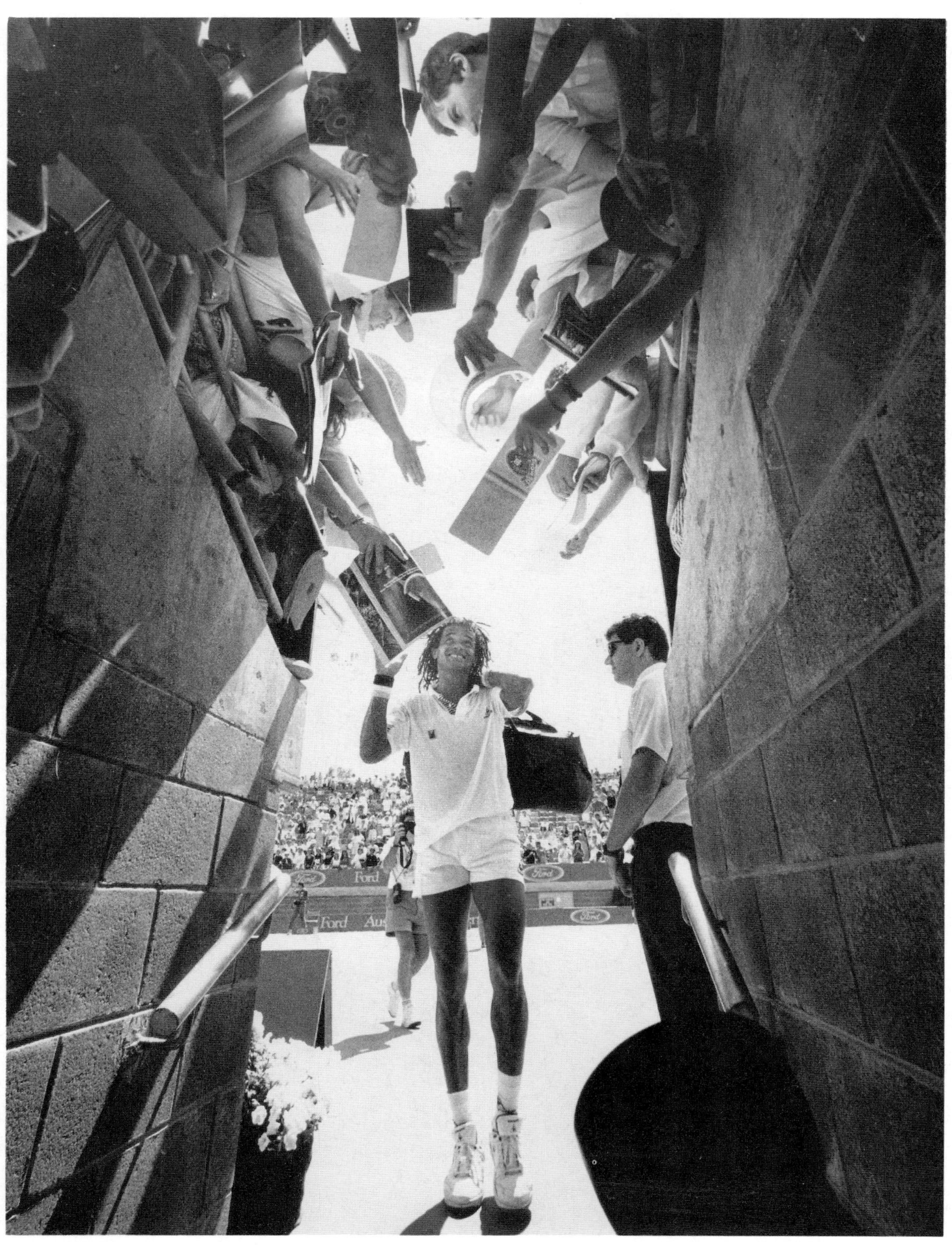

French tennis player Yannick Noah encounters fans on leaving the outside court of the National Tennis Centre, January 1990. (400 ASA film, 15mm lens, 250th/second, aperture f5.6)

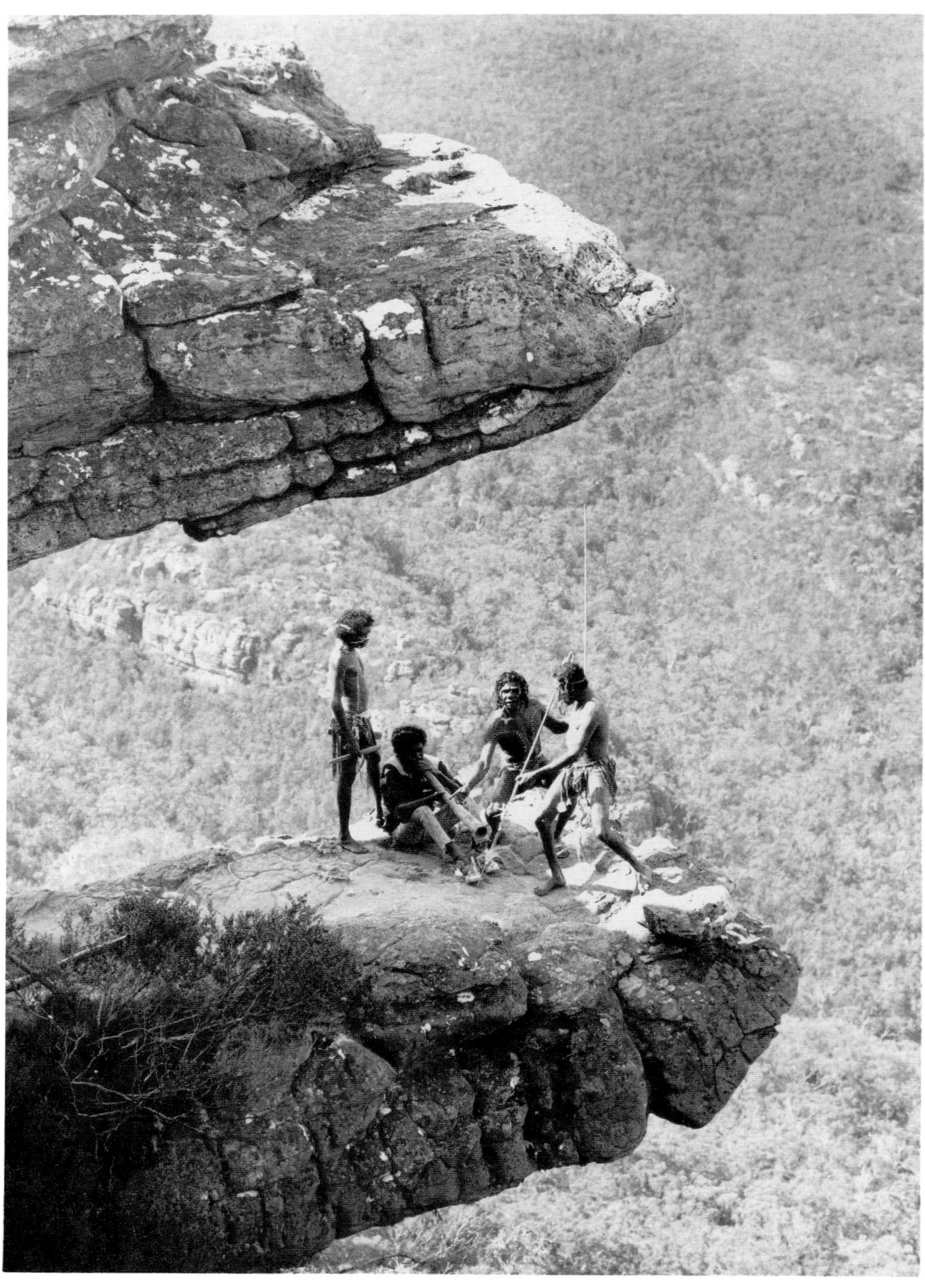

Aborigines performing at the Balconies in the Grampians, 1991. (400 ISO film, 135mm lens, 250th/second, aperture f11)

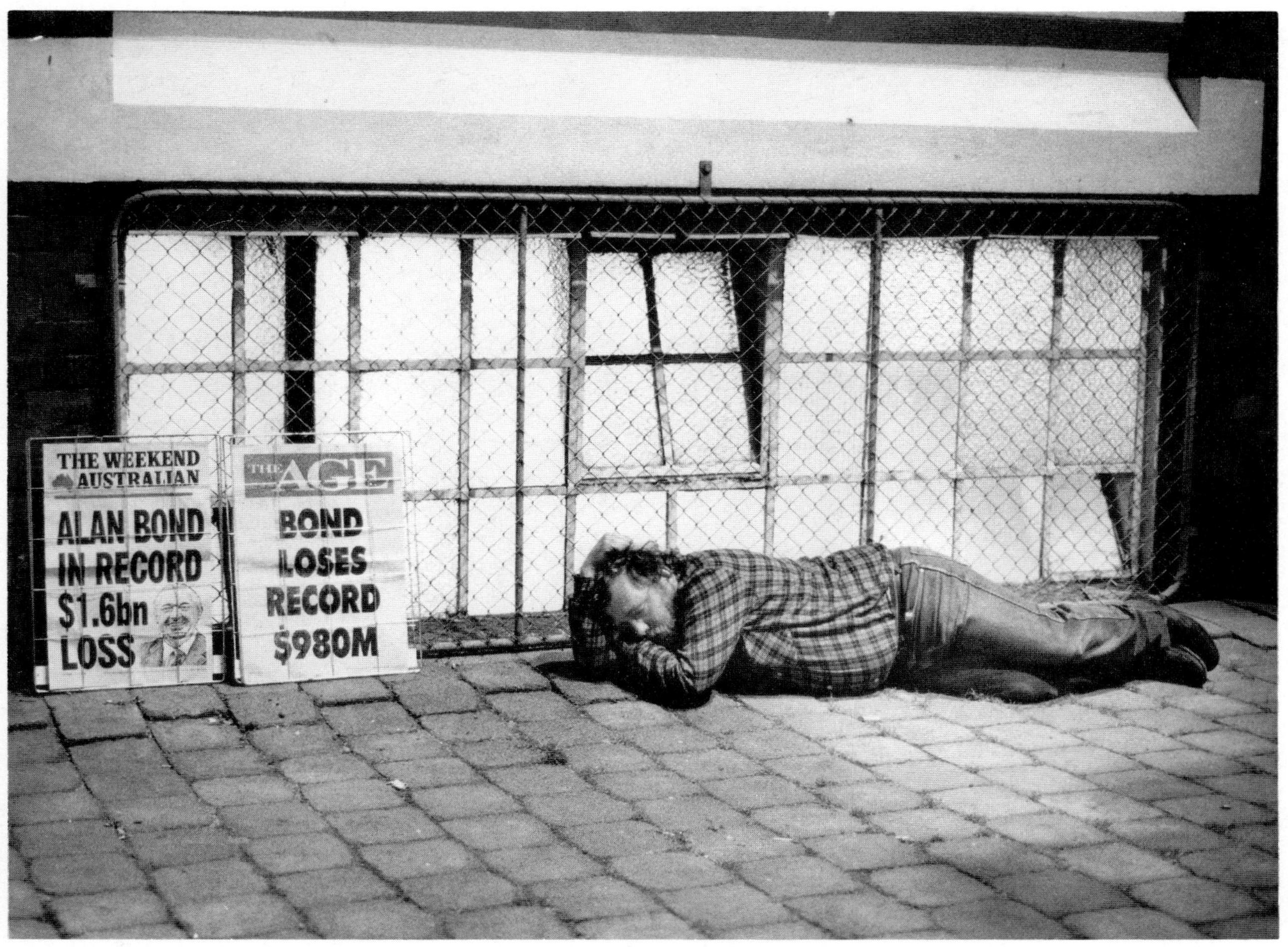

While Alan Bond loses (either $980m or $1.6bn according to which paper you read), this man sleeps on the footpath, October 1988. (400 ASA film, 85mm lens, 30th/second, aperture f5.6)

Joe Sabljak

Joe uses light to exaggerate the three-dimensional roundness of form and exploits background to make the subject stand out.

'If it's a black person, I'll look for a light background. With a white person, I try to find a dark background. I'll use anything that will produce a good shot. It's an on-the-spot decision.

'If you could convince the subject that it will make a good shot, you'd ask them to stand on their head. I once managed to get Steve Crabbe in a toilet at the launch of a water conservation campaign.'

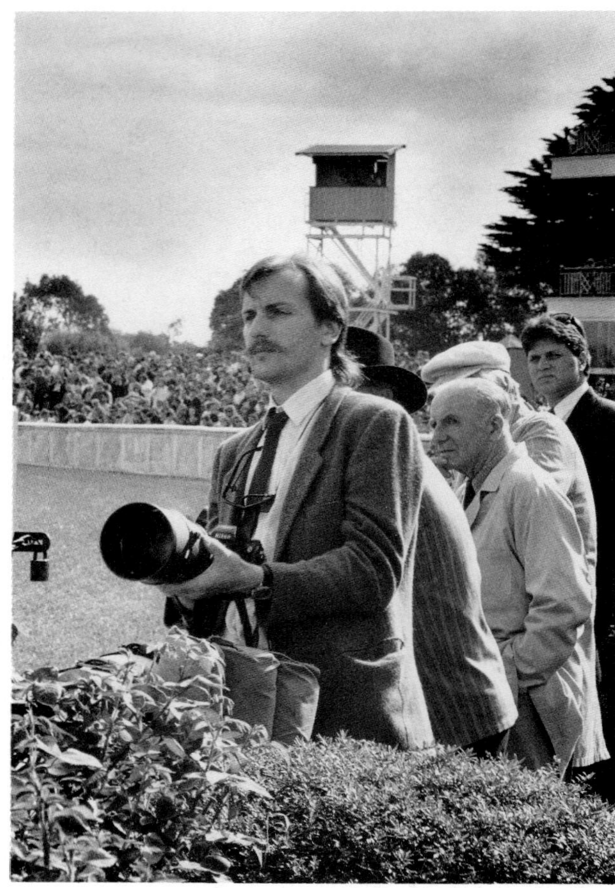

Photo: Kathleen Whelan

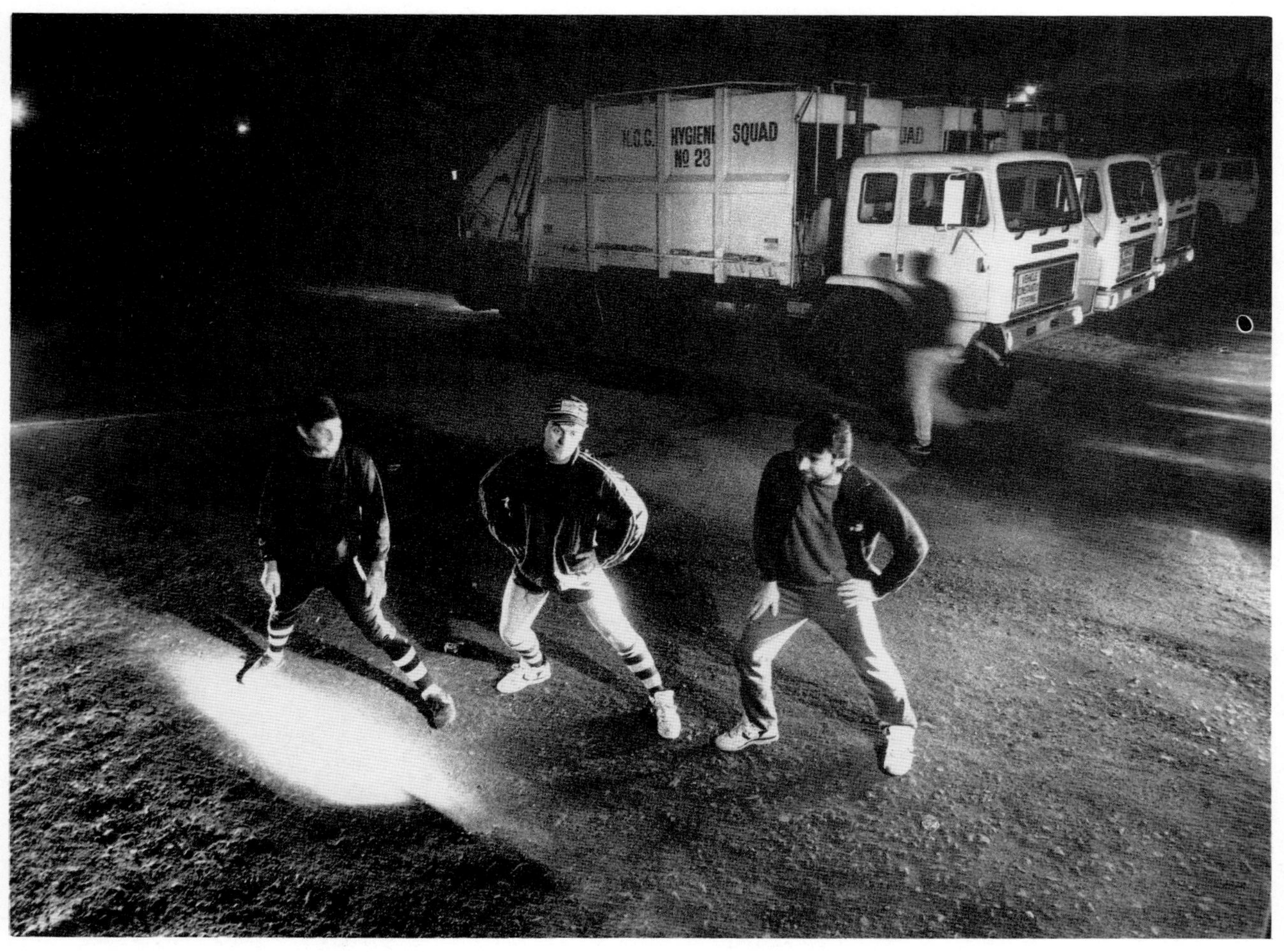

Hawthorn garbos doing warm-up exercises before they start work. (Nikon F4, T-max 3200 film, 20mm lens)

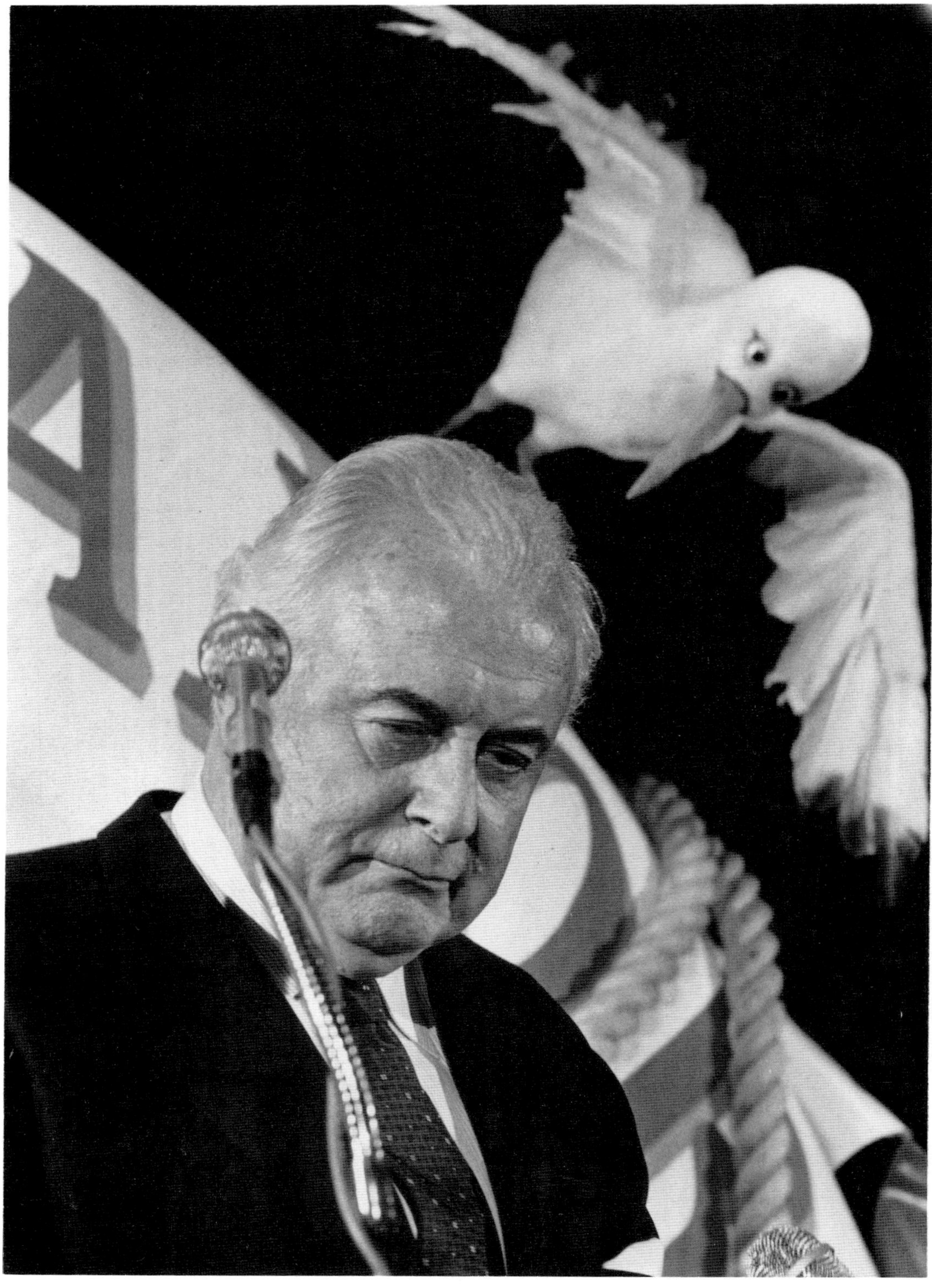

Former prime minister Gough Whitlam at the launch of The Pirates of Penzance

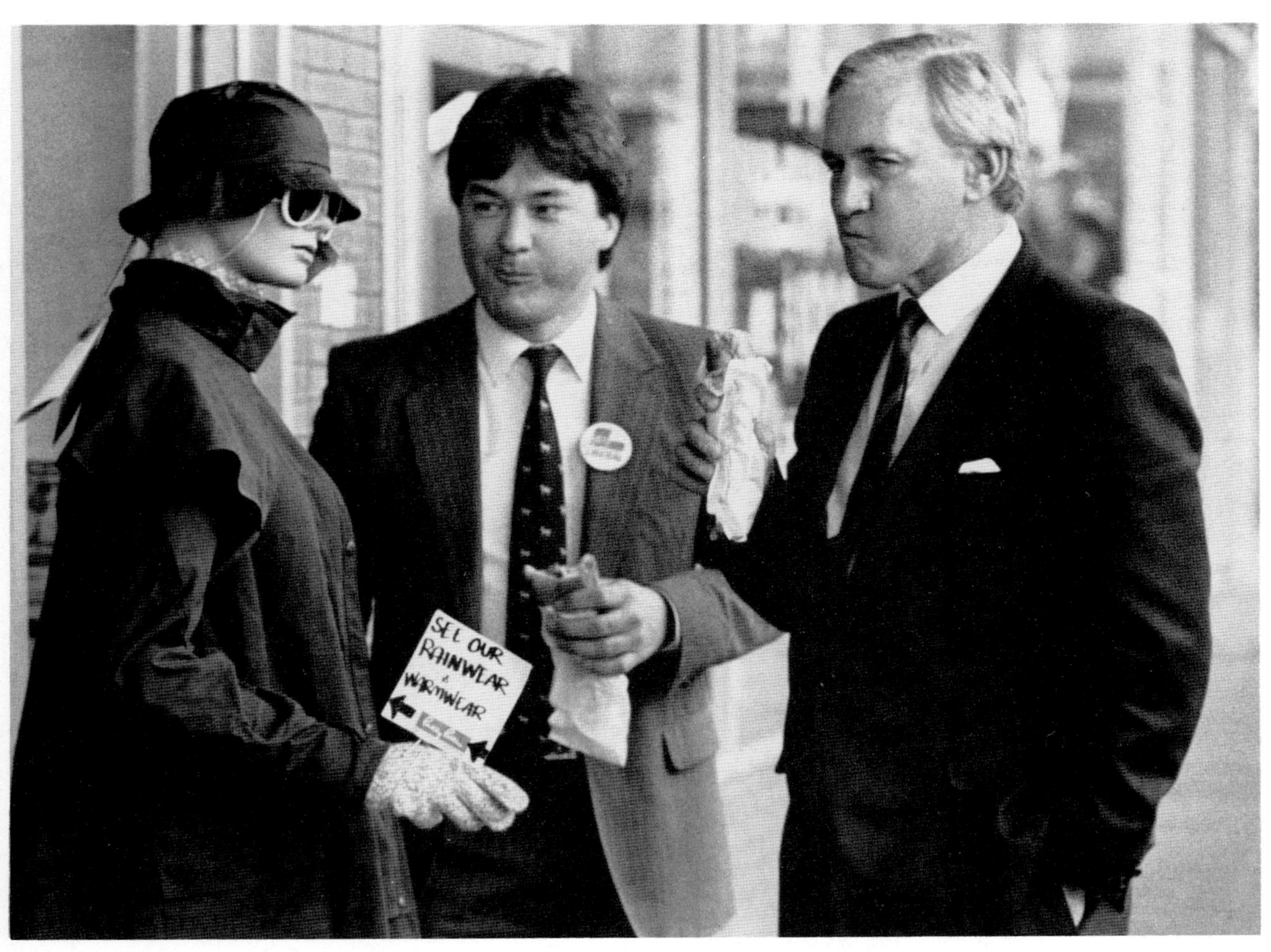

Andrew Peacock with the local candidate for Box Hill during a federal election meet-the-people walk. (Nikon F3, Tri-x film, 180mm lens)

Sandy Scheltema

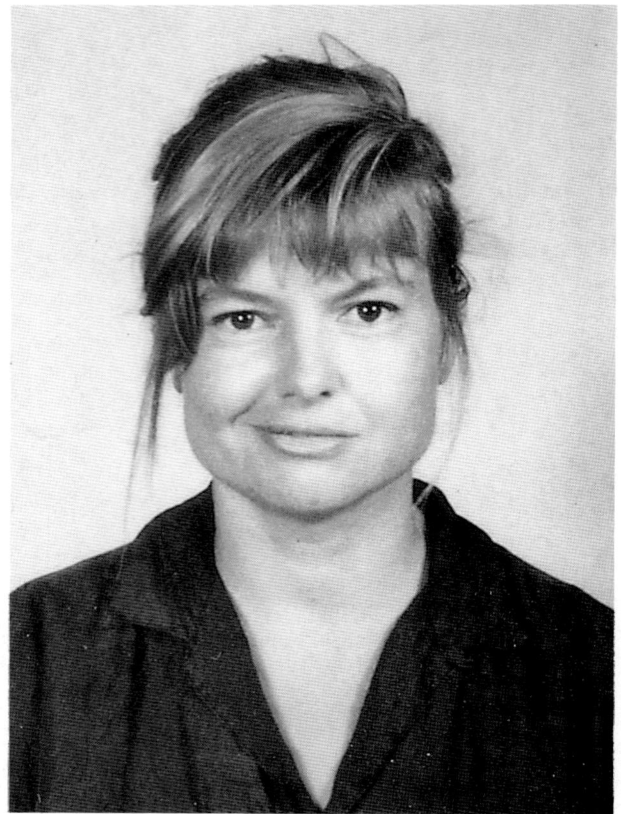

Sandy Scheltema is interested in documenting humanitarian and environmental issues and those of social justice and human rights. She organises feature stories and pictures several times a year. Working on features often allows more time than daily news jobs and allows her to photograph different aspects of a place and its people and gives her greater control of light.

When working as a freelance photographer in San Francisco, she organised articles which were published in the Age *Good Weekend* magazine. One was shot in Chile and dealt with the indigenous people and the effects of the Pinochet government. The other was photographed in Southern California and looked at Mexican workers suffering from cancer as a result of pesticide sprays.

When she gets an idea for a feature or picture story she approaches the picture editor and the journalist to develop the idea further. In 1990 in conjunction with journalist Kay Ansell she worked on two environmental pieces and several 'holdable' picture stories in far North Queensland during a two-week assignment. In 1991 she organised a story and photographs for the magazine on the High Country Cattlemen's supposed last muster on the Bogong High Plains. (This involved five days of photographing while riding a horse through scrub with two Nikons and several lenses strapped to her body!) Some of these photos were later shown in an exhibition and made into colour posters.

In 1992 she worked for a month in South-East Asia and the Pacific, funded by a Department of Foreign Affairs grant designed to foster understanding between these countries and Australia. The work depicts life in Indonesia and environmental problems in Samoa.

'I started working as a press photographer when I was 17 for two weekly newspapers near Sydney. It taught me a lot about working with people and how to try and make them feel comfortable about being photographed. I like to spend some time with people before I photograph them so I can get a portrait more likely to reveal their true character.

'Working for a small newspaper put me in touch with a whole range of people I otherwise would not have encountered and meant becoming involved with whatever was happening in the community. It also taught me the basics of press photography (such as not to leave a week's worth of captions a long way from the office the night before publication). Press photography taught me to be prepared for any kind of eventuality and to try and work fast under often difficult circumstances. You often have to make the best of poor lighting and awkward backgrounds and learn to turn them to your advantage.

'I have worked in many different facets of photography: as a stills photographer for a David Bellamy documentary, in a fashion and advertising studio, as an assistant to a photographer producing photographs for the *Wall Street Journal*, as a photography tutor for unemployed youth, as a freelance photographer for AAP Reuters, and for Greenpeace. Of them all, press photography is to me the most unpredictable and challenging.

'I have been inspired by the work of such photographers as Brazilian Magnum photographer Sebastian Salgado and Eugene Smith, both photographers with a social conscience. Salgado believes his photos of people performing manual labour are documenting a vanishing world. He does so with an art; a style of black and white photography that seems to be slowly vanishing from the daily newspaper world. His photographs are beautiful — great images that provoke a greater understanding. Eugene Smith was another great black and white photographer whose work was published in *Life* magazine and set a standard for that type of photography: "I have tried to let truth be my prejudice, it has taken much sweat, it has been worth it" '

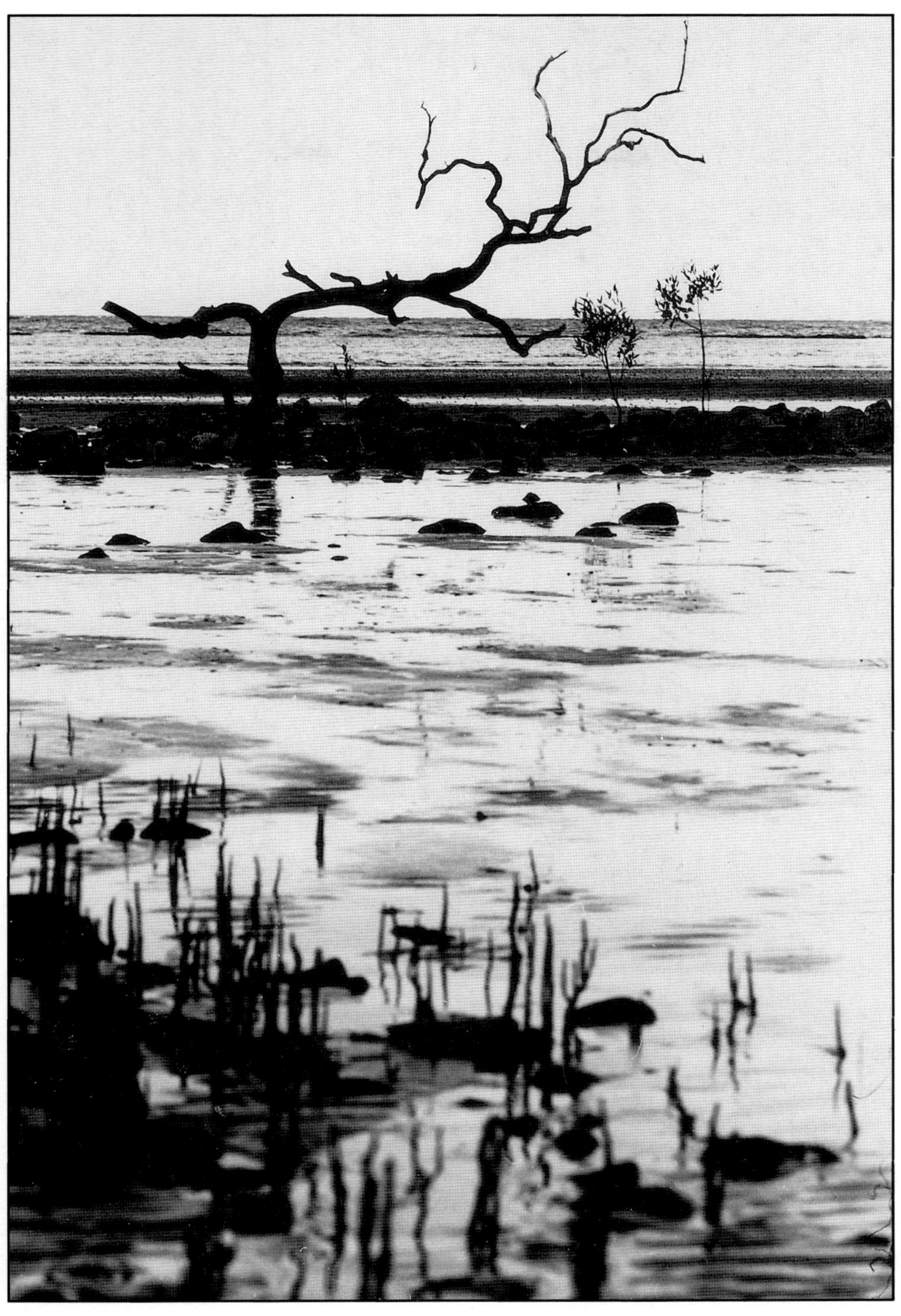

Cape Tribulation Dawn. An early morning walk on the beach while on assignment in far north Queensland produced this shot which was used in conjunction with an environmental piece on the Cape Tribulation Road. 1990

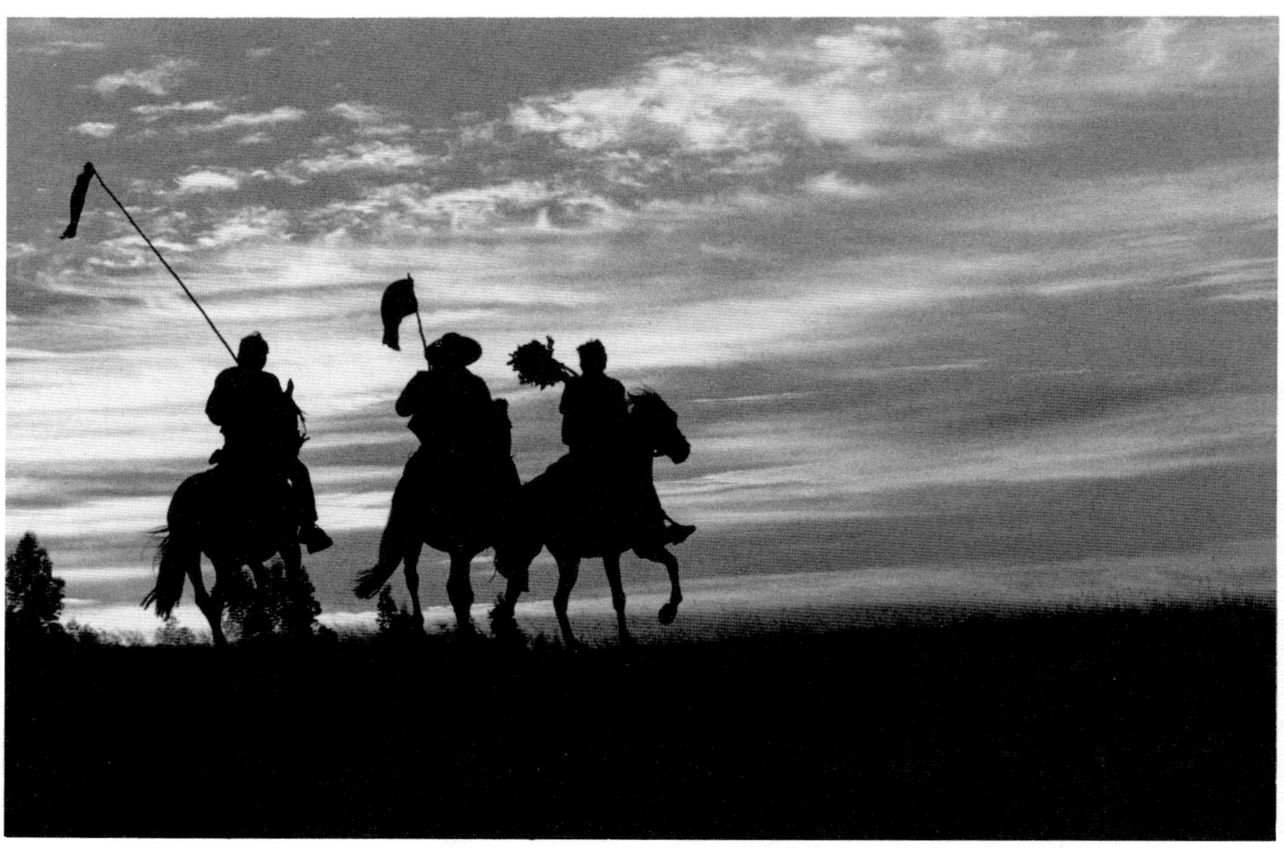

Chilean Mapuche Indians in a pre-dawn ceremony, 1989

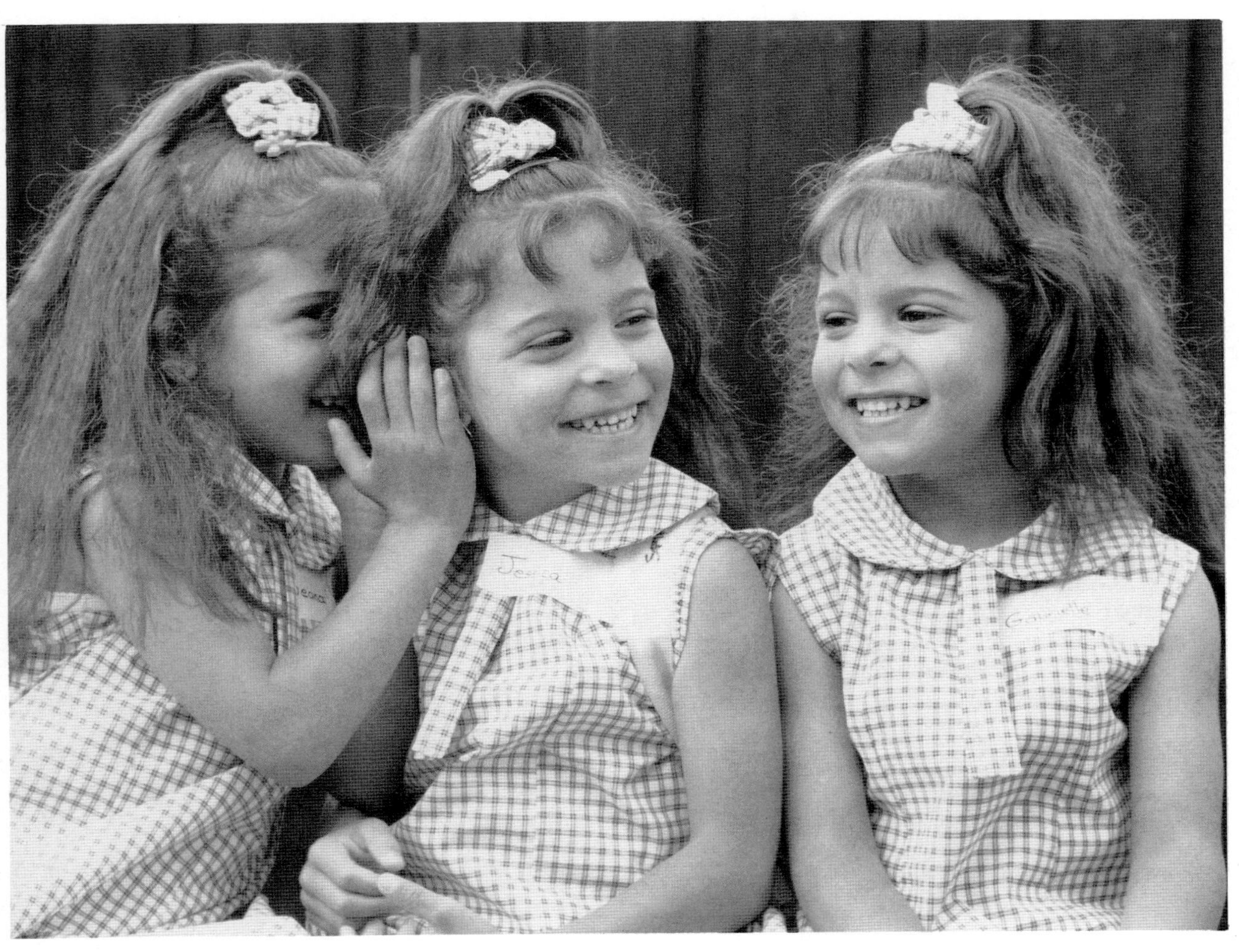

The caption to this photograph read, 'Promise not to tell: Deanna, Jessica, and Gabrielle Spinelli, aged five, whisper together during a quiet moment on their first day at school'. These little girls were a joy to photograph. I asked them to tell a secret, so they wouldn't stare into the camera with a fixed smile. They were delighted to oblige

Cathryn Tremain

Since 1987 Cathryn Tremain has been the principal fashion photographer for the *Age*. She works with Fashion Editor Jan Phyland who chooses the clothing and accessories that are included in the two large Tempo fashion supplements that appear each year. She photographs the models in a professional photographic studio and aims for a simple composition devoid of background distractions. She uses the rectangle of the frame to emphasise strong shapes.

'I began my career in 1979 as a cadet photographer on the Albury *Border Mail* and joined the *Age* in 1984. The following year I won first prize in the human interest section of the Rothmans National Press Photo Awards and a merit award in the Nikon National Press Photo Awards.

'With fashion photography I usually shoot in 50 ISO Fujichrome slide film. The lower ISO enlarges better and has more intense colour. The studio lights are often flash units. Exposure is crucial to transparencies — I can determine correct exposure through the flash meter.

'The 1991 supplement used tungsten lighting with softboxes and reflectors. I used an 80A filter to compensate for the orange tinge on the daylight film. Tungsten lighting is more subtle than flash.

'I attempt to portray the personalities and emotions of my subjects whereas a journalist usually deals in facts and analysis.'

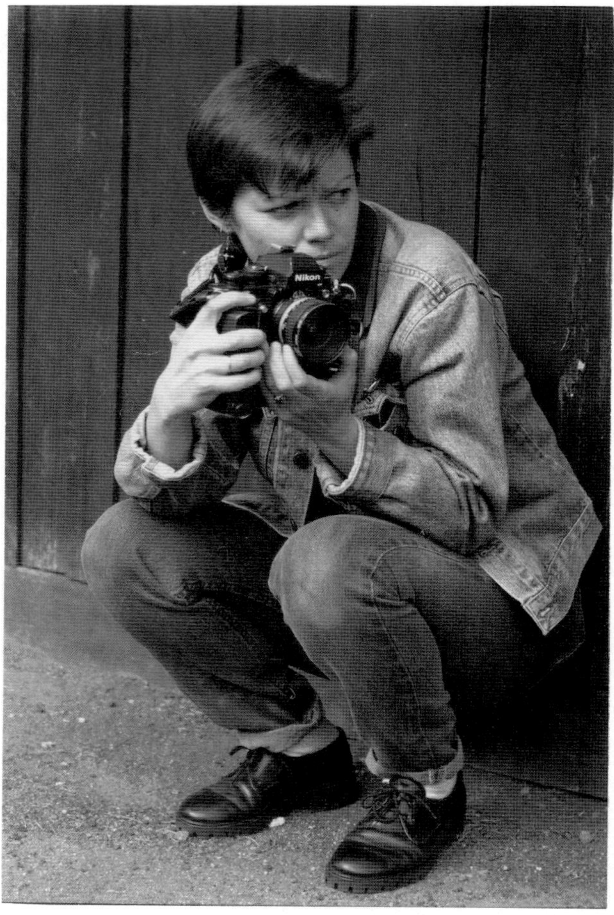

Photo: Kristine Beach

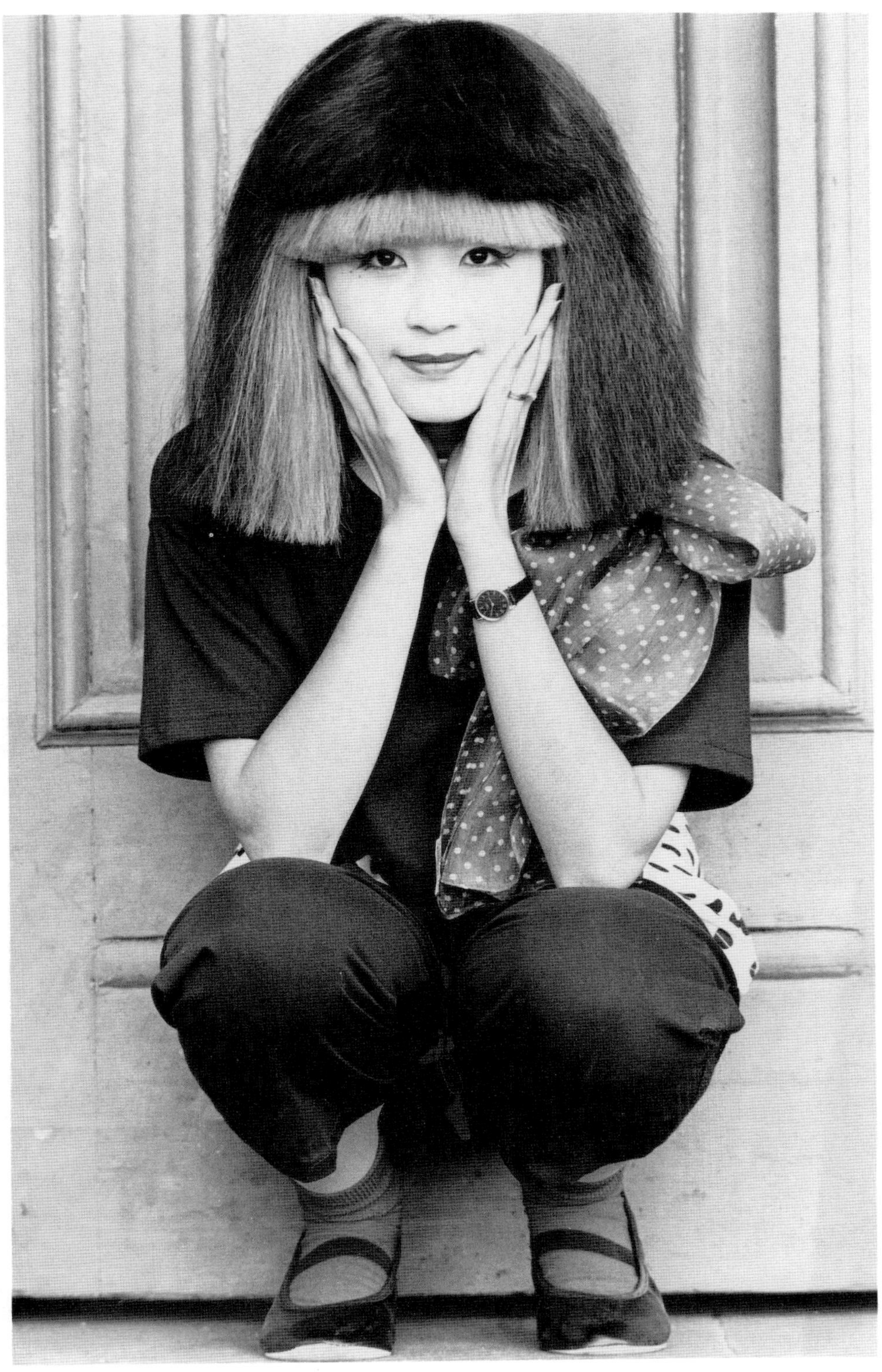

China doll. Not long in Australia, this young Vietnamese girl shows the hairdressing skills she has acquired since attending school in Australia. She reminded me of a tiny porcelain doll

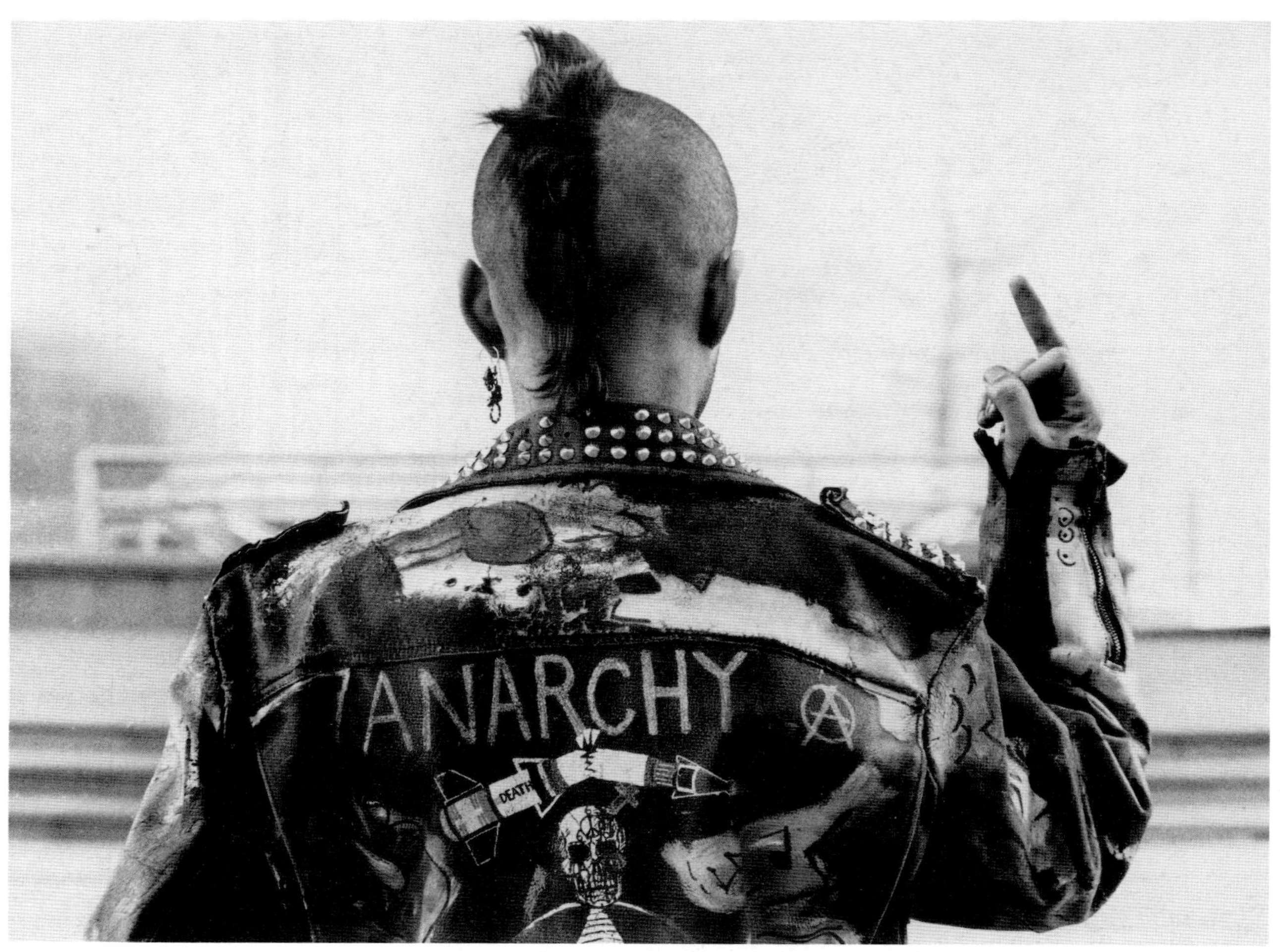

While on an unrelated assignment I came across this punk who, unimpressed by the thought of having his photo taken, turned his back on me — which made a better picture.
(Nikon F3, 800 ASA Tri-x film, 135mm lens)

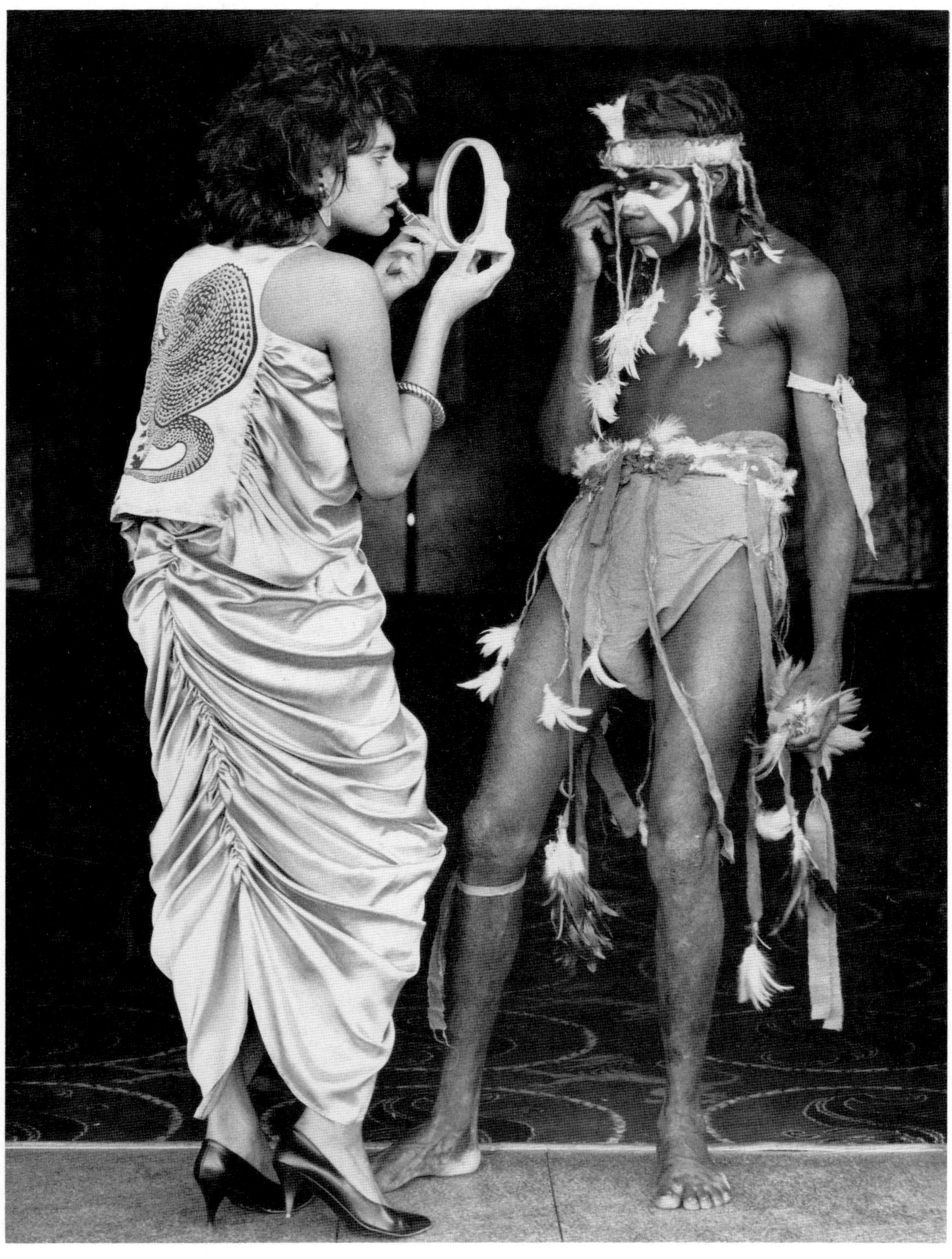

I was asked to cover an Aboriginal fashion parade and came across a model and dancer sharing a mirror to do their make-up in preparation for the show. (Nikon F3 camera, 800 ASA T-max film, 85mm lens)

William West

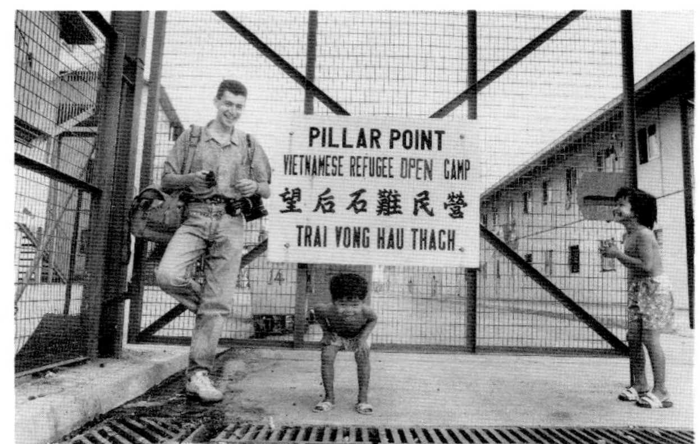

William West worked as a press photographer in New Zealand for four years before joining the Melbourne *Herald* and, in 1989, the *Age*.

William sees the broader perspective with his 20mm lens. He attempts to captures the interaction between people, how they relate to each other. He explores human beings and their forms in action, as can be seen even in the portrait of himself.

'The highlight of the job is the big events or the hard news. You don't have to set it up, just be amongst it and find the best photograph. You are competing with lots of other newspaper photographers and have to make sure that you've got a better photograph. I really enjoy the high pressure.

'Of course, there aren't enough big events to go around, and I like the challenge of different jobs — from arts to sport, to a fire. The arts, particularly ballet, always make a good photo, and there they usually have a clean background to emphasise the figures. The background is 50 per cent of any photograph.

'I try to take a more documentary approach to press photography. I look for something a tiny bit off-beat. A lot of the time it is a matter of keeping the camera up to the eye when everyone thinks that it's all over. The *Age* is good to work for in this respect because there is no set style or formula as is the case with some newspapers.

'Lighting is the first thing that I consider when approaching a job. That determines which film to use, flash or not. I use flash usually as a last resort.'

'As for film, I prefer Fuji Neopan Professional Black and White, which the *Age* doesn't use. T-Max is good in low light. For outdoor summer lighting, I use FP4 rated at 320 ISO. It has beautiful tones and is especially good on details in harsh lighting.

'I enjoy the travelling, from following Andrew Peacock around during his campaign in the last election to spending three weeks in Russia in 1988. It's a real challenge to get the pictures back to the paper in time.

'The most disappointing aspect of the job is not getting your work published. Only about three quarters gets printed. You get used to it after a while, unless it's a bloody good photo.'

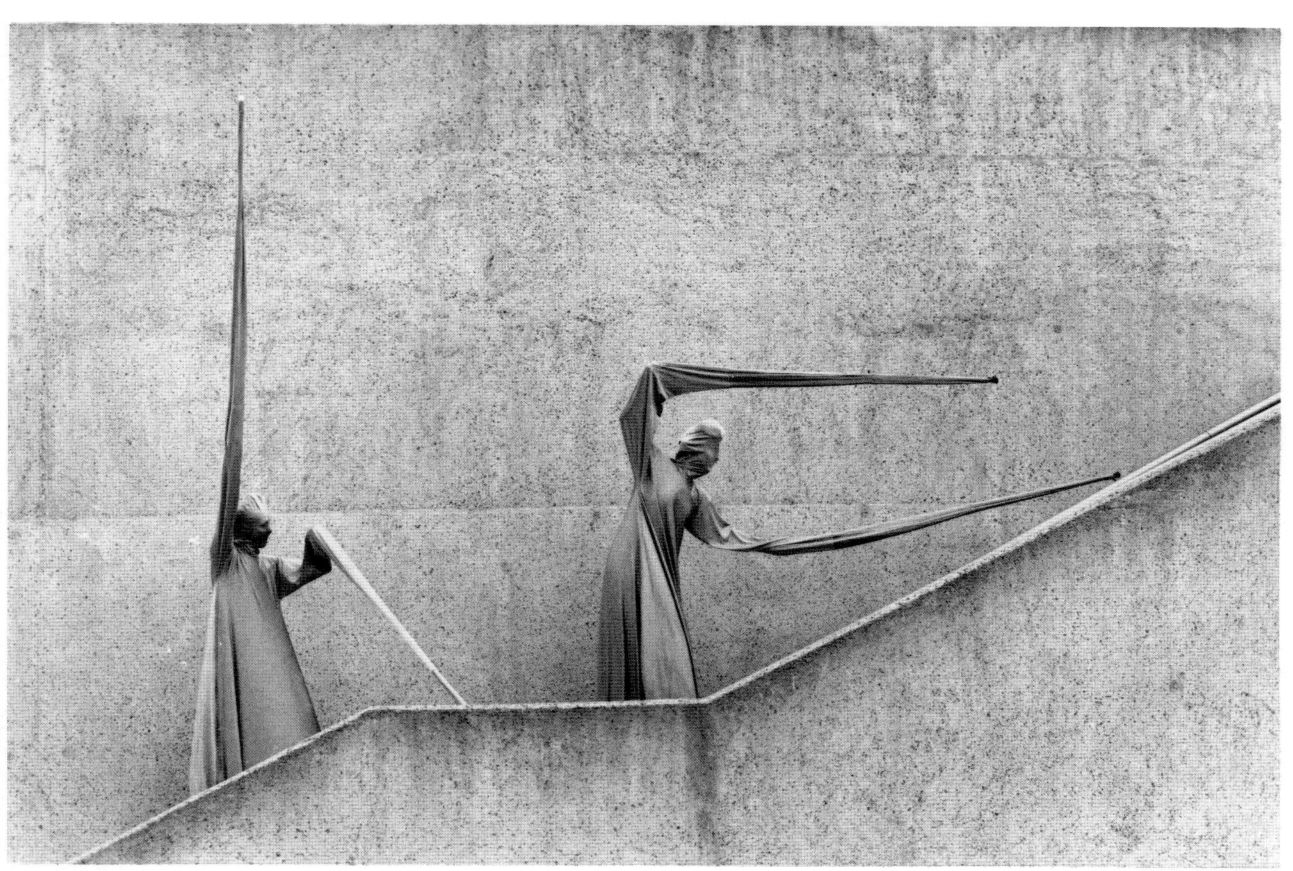

An experimental dance group performs outside the Arts Centre during the 1989 Melbourne Arts Festival. (Nikon F3, 85mm lens)

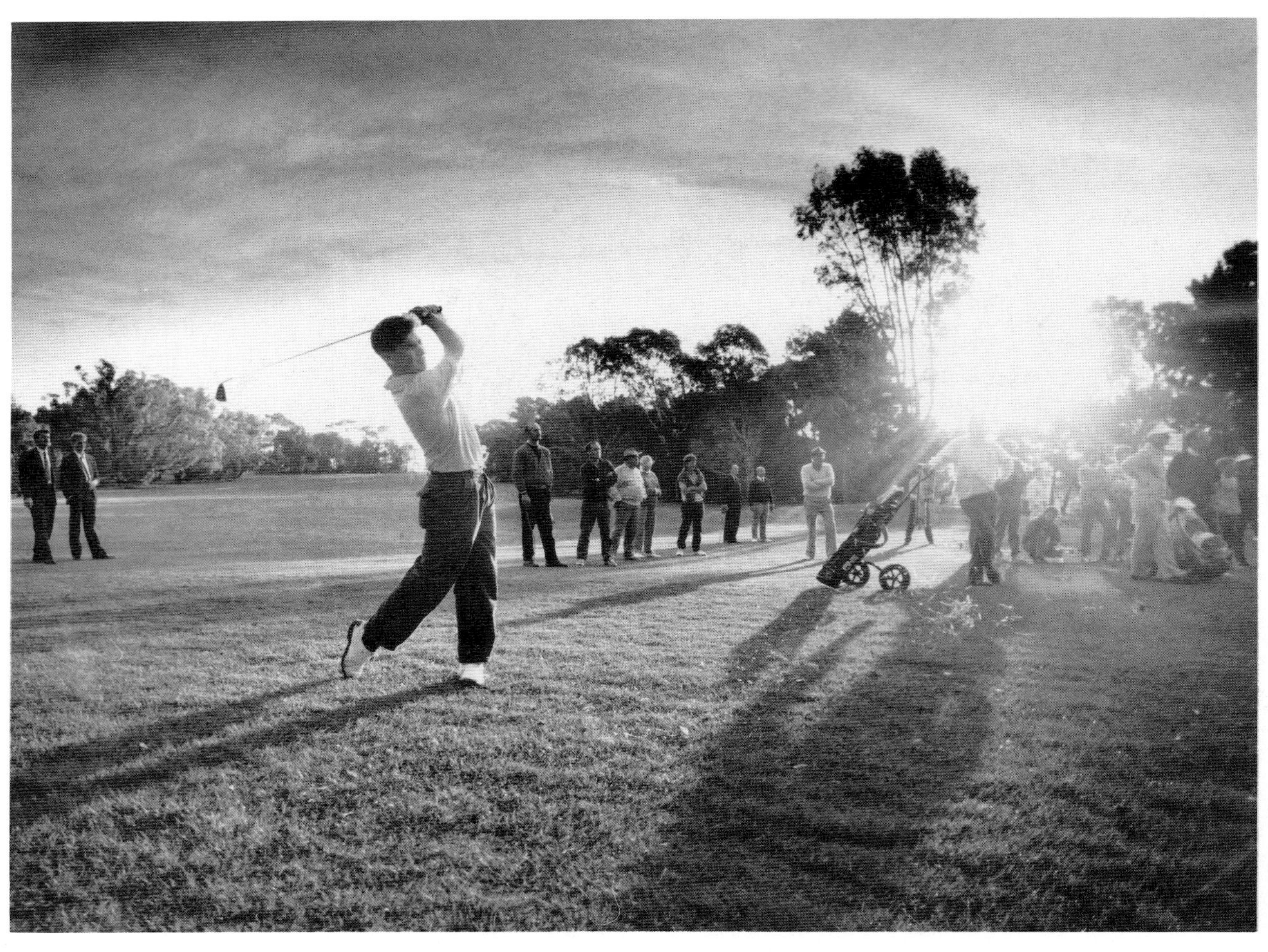

Final of a club competition, Melbourne 1990. It was late in the day and the sun was setting. I like the picture because it was a very different pin shot, one that coincidentally proved to be decisive in winning the club title

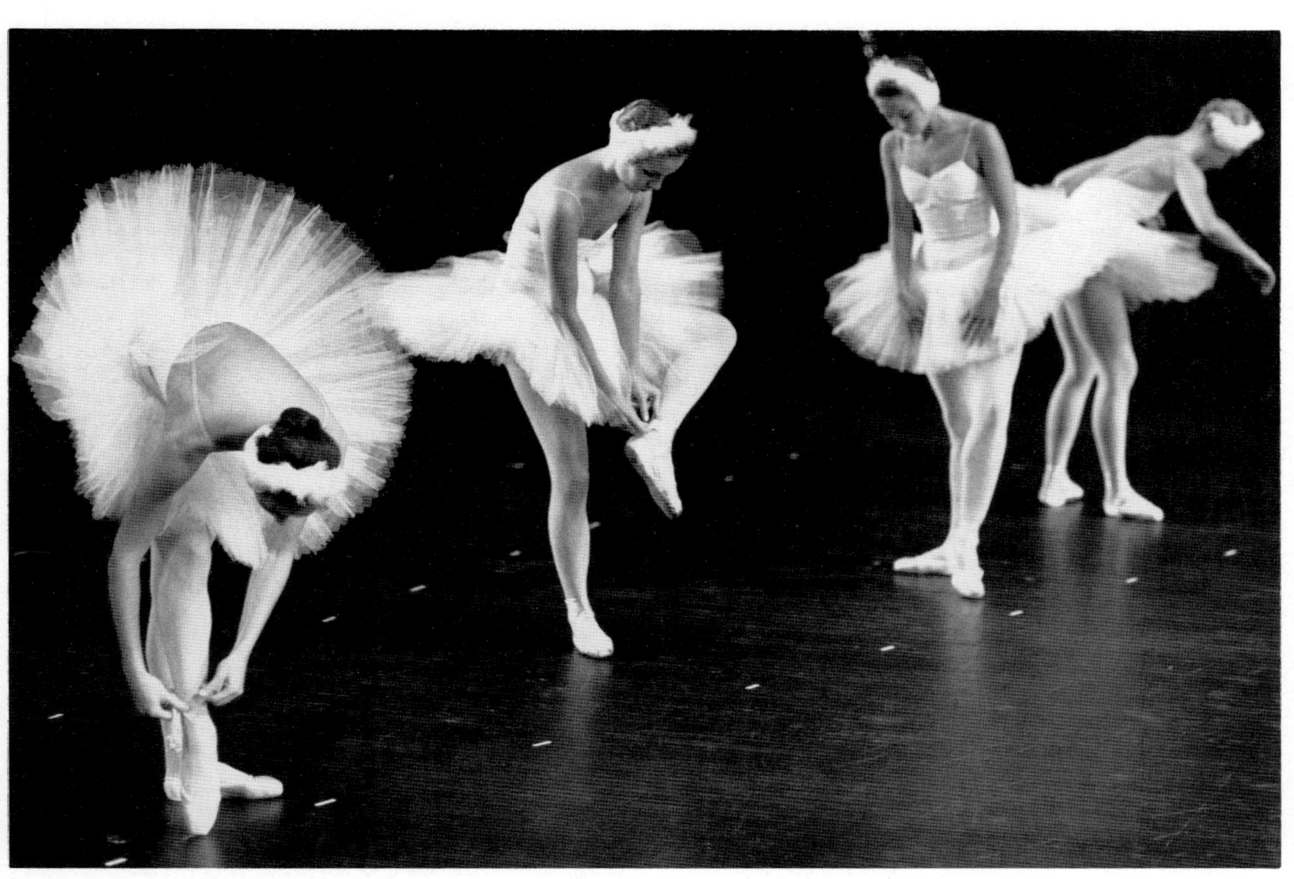

My favourite shot. It was taken during a press call for the Kirov Ballet at the Melbourne Arts Centre, September 1989. While everyone else was getting nice photos during the press call, I took this during a break in the dancers' run through. They are all attending to something different. (Nikon F3, 35mm lens)

Mark Wilson

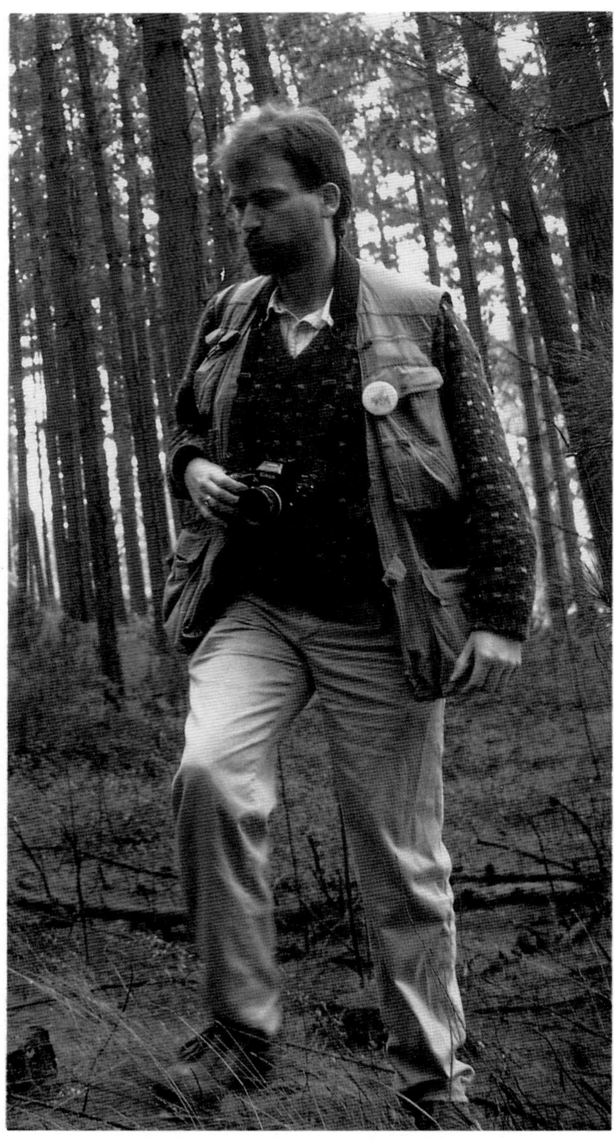

Photo: Kathleen Whelan

John Lamb describes Mark Wilson as a young creative photographer who works hard at getting a very good picture. Mark's favourite work is bush photos and outback jobs. He tries to capture the fleeting moment — he is the onlooker, the quiet observer.

'Here you learn photography through the school of hard knocks. I began as a press photographer at the age of 18 at the Warrnambool *Standard* and have been at the *Age* since 1985.

'I am always surprised at how cooperative people are when you say that you are from the *Age*. It's best to show up in person to arrange a picture, rather than to do it over the phone. And it's always preferable to work with a journalist through an interview.

'I prefer to sit back and watch, like the proverbial fly on the wall, to observe and see what the people are, rather than create what I want them to be or think that they are.

'With politicians, after a while you can learn enough about their personalities to wait for the right expression. Bob Hawke is not good to photograph. He shows what he wants to show; his expressions are very controlled.

'The visually interesting ones are a delight. Malcolm Fraser was intriguing because of his size. He is very large.'

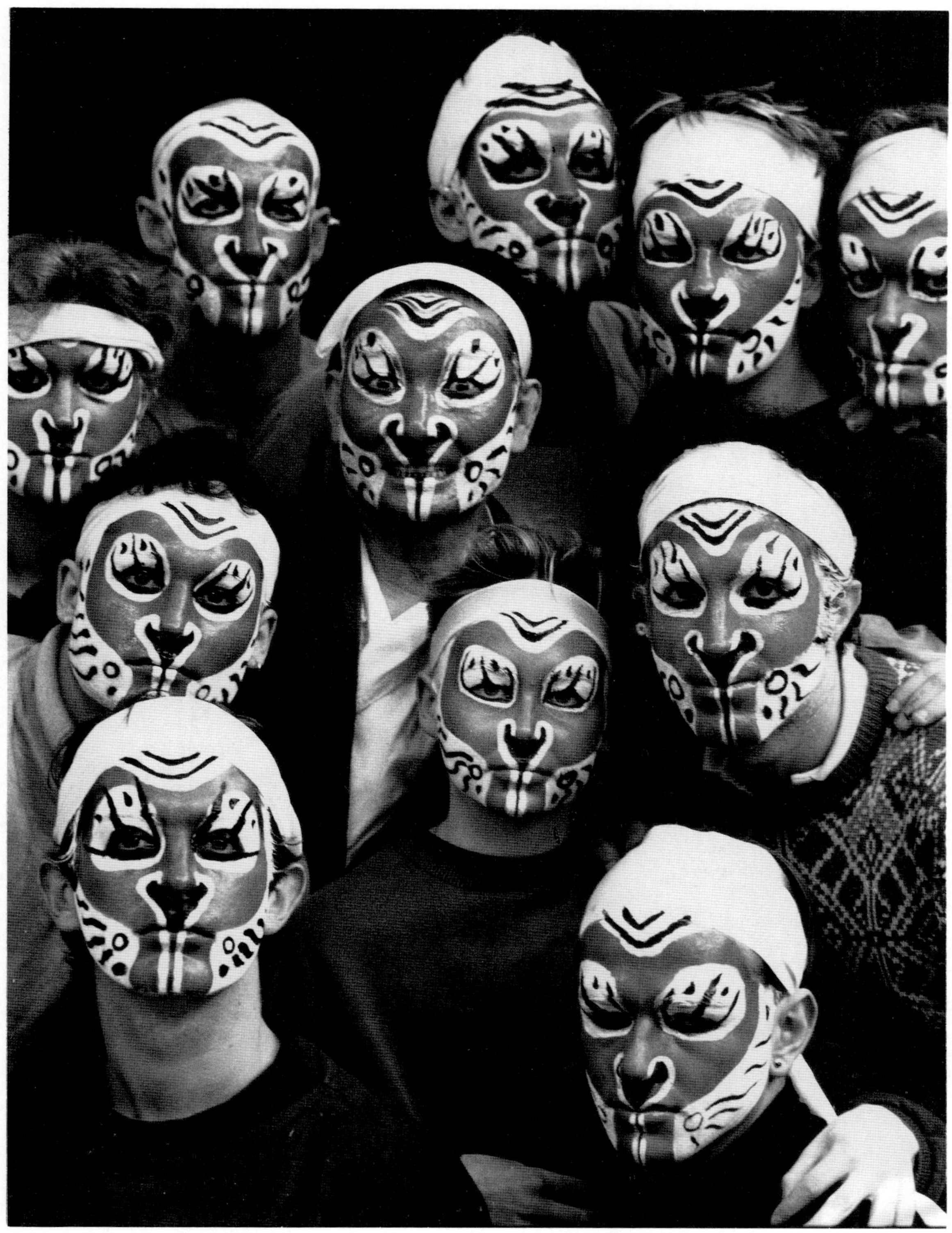

Acting students of the Victorian College of the Arts working with Zhou Yunliang, deputy director of the Beijing Opera Company, August 1989

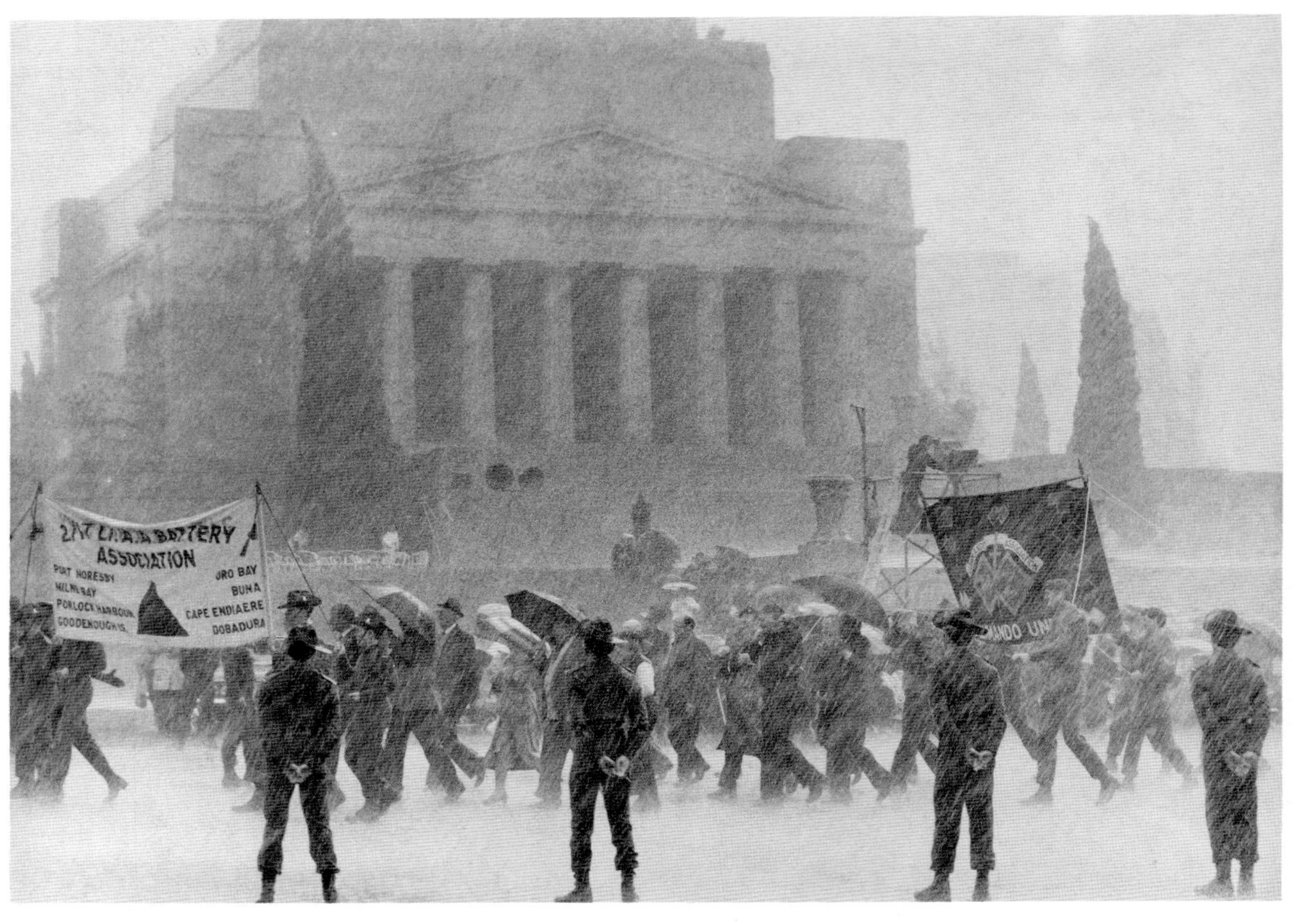

Anzac Day, 1986. They marched on regardless. The War Memorial, Melbourne, is in the background

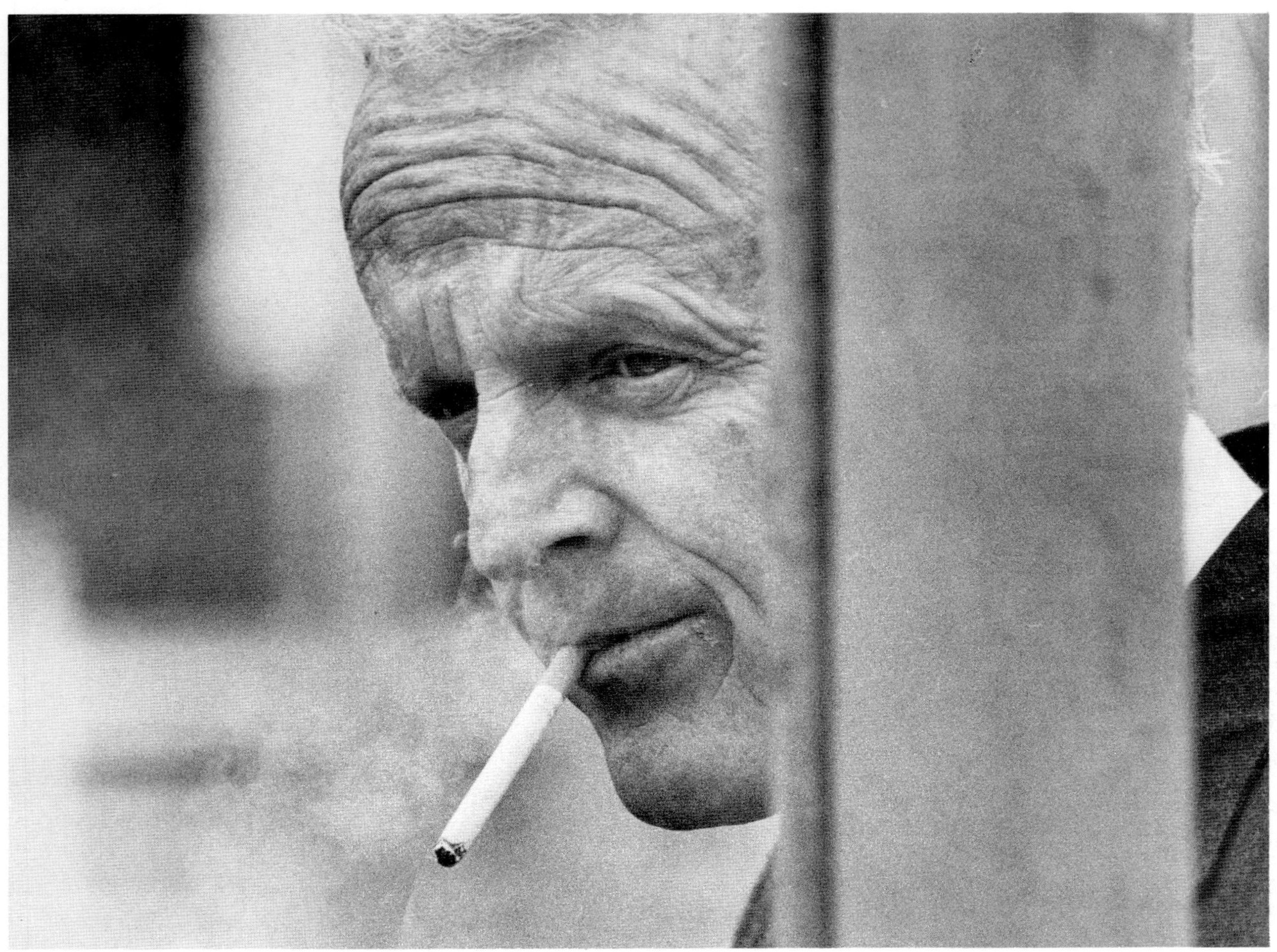

Senator John Button, September 1986

John Woudstra

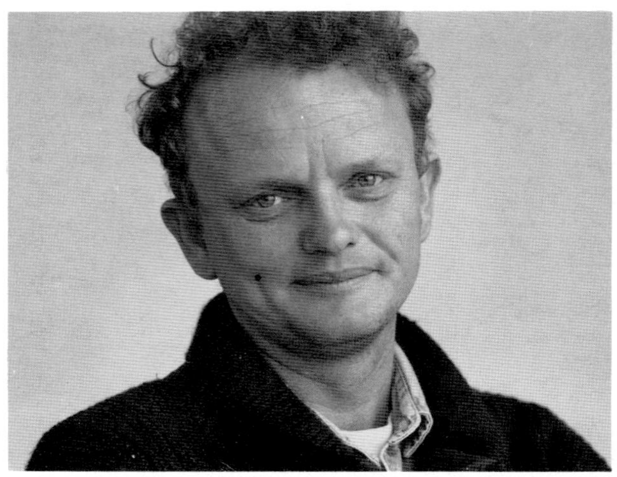

John Woudstra has been a press photographer for 15 years, working for both provincial and metropolitan newspapers.

'Arts stories are good to photograph because professional artists are used to performing in front of the camera and are much more relaxed.

'I prefer black and white film for its impact, although it's harder to get a great shot. Colour enhances a photograph. 'If possible, I use the slower films to minimise grain and maximise clarity. Unfortunately, in press photography, you usually have to go for the quicker films like T-Max 400 or 800 ISO.

'Press photography demands patience. We always seem to be waiting; watching and waiting. The old saying is that all it takes is being in the right spot at the right time. But getting to the right spot can take hours and, once there, the right time can mean a wait of several more. This can be stressful as deadline approaches. If you miss the edition you may as well not be there. Yesterday's news is yesterday's news.

'Each day, as you view the results, there's always an element of self-criticism about what you could have done to improve the shots. You never stop learning.'

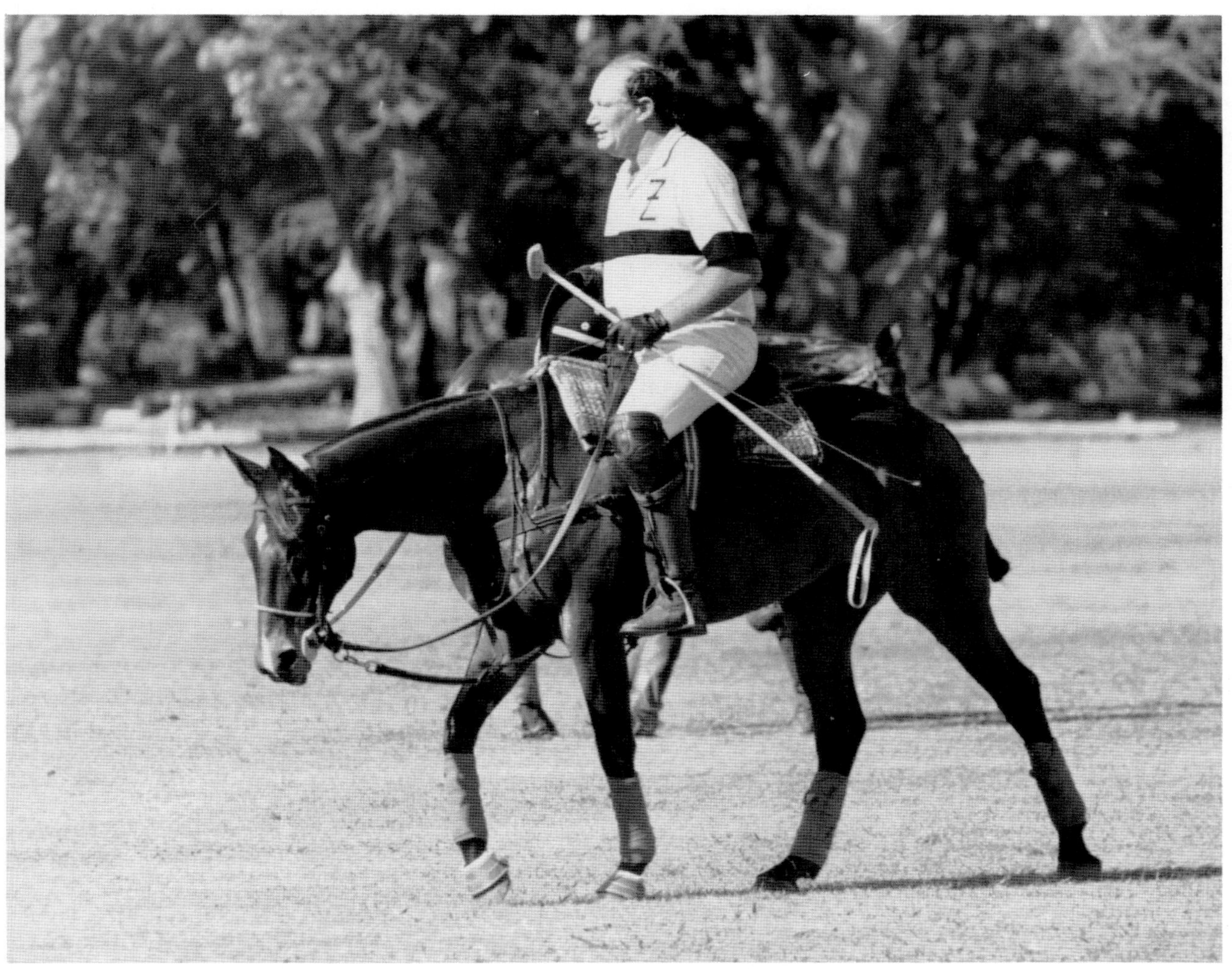

Kerry Packer and pony at a polo match

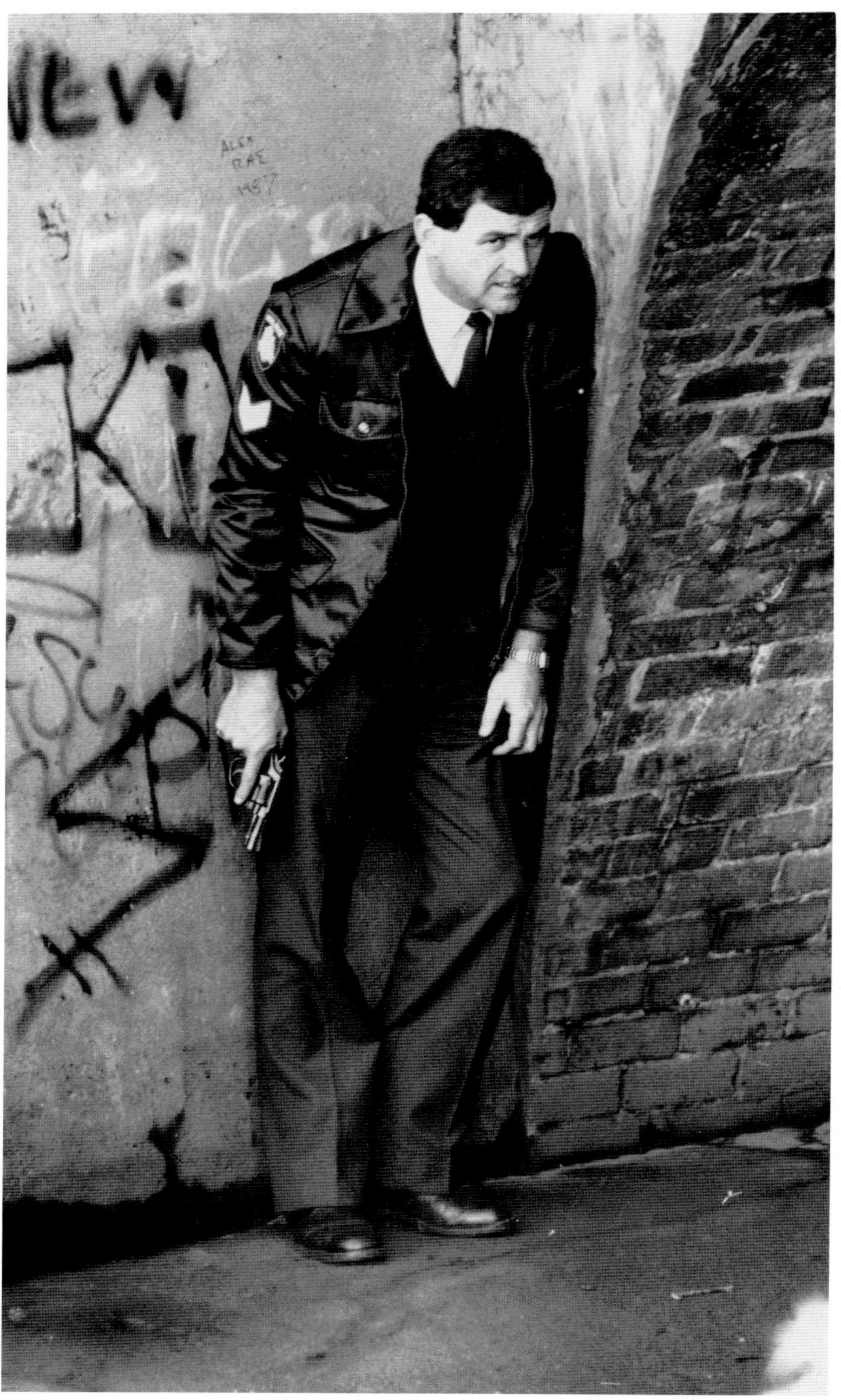

Sgt Mark Bowden hunting Walsh Street killers

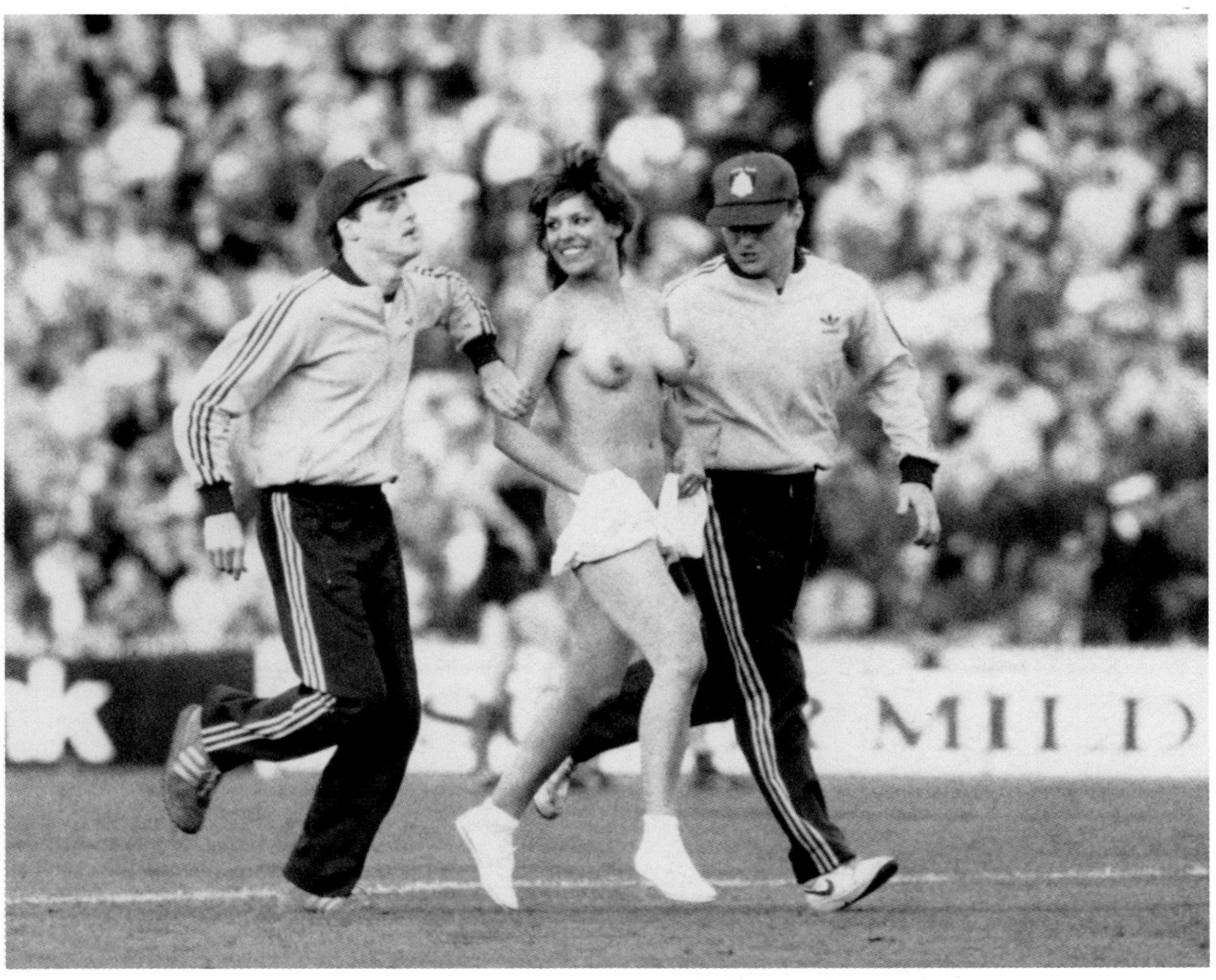

Streaker at Aussie Rules Grand Final

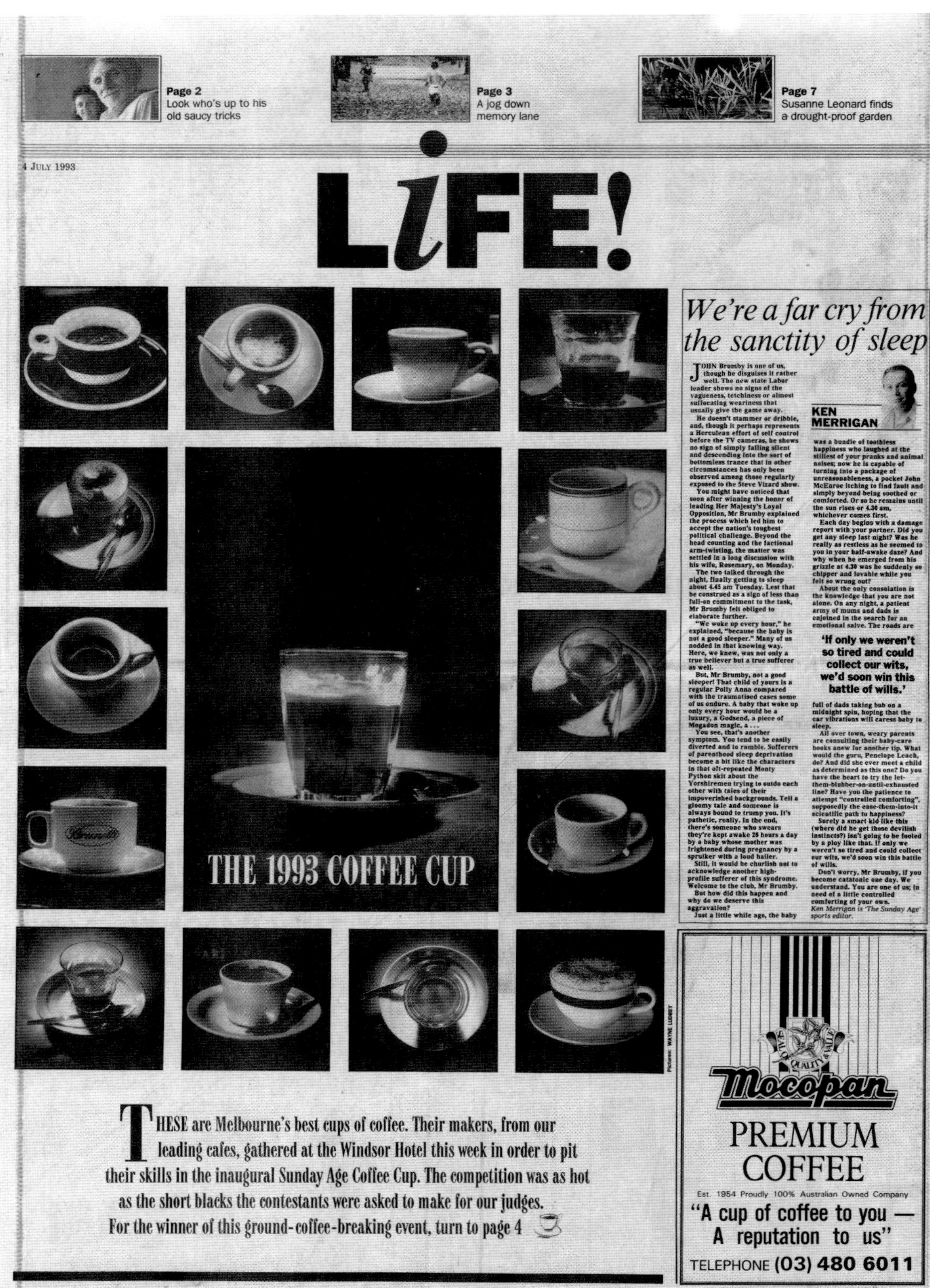

Page 2
Look who's up to his old saucy tricks

Page 3
A jog down memory lane

Page 7
Susanne Leonard finds a drought-proof garden

4 July 1993

LIFE!

THE 1993 COFFEE CUP

Pictures: WAYNE LUDBEY

THESE are Melbourne's best cups of coffee. Their makers, from our leading cafes, gathered at the Windsor Hotel this week in order to pit their skills in the inaugural Sunday Age Coffee Cup. The competition was as hot as the short blacks the contestants were asked to make for our judges.

For the winner of this ground-coffee-breaking event, turn to page 4

We're a far cry from the sanctity of sleep

KEN MERRIGAN

JOHN Brumby is one of us, though he disguises it rather well. The new state Labor leader shows no signs of the vagueness, tetchiness or almost suffocating weariness that usually give the game away.

He doesn't stammer or dribble, and, though it perhaps represents a Herculean effort of self control before the TV cameras, he shows no sign of simply falling silent and descending into the sort of bottomless trance that in other circumstances has only been observed among those regularly exposed to the Steve Vizard show.

You might have noticed that soon after winning the honor of leading Her Majesty's Loyal Opposition, Mr Brumby explained the process which led him to accept the nation's toughest political challenge. Beyond the head counting and the factional arm-twisting, the matter was settled in a long discussion with his wife, Rosemary, on Monday.

The two talked through the night, finally getting to sleep about 4.45 am Tuesday. Lest that be construed as a sign of less than full-on commitment to the task, Mr Brumby felt obliged to elaborate further.

"We woke up every hour," he explained, "because the baby is not a good sleeper." Many of us nodded in that knowing way. Here, we knew, was not only a true believer but a true sufferer as well.

But, Mr Brumby, not a good sleeper! That child of yours is a regular Polly Anna compared with the traumatised cases some of us endure. A baby that woke up only every hour would be a luxury, a Godsend, a piece of Mogadon magic, a . . .

You see, that's another symptom. You tend to be easily diverted and to ramble. Sufferers of parenthood sleep deprivation become a bit like the characters in that oft-repeated Monty Python skit about the Yorshiremen trying to outdo each other with tales of their impoverished backgrounds. Tell a gloomy tale and someone is always bound to trump you. It's pathetic, really. In the end, there's someone who swears they're kept awake 28 hours a day by a baby whose mother was frightened during pregnancy by a spruiker with a loud hailer.

Still, it would be churlish not to acknowledge another high-profile sufferer of this syndrome. Welcome to the club, Mr Brumby.

But how did this happen and why do we deserve this aggravation?

Just a little while ago, the baby was a bundle of toothless happiness who laughed at the silliest of your pranks and animal noises; now he is capable of turning into a package of unreasonableness, a pocket John McEnroe itching to find fault and simply beyond being soothed or comforted. Or so he remains until the sun rises or 4.30 am, whichever comes first.

Each day begins with a damage report with your partner. Did you get any sleep last night? Was he really as restless as he seemed to you in your half-awake daze? And why when he emerged from his grizzle at 4.30 was he suddenly so chipper and lovable while you felt so wrung out?

About the only consolation is the knowledge that you are not alone. On any night, a patient army of mums and dads is enjoined in the search for an emotional salve. The roads are full of dads taking bub on a midnight spin, hoping that the car vibrations will caress baby to sleep.

'If only we weren't so tired and could collect our wits, we'd soon win this battle of wills.'

All over town, weary parents are consulting their baby-care books anew for another tip. What would the guru, Penelope Leach, do? And did she ever meet a child as determined as this one? Do you have the heart to try the let-them-blubber-on-until-exhausted line? Have you the patience to attempt "controlled comforting", supposedly the ease-them-into-it scientific path to happiness?

Surely a smart kid like this (where did he get those devilish instincts?) isn't going to be fooled by a ploy like that. If only we weren't so tired and could collect our wits, we'd soon win this battle of wills.

Don't worry, Mr Brumby, if you become catatonic one day. We understand. You are one of us; in need of a little controlled comforting of your own.

Ken Merrigan is 'The Sunday Age' sports editor.

CHAPTER 4

THE SUNDAY AGE

The approach of the *Sunday Age*

by Leigh Henningham, Pictorial Editor

The *Sunday Age* approaches photography differently to a daily paper. The philosophy behind the photography is to approach assignments with a magazine style.

Our three photographers, Chris Beck, Mario Borg and Wayne Ludbey, have personal and distinctive styles which can set the tone for the newspaper. When photographing subjects their minds are not focused only on the obvious but also on the interpretation of the subject and his/her/its mood and emotion. This can often mean photographing beyond the boundaries of the central theme. The peripheral is often taken for granted and never explored with the camera.

The pictorial department of the *Sunday Age* is attempting to break from the traditional expectations of newspapers and maintain a unique visual quality throughout.

This front page of the Sunday Age *contains nine photographs in all: three enticing readers to turn to features within the paper; three adorning an advertisement; one illustrating a story about the resignation of the leader of the Victorian opposition; and two illustrating the leading article. Their impact on the reader is immediate, even outweighing that of the text*

Fifteen shots of coffee cups from a variety of angles, coupled with imaginative layout and use of type, make an arresting front page for the Life section of the Sunday Age

Chris Beck

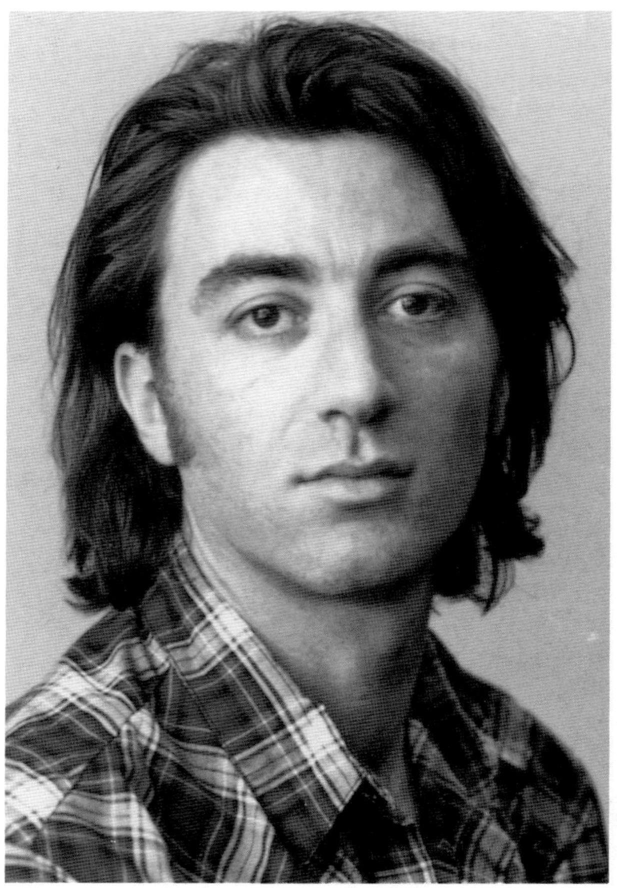

'I began freelancing in photography when I was 20, which meant that, apart from pop music photos, I didn't have much work. At that stage, graphic art orientated photos appealed to me. One year of a photography degree at Prahran College changed that. As part of the course we studied photojournalism and my attitude toward the medium changed.

'The emotional work of Bruce Davidson, the pathos of Elliot Erwitt's photographs, the incisive and simple portraits of Bill Brandt, led me to leave the course and seek out press work. Soon, I was working on local papers. Much of this work involved 100th birthdays and 50th anniversaries.

'After a while, it became repetitious. I also freelanced with Public Relations but wasn't satisfied. I eventually travelled overseas to gain more experience and this helped me to land the job at the *Sunday Age*.

'My heroes have always been photojournalists like Robert Frank and Elliot Erwitt. They travel and document life with a personal style and vision.

'Press photography unfortunately has the stigma of "The Big Picture" — photos of disasters or events. And the safe, recognisable picture will usually triumph over an innovative angle on a subject. Rarely are the nuances and foibles of the everyday represented in newspapers. With the *Sunday Age* there is scope for such photographs, but usually, the obvious will win out.'

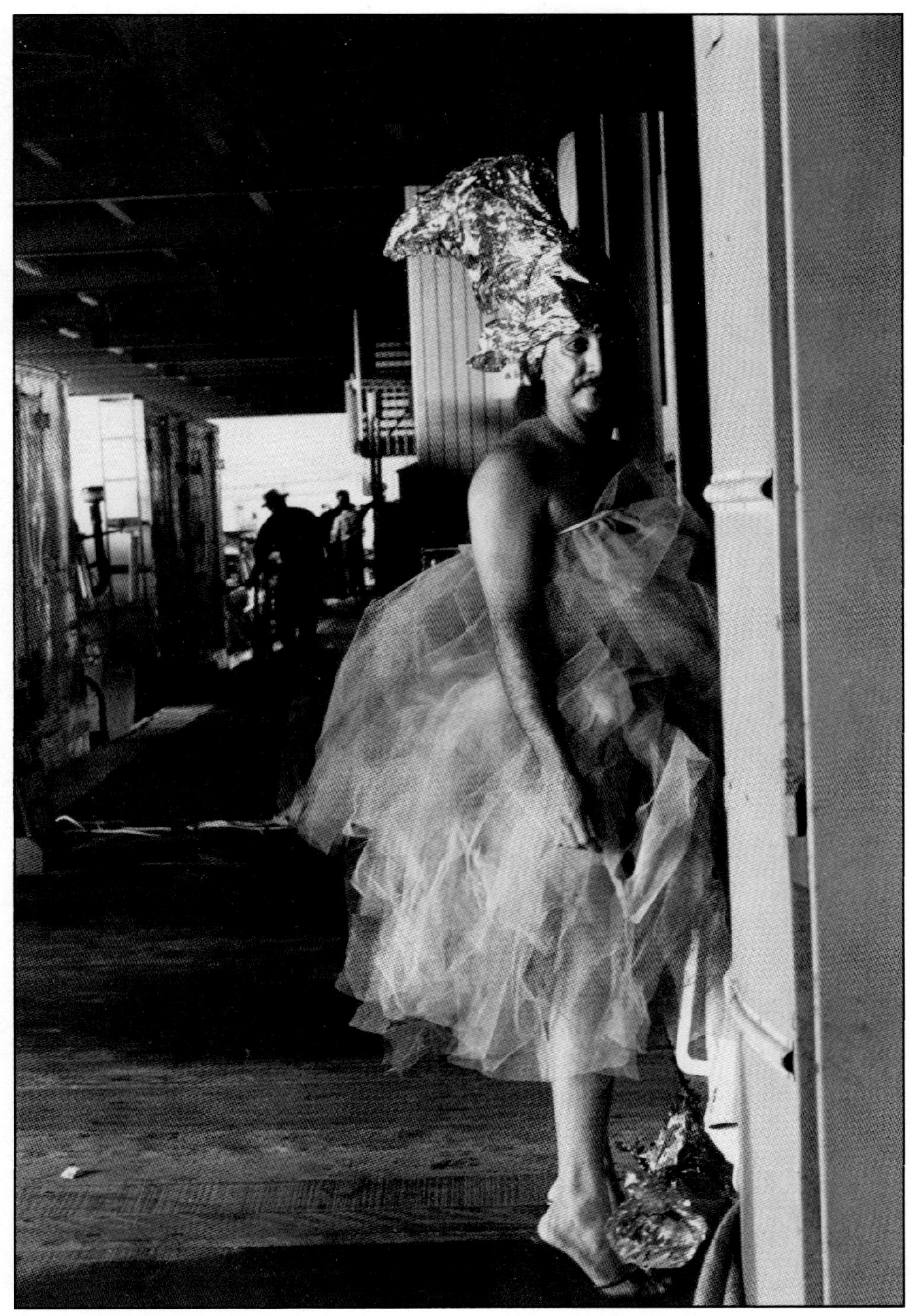

I found this man very early in the night at Port Melbourne Pier where a big celebration was to take place. There was hardly anyone there, and he felt slightly uneasy. Had he been camping it up there would have been no picture

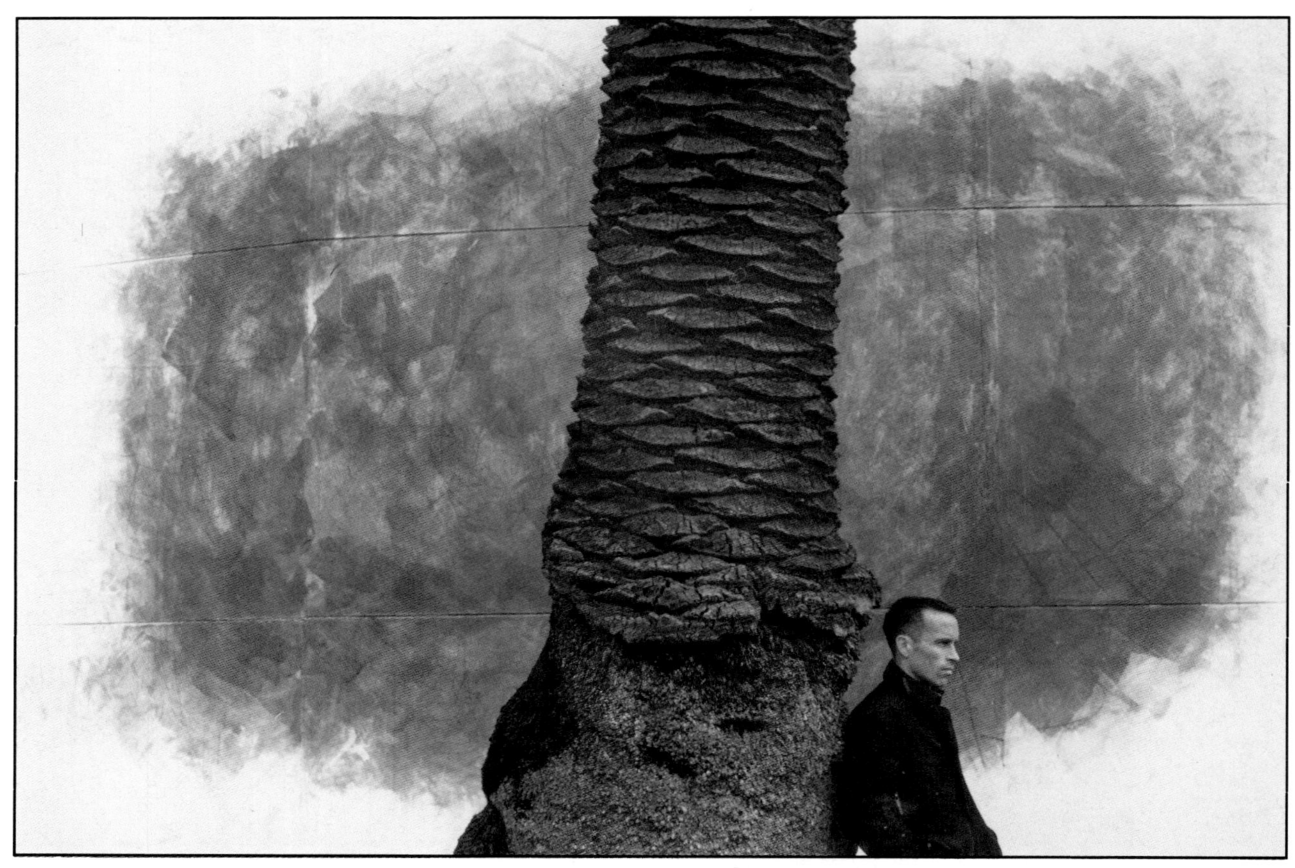

Mark Seymour of the rock group Hunters & Collectors

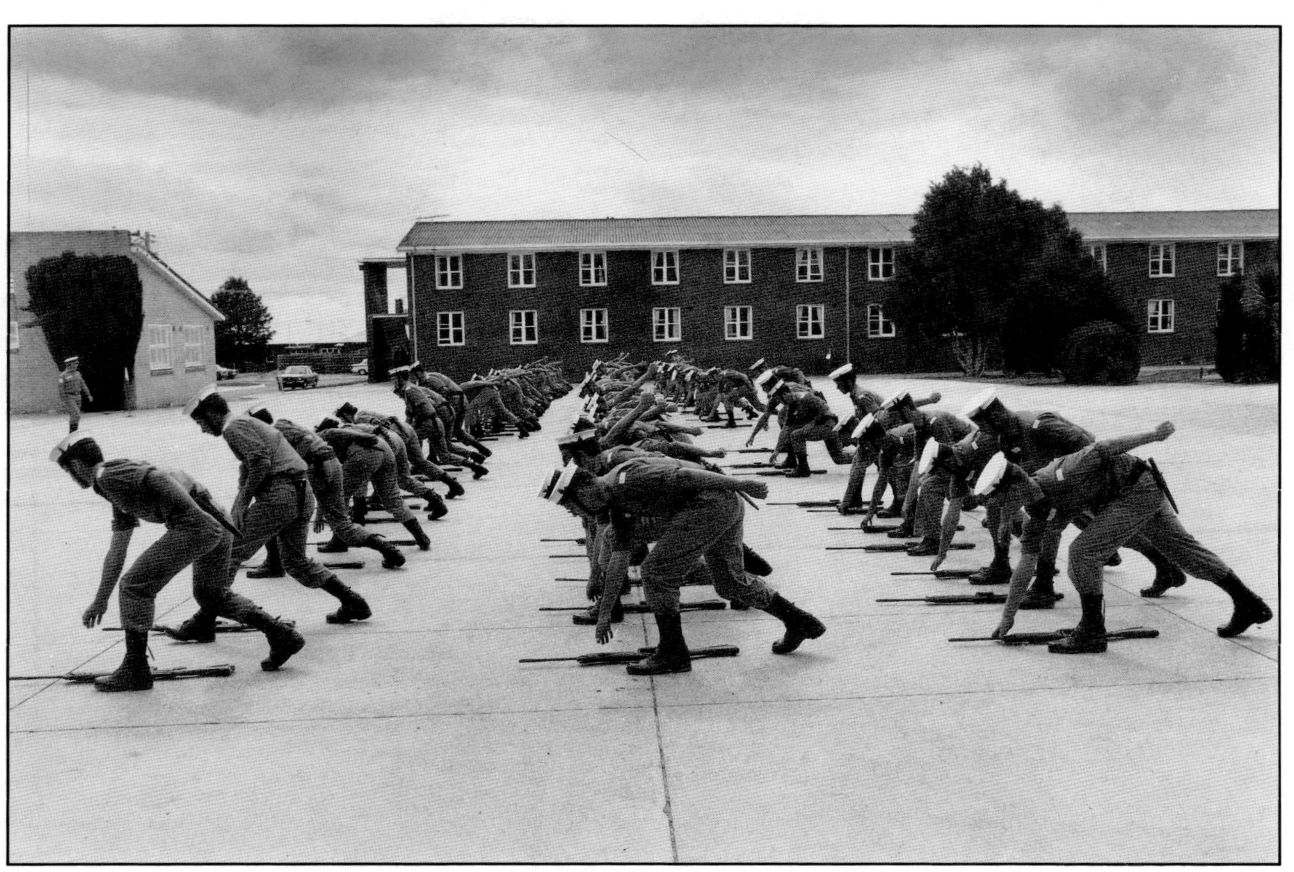

The Navy barracks for new recruits at Hastings. This shot was taken during the Gulf War

Mario Borg

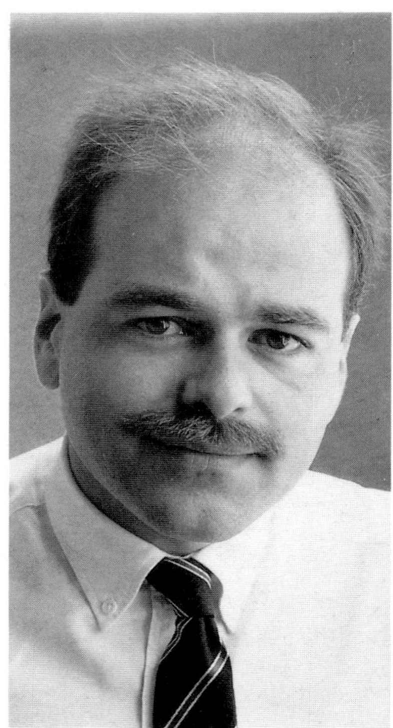

'I began my newspaper photography work in 1975 as a cadet at the *Herald and Weekly Times* Ltd. I started at the *Sunday Age* in 1989.

'Photography is about seeing, not shutter speeds and f stops. My ideas about pictures have been influenced by photographers like Andre Kertez, Henri Cartier-Bresson, Elliot Erwitt, W. Eugene Smith, and Don McCullin. Their work was shot exclusively in black and white. Colour sometimes gets in the way of expressing emotion, pictorially. Ultimately, we all bring something of ourselves to the work.

'Most importantly, we must present the story honestly; with no embellishment — we're journalists who use pictures instead of words.'

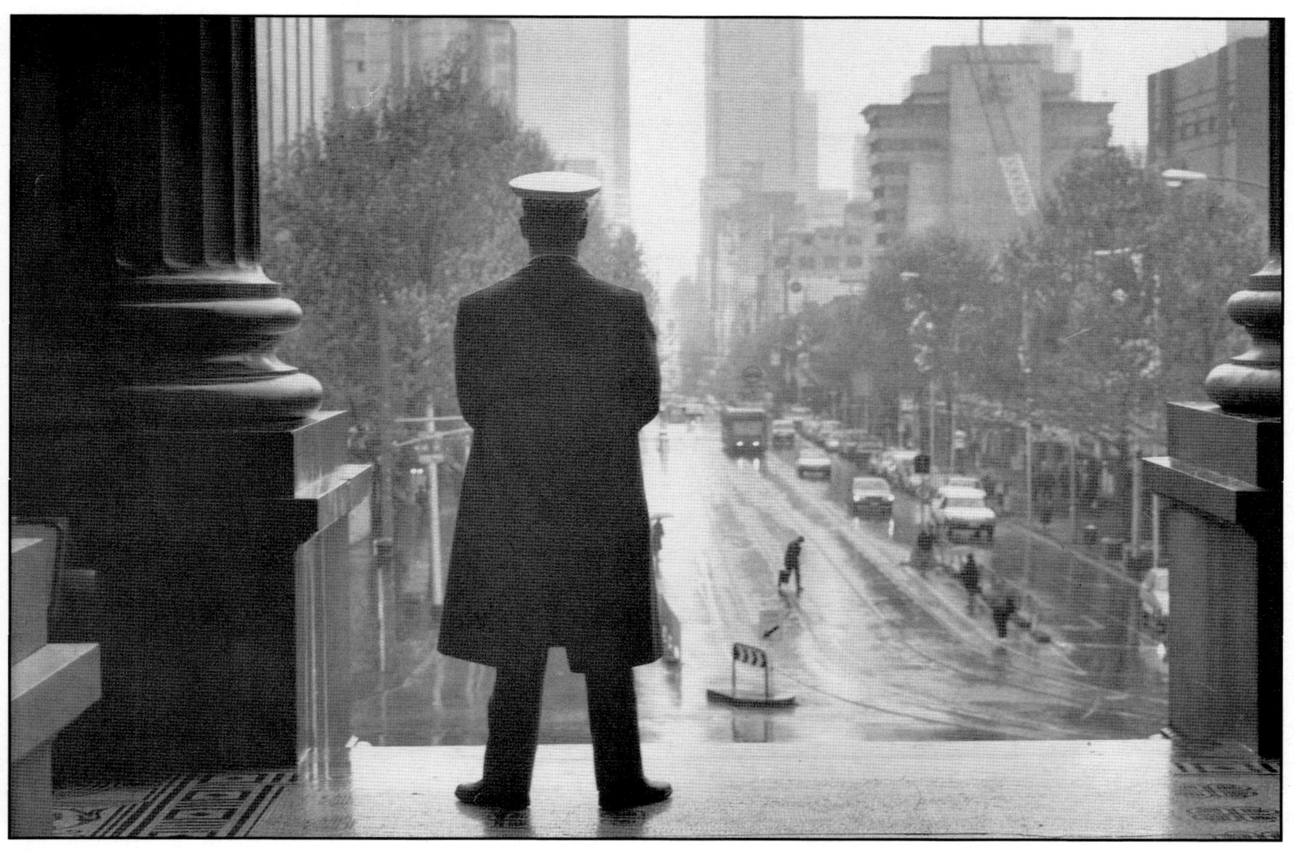

Bourke Street (from Parliament House) on a wintry Melbourne afternoon. 1990

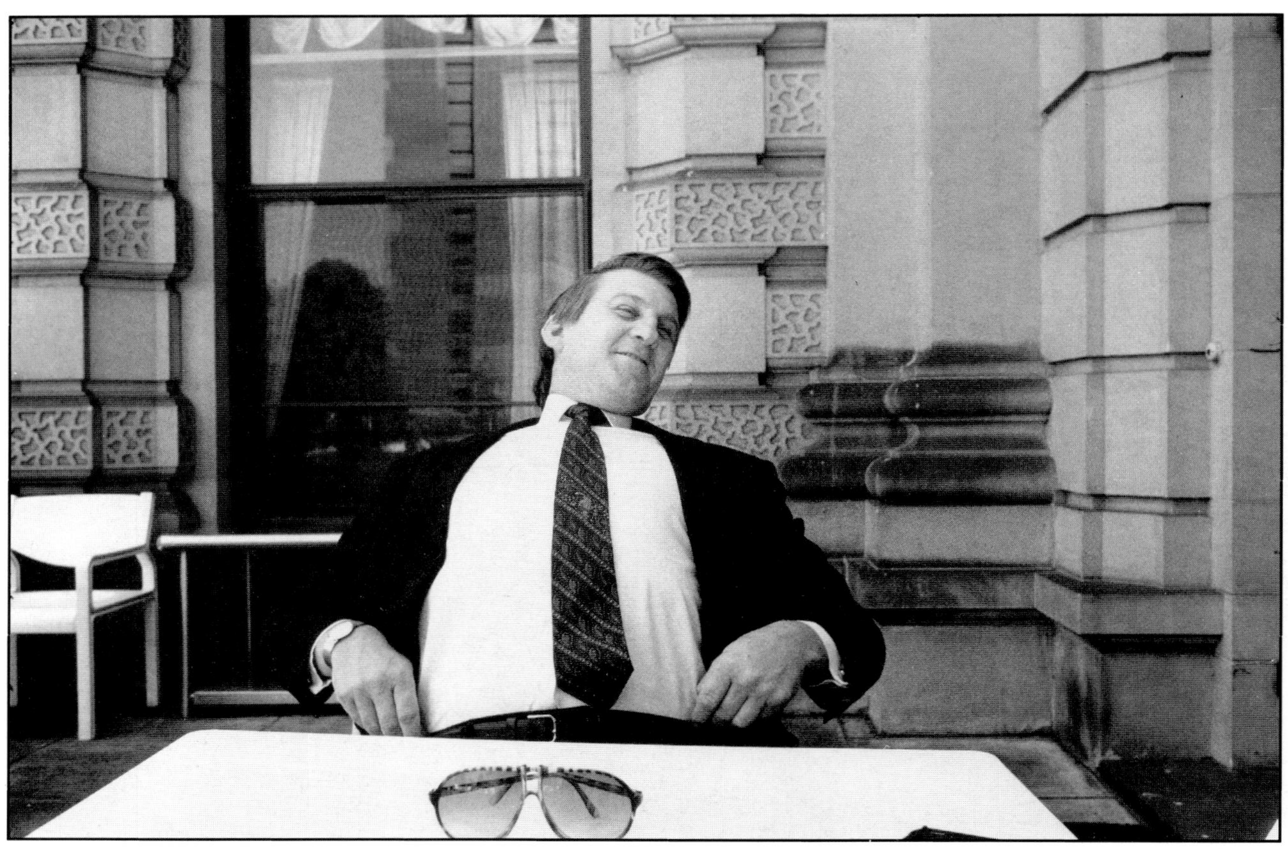

Jeff Kennett at Parliament House, 1991

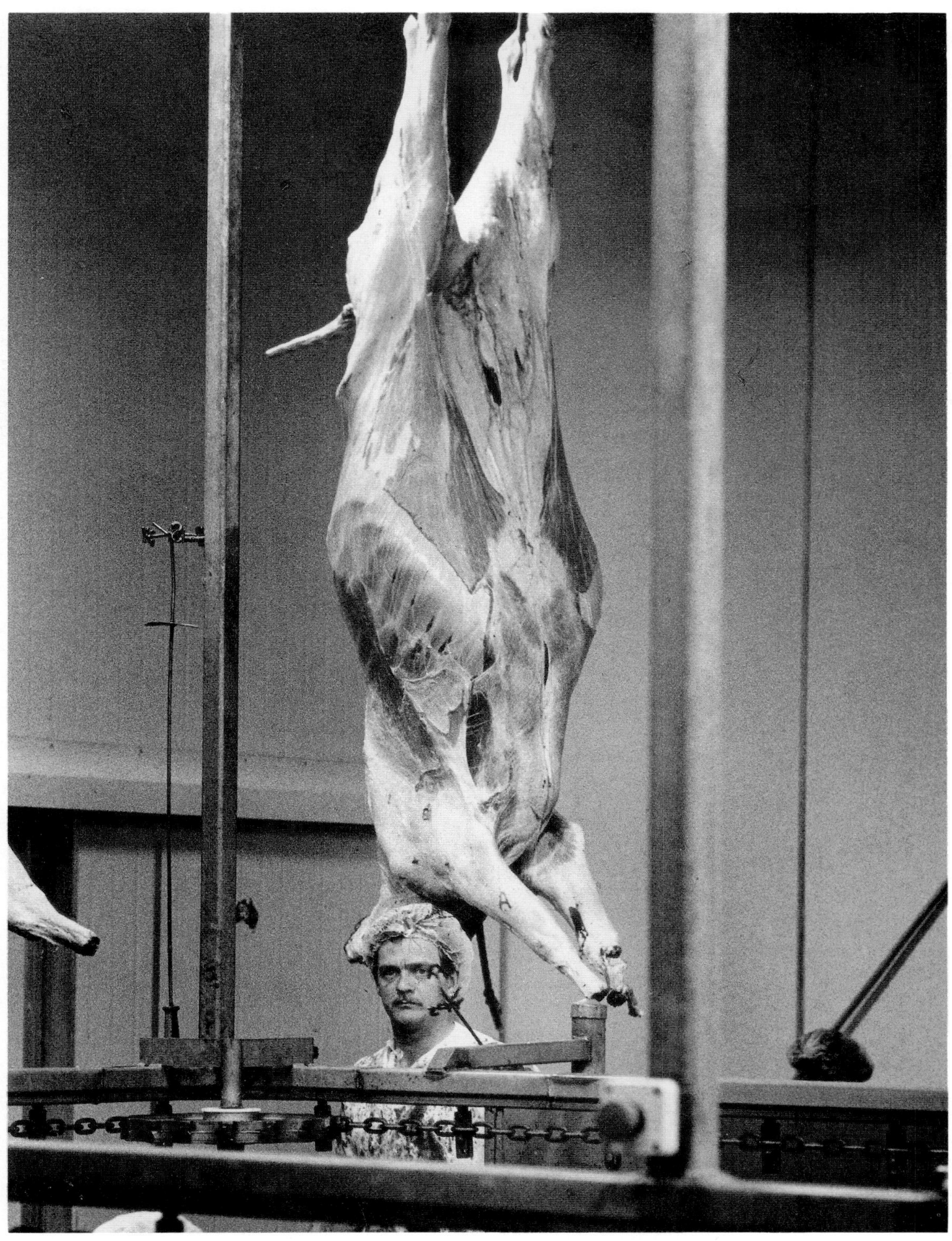

Meat worker at Pakenham Meatworks, 1991

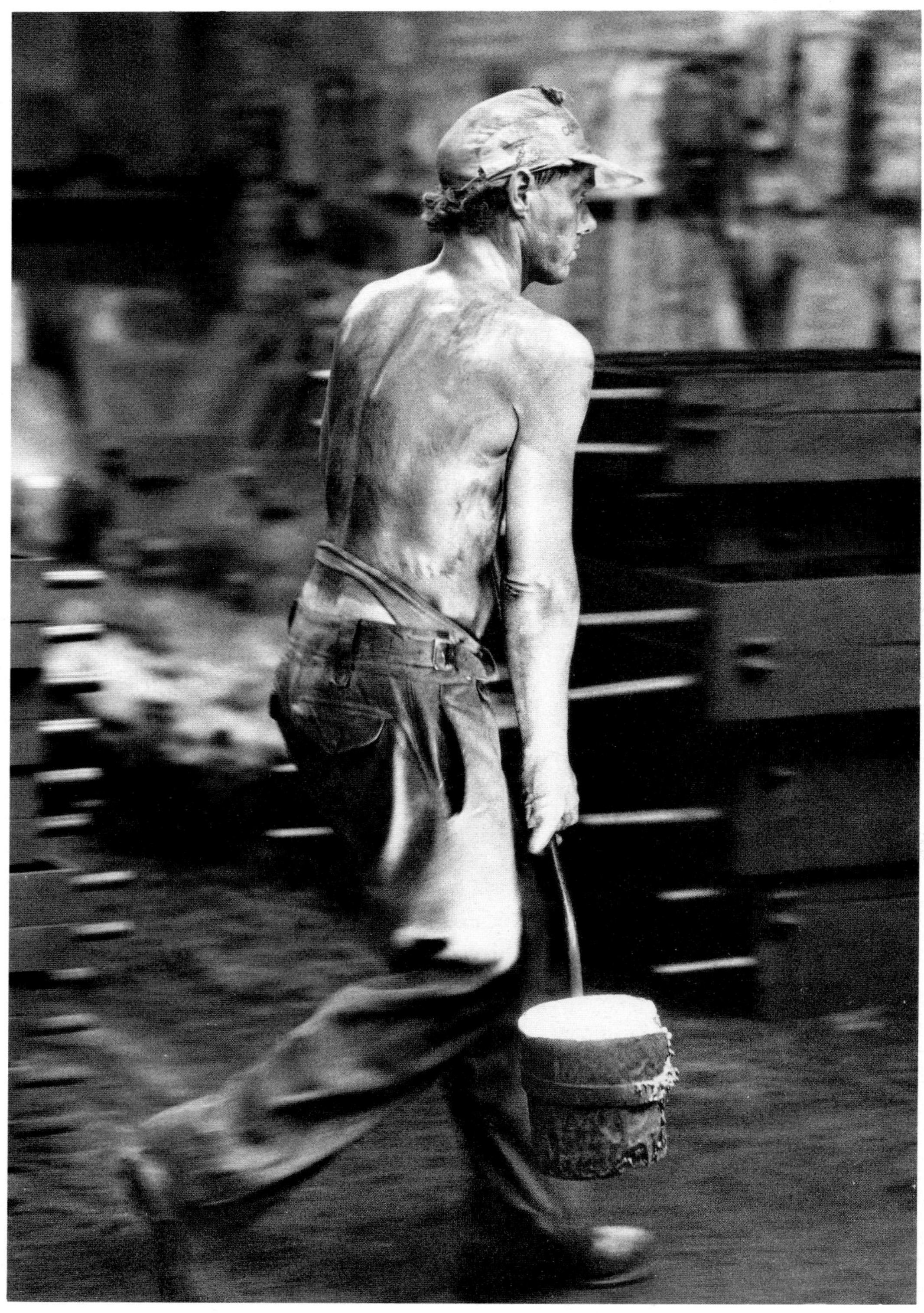

Iron foundry worker Rocky Rizzetti delivering molten cast iron to moulds, 1992

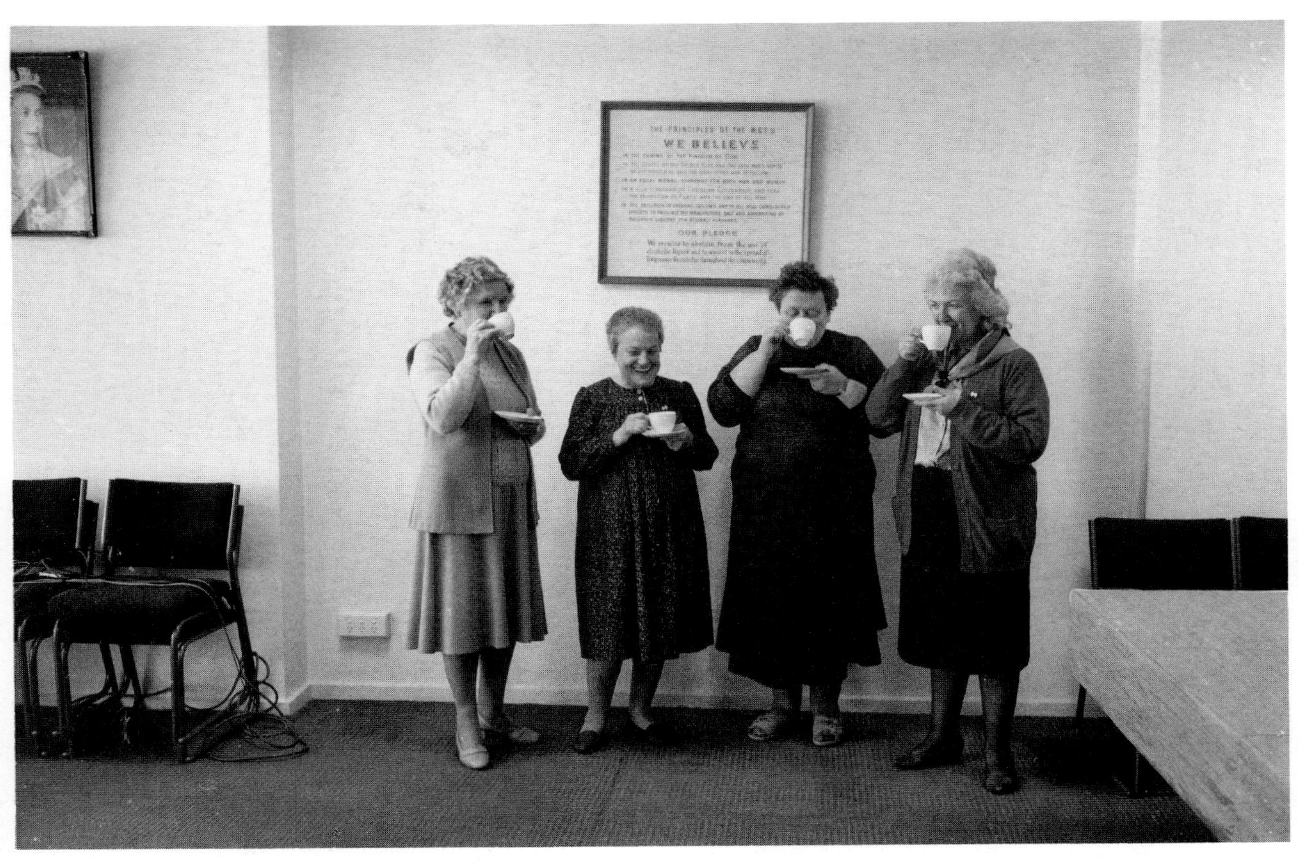

Members of the Women's Christian Temperance Union at their Melbourne headquarters. Pictured are Mrs Lorna Risstion, Mrs Gladys Izzard, Mrs Robyn Welham, and Mrs Jenny Cormack

Wayne Ludbey

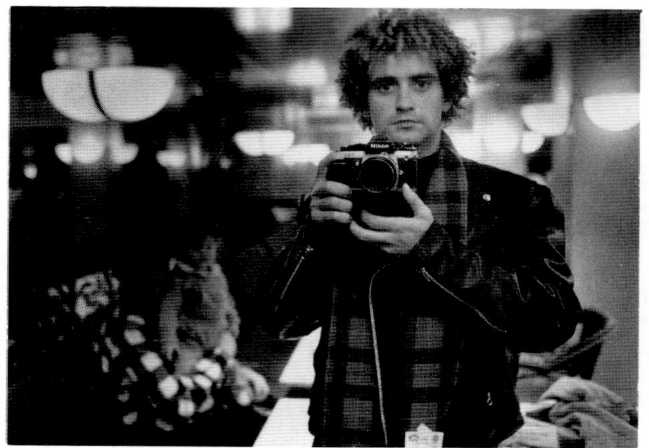

'I began a photographic cadetship with Standard Newspapers, the Melbourne suburban newspaper chain, in 1981. Very character building. The job involved real estate (taking pictures of houses for sale), car yards (pics of cars for sale), city council mayors and other local dignitaries, and the odd diamond wedding anniversary.

'I joined the *Age* in July 1984 as a D grade photographer, which is a rung on the career ladder not far above the poverty line. In five years with the *Age*, the first three were spent covering general news, sport and features, with the last two as the main sports photographer for the paper. I moved to the *Sunday Age* in July 1989.

'Newspaper photography is an instinctive art that has a habit of engulfing those who practise it. The pictures that are expected of a newspaper of this standard just don't happen during normal office hours.

'The fact that we deal with important people on a regular basis does not make us important ourselves — we're dealing with non-transferable celebrity.

'When I started as a press photographer, I relied solely on instinct and used a candid approach to my work. Now I often try to develop my concepts before I use the camera. This helps to determine the content and structure of my photographs. Yet you can't afford to manipulate the subject of your picture beyond a certain point — the name of the game is spontaneity and freshness. We leave the studio shots and epics to Hollywood.'

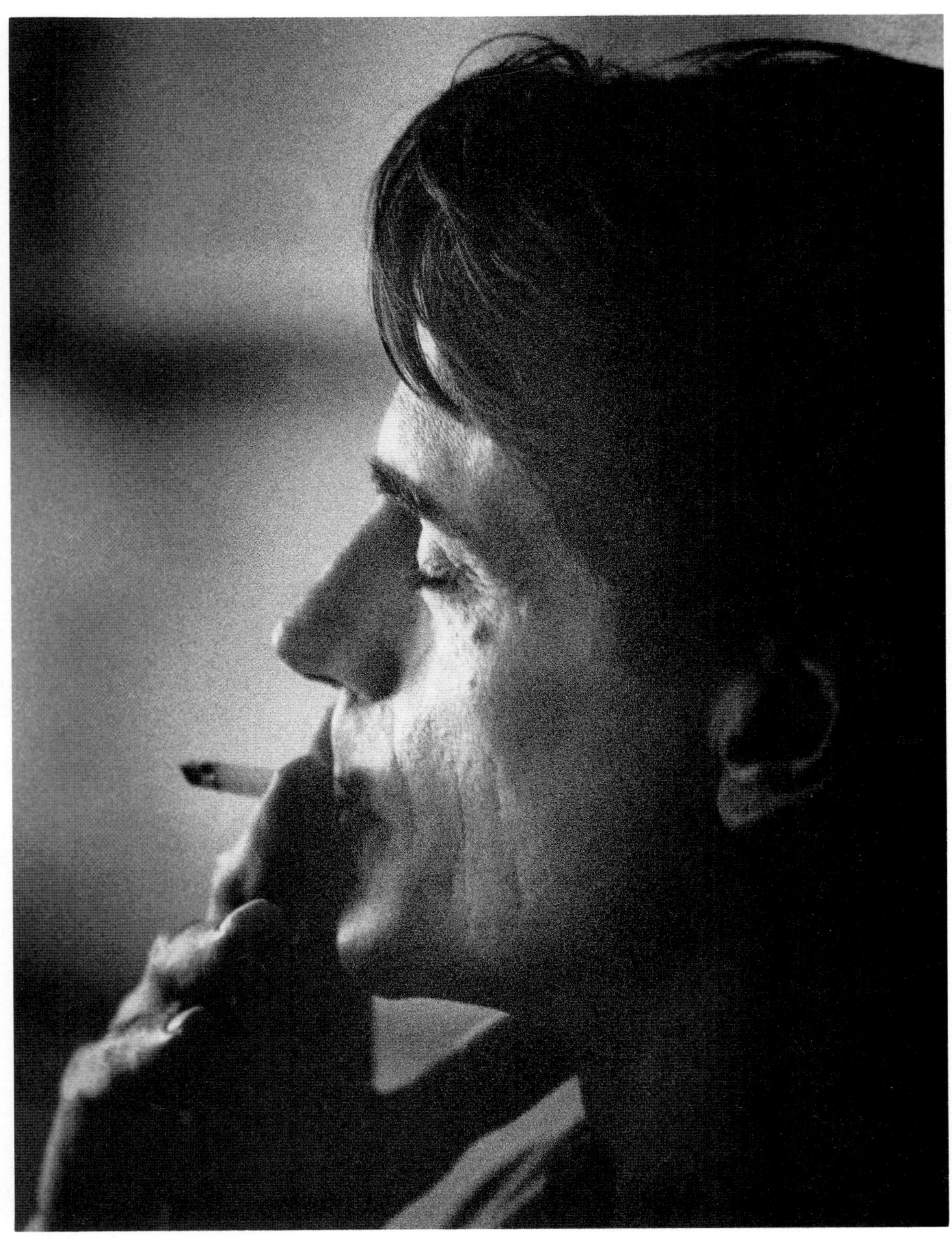

Jeremy Irons. Portrait for a feature article, 1991

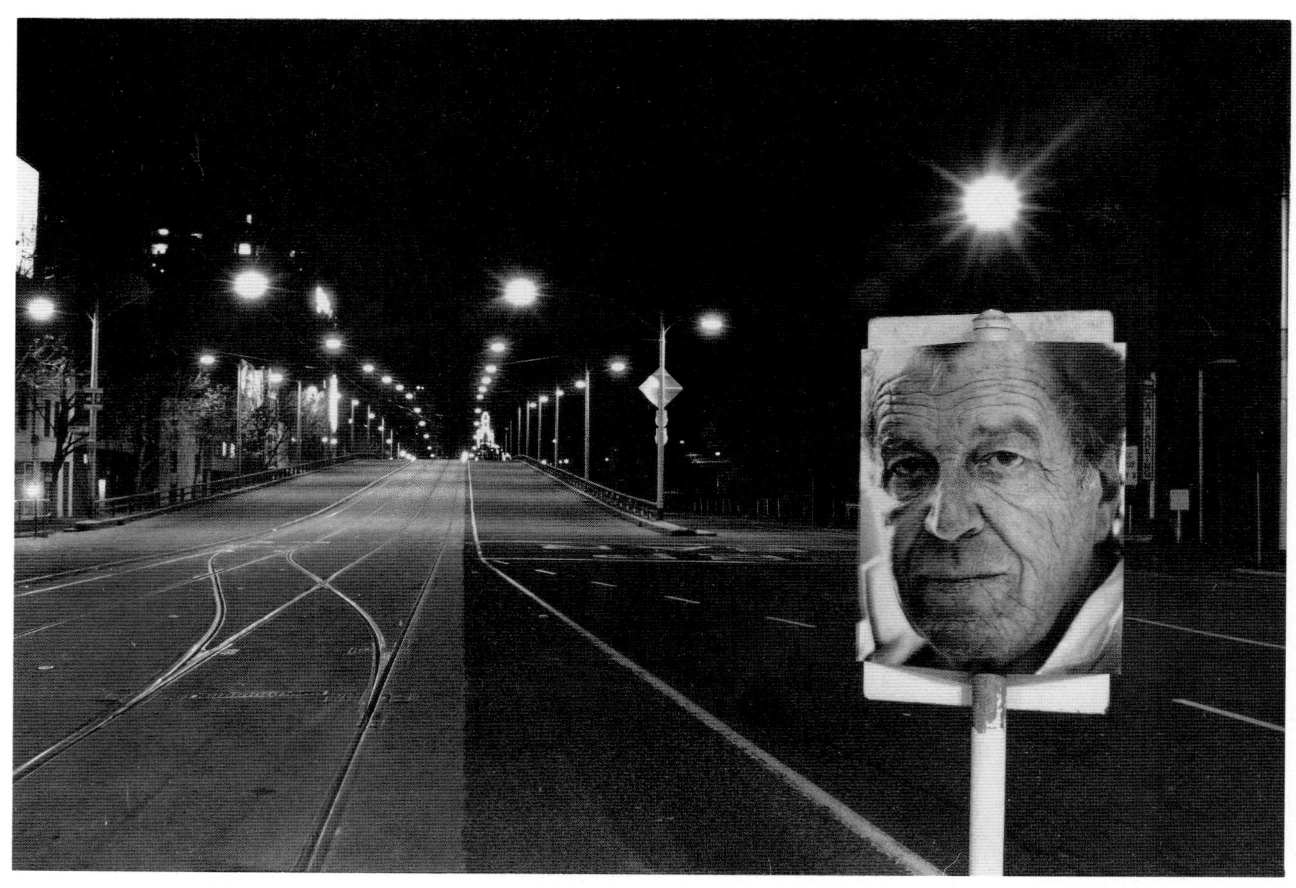

Don Chipp, portrait for a feature article, 1990. My impression of Don Chipp is as an icon. He personifies a set of beliefs that differ from the established

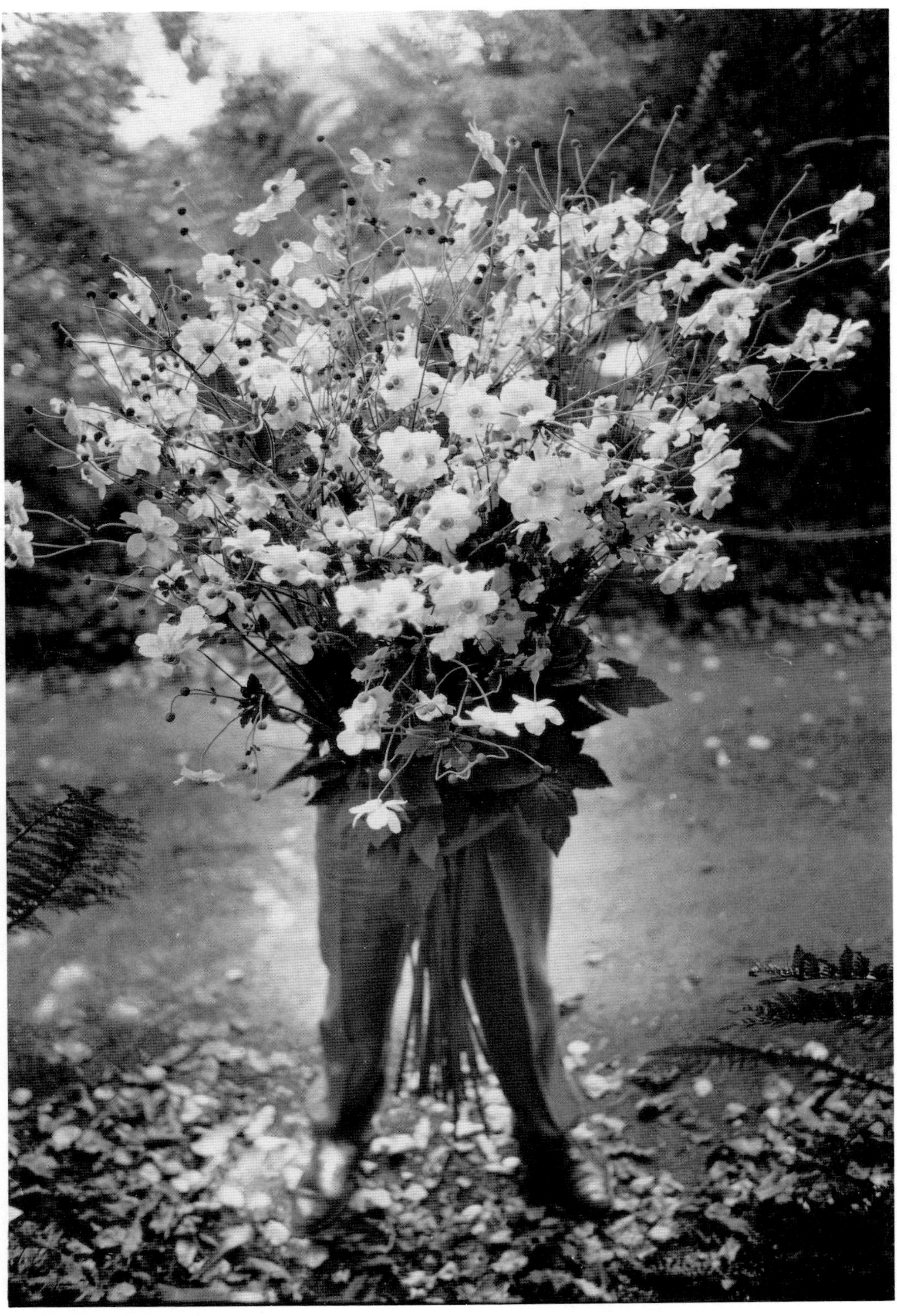

Florist Kevin O'Neill. Portrait for a feature article, 1991

CASE STUDIES

Geoff Ampt Binoculars

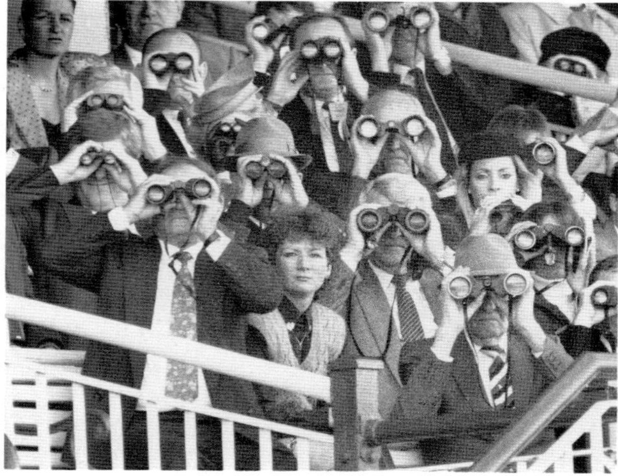

Image The strength of this photograph lies in trainer Flo Kennedy, the woman without binoculars. The railings give added impact by framing and containing the group.

Statement Humour is the overriding element. The absurdity of the myriad of binocular eyes is emphasised by the intensity of the strapper's gaze on her horse. As Australians, we are aware of the role that horse racing plays in our national self image.

Camera use Geoff uses a very long (600mm) lens to capture racing horses at a distance. But here it is his ability to find interesting photographs away from the track that is apparent. By being perceptive and recognising the potential humour in the scene, he has captured a moment others could well have missed. His position is below the stand. The relatively short depth of field with an aperture of f4 has emphasised Flo Kennedy; the people at the the top back are fading in definition and clarity of focus.

Design Repetition and rhythm are the strongest design elements in this photograph. The viewer's eye is led from binocular to binocular always coming back to the focal point — the one person whose face is unobstructed. The rounded forms of the top of the heads also are repeated. The dynamic diagonal whiter lines of the railing frame the people and draw the viewer into the picture. The horizontal railings at the bottom left direct the viewer's eye back up to the group. Without the contrast of the linear railings, the photograph would appear too confused and busy. Except for the contrast between the soft woollen jumper and the numerous grey suits, textures are not a prominent feature of the photograph.

Print quality The tones range from white to a few small areas of black with a predominance of mid-tone greys. Because of the fast film, the distance, the lens, and the cropping, the grain is quite large but remains in focus and round throughout.

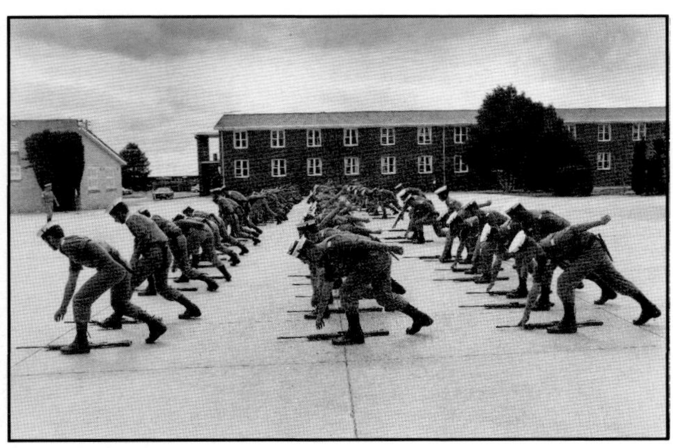

Chris Beck The army

Image At first glance, the photograph's visual strength lies in its design and rigid structure. Its composition is very orderly and symmetrical. The people, the buildings, and the pavement speak of order and regimentation.

Statement After responding to the initial impact of the design, we realise that the three lines consist of army personnel following a regimental routine. The unvarying windows in the barracks reinforce the lack of individuality. The few shrubs amid the concrete appear out of place and insignificant. But, as we examine the human beings, it becomes evident that they are not perfectly synchronised. Each bends at a different angle, has a different head tilt, and is at a different stage of reaching for a gun. The faces are in shadow and unclear.

This photograph's statement will be interpreted differently by different people: those who see war as wrong will have their views reaffirmed by the loss of individuality and futile regimentation; those who feel that we need a strong defence force may be encouraged by the regimented training; those who have an army background may worry at the lack of synchronisation.

Camera use A wide-angle lens is used to capture the entire training scene in detail with a long depth of field so that all are in focus. Chris chose to shoot the soldiers side on, thus, adding depth and a feeling that large numbers were in training.

Design The symmetry and repetition of the design add very cleverly to the statement of rigidity. The contrast between the ground and the three lines of soldiers powerfully draws us into the photograph. The repeating windows and the lack of a human touch in the buildings contributes to the impression. Only one or two shrubs disrupt the totally man-made environment. They too seem unnaturally sculpted. The space in the foreground with the very eloquent line leading us in is balanced by the tones and space in the sky.

After assessing the strong linear design we begin to look at the individuals. Their actions are clear but there is no detail in their faces. We then notice the one man not in line and realise his importance to the design and story.

Print quality This print is clean crisp and detailed. It has a wide range of tones with high contrast separating the people from the background.

Mario Borg Bourke Street

Image The strength and solidity of form in the columns and the policeman's stance create a powerful contrast to the grey, wintery Melbourne streets.

Statement The unidentifiable policeman's seemingly immovable stance possesses a sense of power and strength. This feeling is enhanced by the huge solid columns, which are often used on government buildings to convey a feeling of permanency and strength. In contrast, the active figures and vehicles in the grey, wishy-washy day are weak and unclear, suggesting their vulnerability.

Camera use Mario has used a slightly wide-angle lens to capture the policeman, columns, and the street. The middle-range aperture (approximately f8) allows the clarity of focus to centre on the figure and diminish in the streets. His camera angle, level with the figure, gives us the feeling of being with

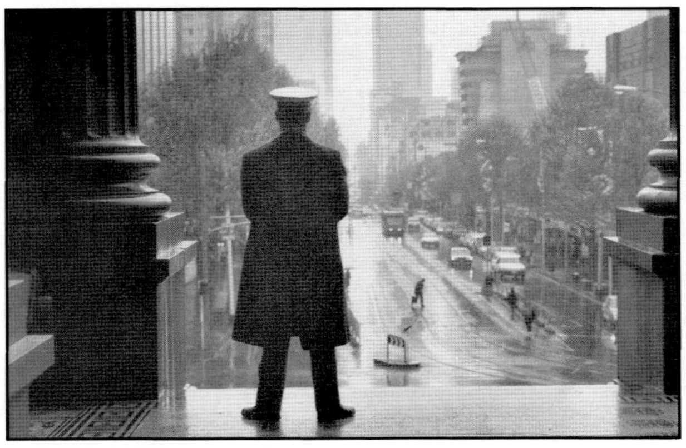

him watching the street and allows the city equal importance in the photograph.

The exposure was calculated to achieve detail in the columns and floor tiles; as a result the city is slightly lighter in tone. If Mario had exposed for the city, all details in the foreground would have been lost.

Design Mario's use of dynamic design and asymmetry is evident. The focal point, the dark policeman, is deliberately positioned on the left of the rectangle and is balanced beautifully by the small figure walking across the tram tracks. This leads the viewer, assisted by the line of cars ending in the tram, into the street.

The light hitting the column on the left creates strong curves which are repeated in the policeman's hat and the right hand columns. The floor plane, with its tiled details and reflections, adds another area of interest for the viewer and clearly separates the policeman and the city street. The textures are smooth and cold.

Print quality Mario has succeeded in capturing the atmosphere of the wet day by using mostly the mid-range of tones without high contrast. The print is clean, clear and the grain is in focus throughout.

Philip Castle The brothel

Image The immediate effect of this photograph is to convey the feeling of being in an uncomfortable situation. The worried expression on the woman's face, combined with the unidentifiable men and the house interior, make the viewer a voyeur: an unwelcome onlooker.

Statement/story The mystery of the conversation and the details of the relationships is the overriding statement/question of this photograph. The imposing male figure so close to the camera gives the viewer a feeling of being there, of being very close to the people. The smoke disguises both men's faces. The poster and the pool table suggest that this may be a brothel.

Camera use A wide-angle lens has been used selectively to focus past the man playing pool. The intricate details of the room are captured by using the available light from the ceiling lamp without the assistance of flash.

Design Philip draws us into the scene by framing the man so that only part of his head and arm are in

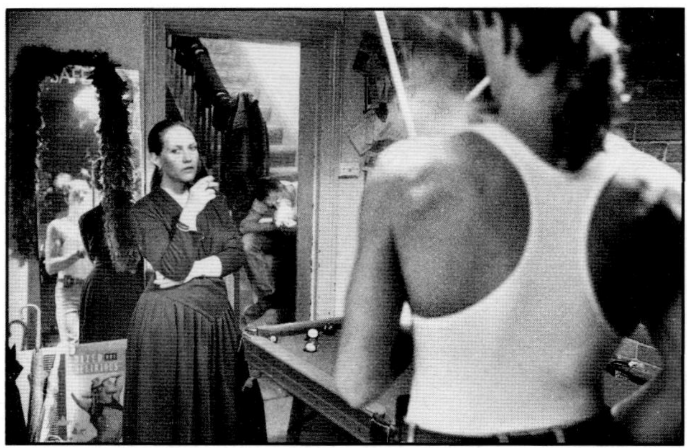

view. By not focusing on him, we feel even closer to him, as if he were too close to photograph. This huge figure is balanced by the clarity of the woman and the honesty of her expression.

The viewer is moved around the whole frame by the repetition of white tones: the white of the singlet is repeated in her skin, in his reflection in the mirror, as well as in the light from the man on the steps lighting a cigarette. The curved shape from the singlet also leads our eye to the pool cue, which draws us back into the middle. The lines of the door, the pool table, the umbrellas, the cue, and the position of the woman's arms are all in varying and often opposing directions, creating a sense of tension within the design.

The variety of textures and surfaces are many, and there are many detailed areas of interest: the door, the umbrellas, the poster, the reflected image in the mirror, the pool table framed by the man's arm. Each would be an intriguing photograph in its own right.

Print quality Quite high contrast and harsh, with details in all areas and a lovely and wide variety of tones ranging from a rich black to a pure white.

Ray Kennedy Aboriginal children race cars at Kintare, Northern Territory

The photograph accompanied a series of stories by journalist Janet Hawley on the Midnight Oil and Warumpi Band tour through koori settlements. In one area, Kintare, they found an additional story: the community's efforts to discourage petrol sniffing among young people. This had once been a problem, but Ray Kennedy's photograph shows the positive results of the campaign.

Image The impact of this photograph is immediate — children running into you, the viewer. The cars almost hit us. The stark clear sky emphasises the figures and gives crisp edges to their bodies. This sharpness allows the viewer to concentrate on the children's expressive faces. The photographer has achieved this effect by positioning himself and the camera angle so that he eliminates the more complicated tones of dirt and houses and emphasises the clear, even tone of the sky.

Statement The central theme behind the image is one of happy children playing and being ingenious in the face of poverty. Their clothes, the lack of shoes, and the very non-commercial toys suggest their poverty. Their ingenuity is apparent in their making movable cars from tin cans and fencing wire. Clearly, they are enjoying themselves, perhaps leading the reader to conclude that the most expensive toy is not necessarily the best. The camera looks up to the children, not down on them. They thus appear strong and in control of the situation. A shot from above might have suggested that they were meek and mild. The viewer is also aware that the photographer does not intimidate the children, who look directly at him without any trace of fear.

Camera use Ray Kennedy chose a wide-angle lens which appears to squeeze the children into the frame, bringing them closer to the viewer. The unusually long depth of field, achieved by using a small aperture, between f11 and f22, allows both the cars and the background to be in acceptable focus. The viewer thus has some knowledge of where the children live and play.

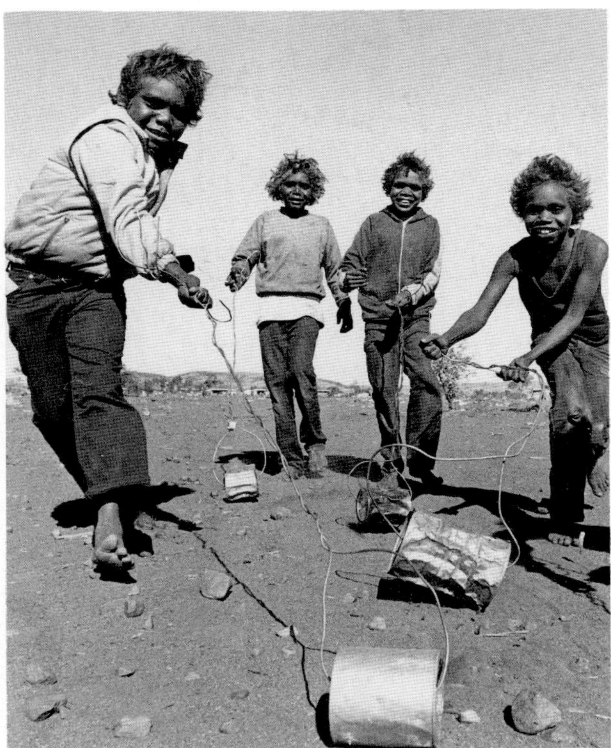

The intense midday sun is very evident. Kennedy positioned himself and the children in such a way as to prevent the strong shadows obliterating their faces. Kennedy used fast film (400 ISO) which needs less light for exposure. He could keep the lens stopped down for the longer depth of field and still use a slightly faster shutter speed (250th of a second instead of the 'normal' 60th) to capture the motion of the children moving towards him. Rather than 'setting up' the shot, Kennedy has allowed them to be themselves.

Design The overall shape of the photograph is a rectangle divided a bit above centre by a light tone above and a softer grey below. The subjects (children and cans) form a lopsided triangle whose apex is the large can in front.

Angles and points always add energy and direction to an image. From the apex the viewer follows the shadow line to the boy on the left. The curve of his body quickly takes our eyes to his strong round face sculpted in light. Responding to repetition, we then move to the other children's faces which are similar in form. Innate curiosity about other humans and their feelings keeps us 'reading' and comparing faces and expressions.

Repetition is a feature of the cans and wires.

The viewer's eyes jump from one to the other. Because the cans are placed one behind another, there is an illusion of perspective and depth. Placing the first can so close to the edge of the rectangular shape (the edge of the viewfinder) creates tension and suggests that the can is about to jump out of the frame or into the photographer. The positioning of two children on the outside edge of the frame adds to the tension.

The triangular negative spaces between the children emphasise them, again giving an ordered sense of repetition. The negative space in the top right-hand corner provides a feeling of open space and a much needed rest for the eyes. It helps to balance all the action.

The textures are many and varied — from soft skin to crumbling dirt, to the fabric of the clothes and the cans. Some textures, more crumpled than others, are clear and allow the viewer's eyes to 'touch' the surfaces.

Finally, because the photograph is well-balanced or composed, the image sits comfortably on the page.

Print quality A good print usually has deep black, crisp white and many intermediate tones. Ray Kennedy's photograph contains at least nine tones, including strong blacks and whites. All areas, apart from a few dense shadows, are well detailed. The print was well focused when enlarged — the 'grain' is round, in focus, and does not distort or fall-off at the edges. There are rich warm tones throughout.

John Lamb Milky way dreaming

Image This photograph speaks of the warmth of the woman surrounded by a huge art work of which she seems a part.

Statement The woman's arm placement suggests that she is shy, yet she smiles with a genuine warmth. There is a sense of pride in her expression. She is dwarfed by this enormous art work, yet she seems at home with it. From the caption we learn that this is a huge glass mosaic designed from her painting 'Milky Way Dreaming'.

Camera use John has used a wide-angle lens here to capture as much of the artwork as possible. He has chosen a long depth of field (with a small aperture, i.e. f16) to record all the details of the work from the nearest piece of glass to the farthest. He positioned himself on a scaffold in order to get the best view and asked the artist to sit among the work, not only to indicate her importance, but also to give a sense of scale to the mosaic.

Design The artist dominates the design. Her placement is extremely important in the design. She is surrounded by a wonderful array of sparkling bits of glass with many lights and darks.

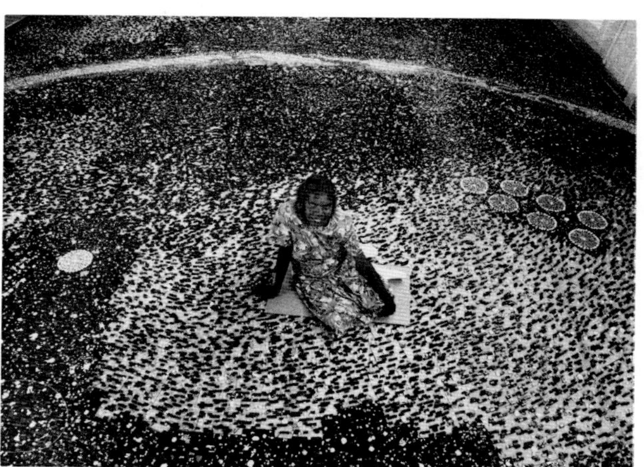

The circular shapes are the next aspect to capture our attention. The group of seven on the right are balanced beautifully by the single one on the left. The flowing sea of the lighter tone draws us gently to the woman then surrounded by the detailed rich black sea of glass, which moves us to the eloquent line which curves back to highlight the woman again.

The use of just a small detail of the door in the top right corner adds a bit of contrast and again helps us to appreciate the size of the artwork.

Print quality Although there is good separation of tones with strong contrast between the blacks and whites, John has achieved details of tone in all areas.

Mike Martin Kids on the train

Image A strong impact is achieved at first glance. The teenager closest to the camera quickly captures our attention and we proceed to inspect the other players with interest.

Statement/Story The statement is one of teenagers rebelliously enjoying themselves on the public transport system in the evening. The alcohol, the girl standing on the seats about to jump for the stirrup, tells us that we are viewing an illegal incident. Yet, it is their open, joyous and defiant attitude, welcoming the photographer that is communicated clearly through the photograph.

Camera use Mike needed a very fast film (ISO 1600) to achieve the depths and details of this photograph. If he had chosen to use a flash, the reflections in the windows would have been obliterated. The passengers at the rear would have been lost through the diminishing light of the flash.

The slower shutter speed, 1/30th of a second, may have been necessary to achieve such a long depth of field (aperture f11) given the limited light. Alternatively he may have chosen that shutter speed in order to capture the motion of the people.

The wide-angle lens with a wide angle of view of about 75 degrees allowed Mike to include the entire width of the train in the frame, giving us the feeling that we are seeing the whole carriage.

Design The first smiling face strikes the viewer instantly. His direct gaze clearly shows that he is communicating with the photographer. From there our eyes follow the rounded forms, the other faces, to learn their feelings in the situation. The lines on the

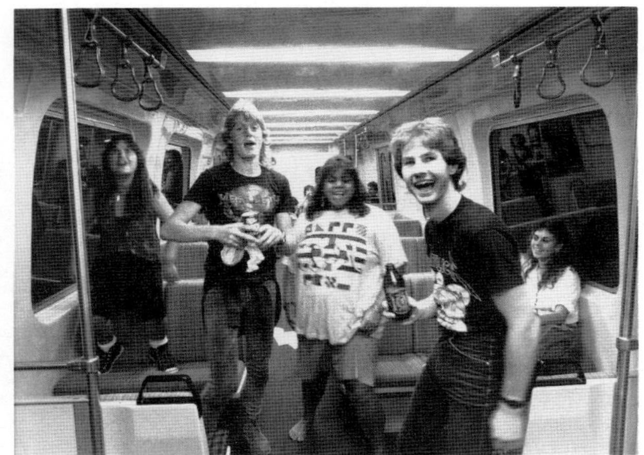

stirrups and the roof line on both sides carry us back into the rear of the train. The lights on the roof also add to the diminishing perspective and entice us to follow. We then begin to peer into the reflections for more clues about the activity and the other passengers' behaviour.

The textures and tones of the clothing and the interior maintain the viewer's interest. Our eyes tend to follow the repetition of strong tones, jumping from one black t-shirt to another and then from white to white on the females. There is a gentle, curved line flowing from the base of the arm of the boy on the right to the middle girl's shoulder and then to the boy on the left whose elbow continues the line.

The two metal poles and backs of the seats help to frame the action and add some space and contrast to the busy action and details.

Print quality The grain is very large due to the fast film. The enlargement is printed with high contrast (about grade 4) to increase the separation between the blacks and the whites, which are rich and clean. With the combination of film and contrast, there is a little loss in detail.

Neil Newitt Pat Cash

Image The viewer is immediately confronted by the strength of this close-up portrait. The eye looks straight at you, while the arm obscures the face. Yet, for most Australians, it is recognisably Pat Cash's sweatband.

Statement The arm wiping the sweat off the brow tells us that Pat Cash is in the middle of a tennis match. There is a sense of a great sportsman fighting to win.

Camera use The 800mm lens is able to capture such a close-up from quite a distance. Precise focusing was required to keep the arm and head crisp while the fingers begin to fade and the background is unrecognisable.

Within the frame, Neil, by cropping the top of the head, draws us into the eye of the subject, creating a bold and strong composition. The powerful curve of the arm balances the angle of the head and headband. Such close cropping and the short depth of field allows nothing to distract from the eye and arm.

The black and white checks add a contrast to the grey tones of the skin. The white is repeated in the shirt. The textures are rich, the hair on the arm with light falling on it provides a tonal contrast to the shadowed face. The linear shadows falling on his face from his hair again highlight and lead us to the eye.

The negative space around the hand allows the viewer to rest and balances the action of the arm.

Print quality This print is beautifully done and uses a wide range of tones (at least nine) ranging from black to white. Details are crisp and the print is clean. No scratches or spots detract from its impact.

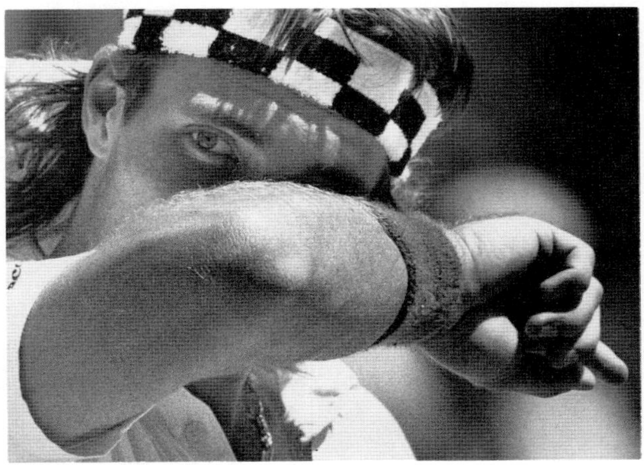

Sandy Scheltema The mangrove tree

Image A peaceful water setting that resembles a Japanese watercolour painting.

Statement The statement is one of mystery and beauty. The grasses in the front are out of focus and dreamlike, while the dead mangrove tree and the rocks silhouetted against the light background become black lines and shapes.

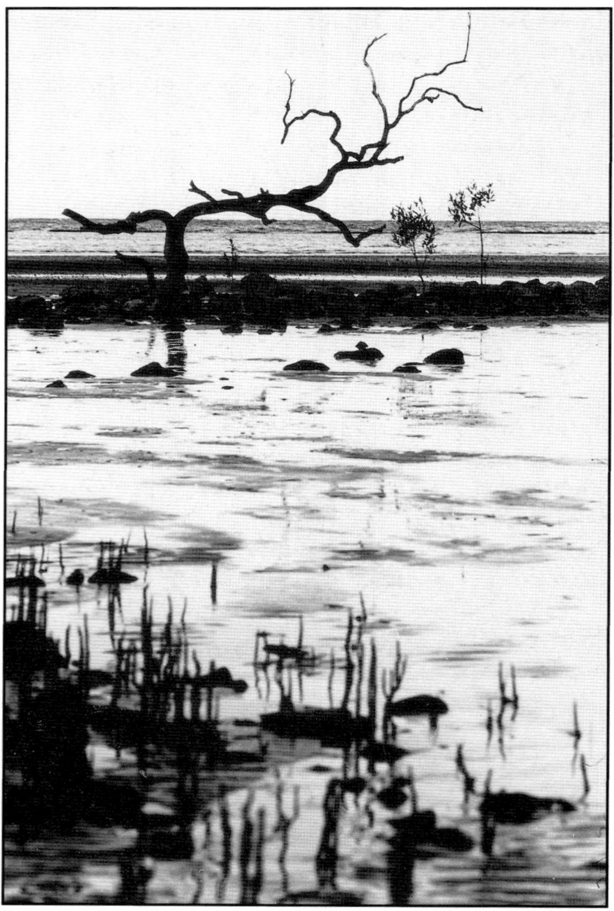

Camera use We wonder where the photographer is standing — is it in the water or on it? Her positioning helps us to feel that we too are in the water. The selective focusing on the dead tree, letting the front blur, helps to add that feeling.

The choice of a slow film has minimised the grain, giving solid blacks and other tones. She may have used a tripod.

Design Lines of black contrasting with the white water and sky are the basis for this design. Sandy has made the tree the centre of interest. Its gnarled and eloquent dead branches direct the viewer across the top of the page to the small live trees, the details of the rocks, and the water in the distance. The black grasses in the foreground have a gentle rhythm that dances our eyes back into the background.

The whites in the water and the negative space are beautifully balanced as are the blacks.

Print quality Printed with very high contrast (grade 4 or 5). Sandy has retained only a few middle tones and concentrated on the rich blacks and whites. The print is clean and crisp.

Cathryn Tremain Aboriginal fashion parade

Image The two figures are strong and clear, silhouetted against a dark background. Their intense concentration on the mirror allows the viewer to feel as if they are unaware of the photographer.

Statement The power of this photograph lies in the two different styles of people, their dress, and their obvious shared concern in their presentation prior to the fashion parade. It shows two differing cultures working together in a very relaxed relationship. Humour is achieved by observing the use of make-up to beautify in varying ways in both cultures.

Camera use Cathryn has achieved the natural expressions by using an 85mm lens which allowed her to stand at a reasonable distance from the subjects and remain unnoticed. The shot is a great example of a keenly observant photographer who always looks for a good picture, even before the main event.

She has photographed from a standing position, which keeps the subjects on her level and gives the viewer the feeling of standing in the same room. By using 800 T-Max film, she was able to maximise the qualities of natural light, which has picked up the textures of the clothes and skin.

Design The two figures are strong, vertical forms that balance each other in the frame. The dark background allows us to view the main subjects without distraction.

The composition is dominated by triangular shapes — the most striking being the dark negative space between the two people. The apex of the triangle meets at the two knees and provides a dynamic interaction between the figures. The viewer's eye travels back and forth from this point. The triangles are repeated in the bend of the arm holding the mirror and in the angle of the man's arm. These triangular negative shapes are again repeated in the dancer's stance and in the base of the woman's dress.

The strong oval shape of the white mirror is the centre of attention, both for the subjects and the viewer of the photograph. The curved lines are repeated in the face paint, the painted design of the back of the dress and in the flowing gathered satin.

The metal line across the bottom and the lighter tone of the floor gives the figures a firm base, separates them from the dark background and adds a linear element to the photograph which is repeated

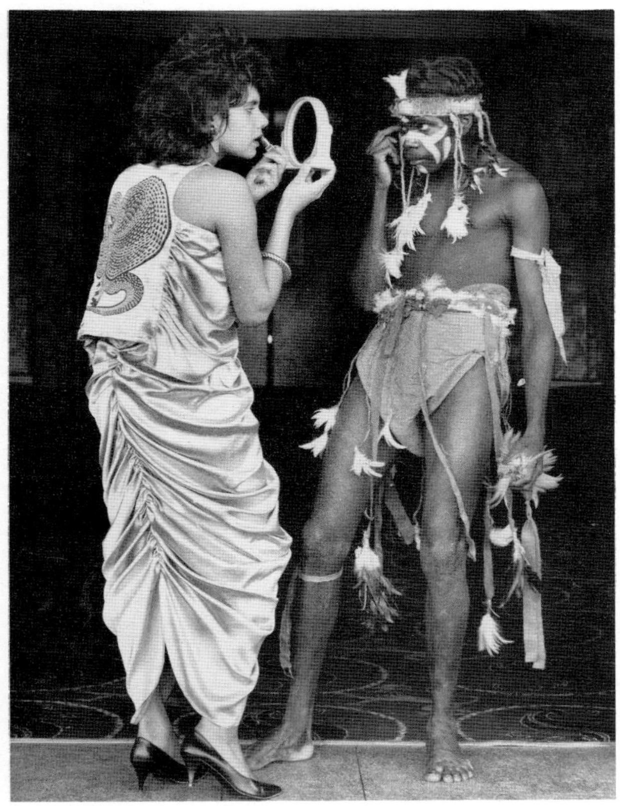

in the bands of fabric and the bracelet. The textures are sensuous, rich and varied. The soft skin textures, the silky satin, the cotton pants, the hair and the feathers contrast with the granite and metal at the base of the photograph.

Print quality Cathryn has achieved a wide range of tones in this print from a rich black to a clean white. The separation of tones is excellent, and the dark background provides contrast. The print is sharp and clear with little fall off in the corners.

William West The dancers

Image We are immediately struck by the doll-like, almost bird-like, figures of the ballet dancers. Their fluffy tutus and varied stances work jointly and singly against the dark floor and background.

Statement It is very unusual to see professional dancers off-guard. Their concern for final touches in their presentation is very evident as each concentrates on something different. No one notices the photographer. Each one's movement is intriguing to study.

Camera use William has used a wide-angle 35mm lens to capture the four figures. He is on the same level as the dancers, which allows viewers to feel as if we too are there.

The relatively short depth of field makes the two dancers on the left appear crisp, while the focus on the figures to the right is slightly blurred and this gives them more of a dream-like quality.

Design The rhythm created by the repetition of the white tutus and head pieces against the dark background brings us across the entire page. The slight overlapping of the two pairs of dancers helps to create a visual line across the entire page. Our eyes go back and forth between them. The interest in each individual's actions then keeps us searching the details.

The soft white textures of the dresses are emphasised by the strength of the linear forms of the legs and arms, with the single leg becoming the centre of focus. The angle of her lifted leg also brings us to the third dancer. The black negative space between them is an interesting shape and allows the viewer to rest. The light falling on the backs and legs gives power to the muscular forms and skin textures.

Print quality Printed with high contrast, the middle range of tones are few, yet the skin is the correct tone for reproduction — not so dark that the faces are obliterated, not so light that details of the muscular forms are lost.

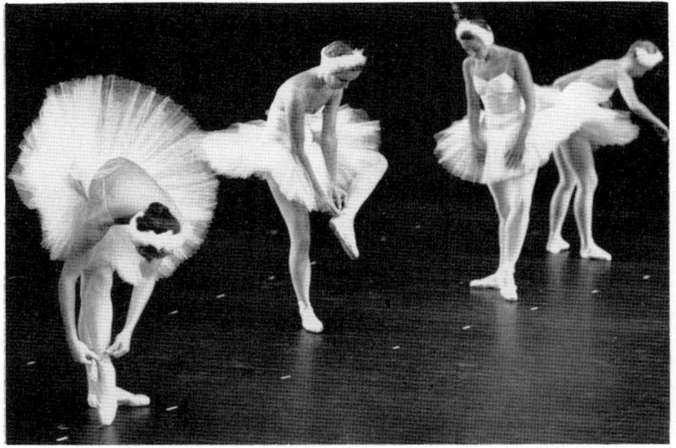

THINGS TO DO

By Clare Gervasoni & Paul Walker

Photography students, particularly Art, Studio Arts, and Media Studies students need to practise many skills and techniques in order to produce quality photographs. But a good photograph also has an added dimension which gives it a 'special quality'. That 'special quality' is often the subject matter, so choose the subject and composition of your photographs carefully.

The following list of 'things to do' encourages you to study the work of professional photographers and should assist you in developing ideas for the production of a quality photographic folio.

VCE Art, Studio Arts, and Media Studies students should find the list useful when completing work requirements. For example, a student undertaking Studio Arts (Unit 3) would be interested in question 16 on conservation of negatives and photographs, whereas a student of Art (Unit 2) may wish to complete question 5 before starting work on a common theme. It is simply a case of completing those questions most appropriate to your studies.

1 When did the the *Age* introduce photography to its pages? How was the newspaper illustrated before then? Outline the changes in the *Age*'s use of photography up until the advent of colour newspaper reproductions. You may need to visit a library or other institution that has archival copies of newspapers.

2 Artists often record the world around them. This is particularly true of photographers. Choose an area of the news of interest to you and collect photographs that illustrate a particular item of news over a period of four weeks. How has the photographer recorded this item visually? What impact does the photograph have on the report? Has the style of recording the information photographically changed during the four weeks?

3 Take any copy of the *Age*. Compare the front page, the back page, a page of the classifieds, and page six. How many photographs are reproduced on each of these pages? What size are the photographs? Has good design sense influenced the layout of each page? Analyse each page critically as a designer would. What advice would you give to the layout artist?

4 Newspaper photographs can lead the reader to an article. Find an article that has 'caught your eye'. Analyse why it did so. Has it been displayed to its greatest effect?

5 Choose a theme common to the *Age* and two other newspapers. Which photograph best captures the 'theme'. Why? Utilise what you have discovered in your own photographs.

6 Find an editorial or piece of text in a newspaper (national or local) that is not accompanied by a photograph. Take a photograph that will illustrate the story.

7 Write a short editorial or article for your local newspaper or newsletter. Take a series of photographs to illustrate what you have written. Choose one and explain why you have chosen it.

8 Find your own 'human interest' photograph in the way that John Lamb does. Are you aware of any people in your community who would make interesting photographic subjects? Children, artists, local identities or the change of the weather are often of 'soft' news value.

9 Within your group choose an editor, a sub-editor, a pictorial editor, and a features editor. Using your photographs from question 6, discuss which photographs should be used in the newspaper, giving such reasons as news value, visual impact, design, and quality of the photograph. Try to reach a consensus. If you can't, remember that the editor has the final say.

10 Analyse a newspaper. Make a list of the different sections (eg general news, sport, business, advertising) and their lengths. How many photographs are included in each section? Are there any general, human interest photos that are accompanied only by a caption? Are the most important news items at the front of the paper? Has a good photograph with a lesser news value been placed further forward than you might otherwise expect?

11 Compare the style of photogaphy in the *Sunday Age* with that in the daily *Age*. How and why does a magazine style differ from that of the daily press?

12 Do you agree with Leigh Henningham, the *Sunday Age* Pictorial Editor, that its photographs are more personal and emotional? Explain using examples.

13 An approach often found in newspapers is to photograph a smiling person facing the camera. Break away from this approach by not simply conveying 'the facts' but by attempting to capture the mood, the atmosphere, and the emotions of a particular event not just the facts.

14 You may find some people do not wish to have their photos taken. What could you say to persuade them to change their mind?

15 What changes can you make to the way you hold the camera and the camera equipment that will make it easier for you take a photograph?

16 Store and file your negatives and photographs to preserve them and make them easily accessible. What archival permanence should your work have if you have processed them correctly?

17 Take a photograph. Make two copies of it on the photocopier, one with low contrast (lighter) and one with high contrast (darker). Is the softer or the harder version more suitable for the image?

18 Print the same negative on grade 1 photographic paper and on grade 4. Explain how the image is altered. Which version is more successful?

19 Using such categories as image, statement/story, camera use, design, and print quality, analyse your own photograph. Alternatively, select a photograph from this book and analyse it.

20 Assess a newspaper page layout and/or photograph in terms of balance. How successful is it? How has this been achieved?

21 Photocopy a newspaper photograph (or use one of your own) three times. Crop each in a different way. What effect does this have on the statement, the image, and the design?

22 Find photographs in books, magazines or newspapers that use natural light and those that use flash. What are the differences? Which do you prefer? Why?

23 Choose a subject to photograph. Vary your angles and your distance from the subject. Describe how each change affects the impact of the photograph, the importance of the subject, and the design of the photograph.

24 Photograph the one object but vary your depth of field by changing the aperture from f2 to f8 to f16. (Remember to vary your shutter speeds accordingly.) What is the effect on your photograph?

25 Photograph an object using a range of lenses (wide angle, standard, and telephoto). Which is the most successful? Why?

26 In this book, the photographers each make a statement about what they are trying to achieve in their work. Choose one or more photographers and study their work. Do you think they have achieved their aims? Use examples from this book or recent *Age* newspapers to illustrate your conclusions.

GLOSSARY OF TERMS

Aperture Opening of the diaphragm covering the lens. The size of the aperture determines the amount of light that enters. The size of the opening is quoted in f numbers. (f2 is a wide opening, f16 is a smaller opening which therefore lets in less light).

Angle of view The angle, measured in degrees, that the lens can encompass — what it 'sees'. A 20mm lens (wide angle) has a wide angle of view of 94 degrees whereas a 300mm lens has a view of only 8 degrees.

Burning in While enlarging from a negative to a print, if one area is too light (too white and lacking detail) the printer may allow extra light to hit the area while preventing light reaching the rest of the print (blocking out) with hands or cardboard.

Depth of field The distance between the closest and furthest points of a subject that are in acceptable focus and appear sharp. A larger aperture opening such as f2 has a small distance of acceptable focus whereas f16, a smaller opening, has a longer distance in focus or a greater depth of field. Increasing the focal length of the lens decreases the depth of field.

Dodging A technique used when printing an enlargement from a negative. A portion of the photographic paper is covered by the hands or by a piece of cardboard on a wire to prevent that area being exposed to light from the enlarger for a part of the exposure time. This area of the print thus remains lighter while the remainder is exposed to more light and thus becomes darker. Burning in is the opposite technique.

Exposure the presentation of a sensitive material, such as film, paper, or plate, to the action of light. The intensity of the light is determined by the opening of the aperture, while the duration of the exposure is controlled by the shutter speed of the camera or the timer on the enlarger.

Fast film Film rated 400 ISO or higher which responds quickly to light and is therefore suitable for use in dimly lit situations.

Film A coating of light-sensitive silver halide crystals on an acetate roll or sheet. The chemical composition of the crystals changes when exposed to light.

f numbers or f stops Numbers used to indicate the aperture or opening size of the diaphragm covering the lens. They are standardised to f1.4, f2, f2.8, f4, f5.6, f8, f11, f16, f22, and f32. The numbers are derived by dividing the diameter of the opening by the focal length of the lens (eg, a 50mm lens has an opening of 25mm when set on f2, but a 2.27mm opening when set on f22. With each numerical increase in f stop from f1.4 the amount of light entering the lens is halved as the aperture becomes smaller.

Focal length The focal length of the lens, when focused on infinity, is the distance from the end of the lens to the film plane. The focal length determines the angle of view (how much the camera 'sees' in degrees). A long focal length (200mm and above) views a small portion of the area; a wide angle (35mm and below) has a wider view.

Flash (electronic) A unit attached to the camera through a 'hot shoe' or a lead which creates a bright flash of light for 1/500 — 1/40,000th second by triggering a high voltage charge between two electrodes within a glass cylinder containing inert gas.

ISO International Standards Organisation. An internationally recognised measurement of film speed (the sensitivity of film to light). The higher the ISO, the faster the film. This has replaced the ASA and DIN numbers.

Lens A contoured piece or element of glass designed to control and intensify light passing through it. Most contemporary camera lenses are composed of three or more individual elements.

Motor-drive An attachment to the camera that enables motorised, rather than manual, film advancement, permitting the taking of as many as six photographs per second.

Panning Moving the camera with the subject, thus blurring the background but keeping the subject in clear focus.

Reflector Any object used to reflect the light toward the subject. There are professional umbrellas in white, silver and gold, but a piece of white cardboard or paper will also redirect and reflect the light.

Resolution The ability of the film or the lens to provide a sharp and detailed image.

Shutter Most cameras have a focal plane or leaf shutter that opens and closes, allowing light to enter and expose the film.

Shutter speed The length of time the shutter opens.

Telephoto lens A lens whose physical length is shorter than its focal length as a result of the coupling of the elements or lenses.

Tripod A three-legged stand which supports the camera.

Tungsten light A source of light resulting from electricity passing through a tungsten wire. Used in household bulbs and studio lights. On colour daylight film it produces a golden, orange cast which can be corrected by using a blue filter (80A or 80B) over the light or lens.